GOUNOD

Gounod at the age of 23 as a student in Rome. Portrait by Ingres, 1841.
(Photo: Stella Mayes Reed.)

GOUNOD

James Harding

*Sir, are you so grossly ignorant of human nature as
not to know that a man may be very sincere in good
principles, without having good practice?*
Johnson to Boswell

𝔰𝔇

STEIN AND DAY/*Publishers*/New York

First published in the United States by Stein and Day/*Publishers*

Copyright © 1973 by George Allen and Unwin Ltd.

Library of Congress Catalog Card No. 72-95990

Printed in the United States of America

Stein and Day/*Publishers*/Scarborough House, Briarcliff Manor, N.Y. 10510

ISBN 0-8128-1541-6

FOR
MICHAEL WISHART
who always travels first-class—
in art as well as life

ACKNOWLEDGEMENTS

Miss Marjory Pegram, who as a child knew Georgina Weldon and was later to inherit her archives, kindly discussed 'Gran' with me at length, as well as letting me see some of Gounod's possessions and communicating to me the contents of a valuable letter Bizet wrote to Gounod. I am also grateful to Edward Grierson, the accomplished biographer of Mrs Weldon. Frank J. Mundy and Anthony J. Charlton, respectively Manager and Deputy Manager of the Royal Albert Hall, offered ready and valued co-operation. Once again I acknowledge with gratitude the assistance of Monsieur André Ménétrat and his colleagues at the Bibliothèque de l'Opéra; the secretarial skill of Mrs D. L. Mackay; and the photographic expertise of Mrs Stella Reed.

CONTENTS

ILLUSTRATIONS

INTRODUCTION

Having chronicled the lives of Saint-Saëns and Massenet, I thought it would be appropriate to complete the trilogy with Gounod. He was, after all, their friend and patron, as he was of Bizet and, to some extent, of Debussy. In spite of the neglect from which he now suffers, he had a considerable influence on the art he practised.

Since his death in 1893 he has been much abused. *Faust*, once the glory of opera houses throughout the world, has slipped from grace. The qualities that enchanted generations of audiences have been cold-shouldered by later ages. This, paradoxically enough, is not a bad thing as the starting-point for a reappraisal. Although *Faust* is a landmark in the history of French music, so far as Gounod's career is concerned it signals a wrong turning. The characteristics that won the praise of contemporaries—its pomp and brilliance—were those most foreign to his true nature. The best things in *Faust* are the quieter episodes where his essentially intimate and lyrical gift was allowed to play freely. The real Gounod is more happily represented by operas like *Mireille* and *le Médecin malgré lui* than by the grandiose affairs that his triumph with *Faust* betrayed him into producing.

At a time when such an example was needed he restored an ideal in French music. Gluck and Mozart gave him his inspiration. He admired in them those features that distinguish his own best writing: pureness, clarity, subtle colouring and refined craftsmanship. He redirected attention to the old French virtues of balance and discretion. At the same time his love of Bach and Palestrina led him to inaugurate the reforms in religious music which were to flower most triumphantly at the end of the century.

Gounod's influence has been potent and far-reaching. It starts with his protégés Saint-Saëns and Bizet, then continues by way of Massenet, who exploited it vigorously. It extends over the years to Debussy's *Pelléas et Mélisande* and is given a concluding polish by Fauré. There is, as somebody once observed, a Gounod slumbering in the soul of every French musician. His Frenchness is inescapable. That may be the reason why he is under a shadow today, for the virtues of elegance and poise are unlikely to be popular in an age that values mass-appeal.

Gounod the man was a bundle of contradictions. His talents were such that he might as easily have become a painter as a composer. In youth he had wanted to be a priest, and throughout the rest of his life he was haunted by religious scruples. One side of his complex personality yearned for the meditative peace of the cloister. The other, just as ardently, hungered after fame and secular excitement. He was perpetually torn between the church and the theatre. The scholar who read and learnedly annotated Saint Augustine was ready to set to music the trashiest libretti if he thought they would bring him success on the stage. The creator of delicate miniatures could also write music of braying vulgarity. An artistic temperament is in itself enough to make life difficult for any man. When the tortures imposed upon it by a religious conscience are taken into account, one is not surprised that Gounod should have been the victim of frequent nervous breakdowns.

The warring elements in his personality made him a doubtful friend and a spiteful enemy. Hypocrisy mingled inextricably with genuine idealism. The promptings of sensuality were a constant trial, and respect for the chastity of his saintly idols failed to overcome his taste for young and pretty girls—the younger the better. True affection was sometimes flawed by envy. He recognized Bizet's talent and encouraged him generously. Then, when the young man produced his masterpiece *Carmen*, some hidden impulse made Gounod shy hastily away from him. It may have been a feeling of insecurity, a weakness in his character that turned him also into the natural prey of dominating women. Several in turn took him under their wing. They all found that, though he was agreeably pliant, his claws were sharp and apt to inflict lasting wounds.

This same insecurity was perhaps the cause of his notoriously excessive politeness. His natural charm was magnified into a compulsion to lavish flattery on everyone he met. A neurotic fear of being disliked made him anxious to secure immediate approval for himself by disarming possible enemies in advance. Like his disciple Massenet, he was to be ridiculed behind his back for the unctuous greetings and emotional embraces he showered on the merest acquaintances. As Chesterfield remarks: 'The world judges from the appearance of things, and not from the reality, which few are able, and still fewer are inclined to fathom.'

When we hear the music of a Wagner or of a Mozart it need not worry us that the one was an unspeakable rogue and the other a weak-chinned creature who delighted in schoolboy obscenities. They become, rather, more interesting, and it is pleasant to realize that artists, even the greatest ones, are fallible human beings. So it is with Gounod. His character was not without a good measure of weaknesses. Yet he went beyond them and wrote music that has its share of beauty.

One last word. This is a biography of Gounod and not a detailed study of his works, though naturally one hopes that it will stimulate interest in his music. Misunderstandings do arise. An elderly criticaster protested that my biography of Massenet told the story of Massenet's life and not 'the eventful history of the Opéra-Comique'. If the arch old fellow is still alive, I have no doubt he will complain that this biography of Gounod does not recount the history of the Paris Opéra. . . .

J.H.

GOUNOD

❦ I ❦

Gounot, Gonnot, Gouniot, Gounaud and Co.

The building known as the Louvre has played, in its time, many parts. It originated during the Crusades, when Philippe Auguste built a defensive wall up to the Seine and added a fortress to defend the districts of Paris which lay on the right bank. The area was already known as the Louvre, either because kennels had been kept there for wolf hunts (*lupara*), or because the fortress was built to a Saxon plan ('lower'). A century afterwards, Charles V turned the simple fortress into a handsome country seat. From then onwards, except for an episode when the English invaded and the Duke of Bedford made off with the contents of the royal library, the Louvre was enlarged, embellished and decorated by successive kings of France. Great architects designed colonnades for it, added whole wings and constructed elaborate façades. Philippe Auguste's fortress became in turn a luxurious retreat, a palace, and a museum for royal treasures. At the end of the eighteenth century it was also a residence for artists. One of the galleries that runs beside the Seine contained the homes and studios of Fragonard, Greuze, Isabey and Vernet. Among the craftsmen who also lived there was the sword-cutler whose sign hung outside at No. 25: GOVNOD FOVRBISSEVR DV ROI.

The name Gounod has an ending frequently met with in the Jura and the Franche-Comté. It was, therefore, from Besançon that the family may well have come. The records of that town preserve details of citizens variously called Gounod, Gounot, Gonnot and Gouniot. They were butchers, vine-growers and tailors. Another Gounot followed the craft of silversmith. His youngest son, Antoine François, was born in 1674. This, it is thought, was the cutler who put up his sign in 1730 at the Louvre, where, since the reign of Henri IV, artists and craftsmen had lived and worked by royal favour.

Antoine died in the early seventeen-fifties. His place in the Louvre and his royal appointment were handed on to a son, Nicolas-François. Nicolas married in middle age. His only child was François-Louis Gounod, later to be the father of the composer of *Faust*. Born at the Louvre in 1758, François as a boy was the playmate of Carle Vernet, the son of the marine painter Joseph, who was a neighbour. The two families were on good terms with each other. On one occasion Joseph Vernet bought a sword from his friend the cutler.

François and Carle went to art lessons together. Their daily routine was strenuous. At five o'clock in the morning they rose to be at their teacher's studio by half-past. Until eight o'clock they sketched a model. For the rest of the day they worked from prints or drawings. From time to time François won medals and distinctions awarded by the Académie Royale de Peinture et de Sculpture. His keenest ambition was to gain the Grand Prix de Rome. While his friend Carle was successful, François was not, and on four occasions he failed in the attempt. Impressed nonetheless by his talent and determination, the authorities made an exception in his favour. In 1787 he was allowed to go to the French Academy in Rome and to study there as a supernumary.

The examples of his work (*envois*) which he sent from Rome for appraisal by the academic committee varied in quality. His delicacy of tone was admired but his irresolute execution deplored. There was, said the examiners, an attractive grace in his productions, but also a coldness which sprang from too close an obsession with antiquity. By 1791 his technique had improved a little. His 'Shepherd at Rest', observed a judge, showed truth of observation and fineness of detail.

In the meantime 'le sieur Gounaud' (the name was to suffer often from the whims of clerks) went to Naples with an architect friend. There the excitements included Vesuvius in eruption, the arrival of the French navy, and a lively encounter with the Neapolitan police. For Gounod and his colleague had been unwise enough to draw sketches of the town. They were taken for spies and marched before an outraged magistrate, who confiscated their subversive drawings.

During the next two years there was political trouble in Rome as well. An enthusiastic body of papal guards proposed to burn the French Academy to the ground and massacre its inmates. There were riots when, in 1793, on orders from the new régime in Paris, the

Bourbon arms were removed from the façade of the Academy. François Gounod and a fellow student discreetly removed to Tuscany, where anti-French opinion was not so strong as elsewhere. They wandered on to Venice, despite an erroneous consular message that 'Gouneaux' and his colleagues were approaching the French border and safety. The Republic of Venice promptly expelled the two artists, who, while tart exchanges flew between embassies, travelled to Genoa. From there they went through Provence and Languedoc, arriving in Paris at the start of 1794. François in time was appointed art teacher at the École Polytechnique.

His parent, old Nicolas, was now in dismal straits. At the Revolution all the occupants of the Louvre had been ordered out. He was allowed to stay on condition that he gave details of the people living in his household. With a fist more used to handling cutler's tools than pen and paper, he indited: 'Sir, Following the Request you made Mee to give you my name, status And my Age, together with That of the Persons who lives with mee, I comply. My name is Gounod artist Patent to the King live in the Galleries of the L'ouvre in my seventy-ninth yeer, And crippled For eighteen years since, Thee names and ages of the Persons who Lives with me are . . . .' The list does not include his wife, who had died in 1786.

The old man lived on in tremulous decrepitude until 1795. Each change of government threatened expulsion from the Louvre, and each political crisis brought with it the fear of homelessness. He was condemned to spend his days in a large wheelchair. On a table fixed to the arms lay the playing-cards with which he trifled away the tedious hours. A dressing-gown of a bold flowery pattern draped his shrunken body, and on his head there flopped a night-cap done up with a coloured silk ribbon. His artist son, fresh from the Italian adventure, nursed him with care and tenderness until the end.

At his father's death François inherited the rooms in the Louvre. They were crammed with the litter of more than half a century's occupation. The furniture was shabby and worm-eaten. Shapeless heaps of books sprawled across the floor. Dust lay thick on plans and drawings scattered at random. Lying among the jumble of objects that cluttered up the place were the dismembered bones of a yellowing skeleton. Not long after François had become master of the house, an elderly cousin died and left him a sum of money enough to produce a modest annual income. In 1796 he resigned his teaching post and made off as fast as he could for Italy.

19

He came back after something less than a year. The fruits of the trip to his favourite land may have been the pictures he showed at the Exhibition of 1799. These comprised a representation of 'Phyllis taking refreshment' and a 'Portrait of a lady with a book in her hand'. Other subjects, presented in the blameless style with which his Grand Prix examiners were familiar, portrayed 'A milkmaid taking her milk to market' and 'A young lady talking to a young gentleman at the window'.

In 1805 the Government decided to unhouse the artists who had lived for so long in the galleries of the Louvre. By way of compensation they were given, François among them, a small pension. With the aid of a cousin he succeeded in clearing out the chaos of seventy-five years. The crumbling furniture, the mildewed books, the splintered skeleton and the grimy papers were thrown on the fire. The cousin who helped him was probably Charles Tardieu, who had married a girl from Rouen and settled there. No doubt François stayed with him for a time in Rouen, since he came to make the acquaintance of Madame Tardieu's younger sister and, soon afterwards, married her.

Victoire Lemachois, born in 1780, was the daughter of a Rouen *avocat*. The Revolution brought disaster to the family. Her father lost his post in the magistrature, and at an early age Victoire was introduced to a life both hard and penurious. When she was only eleven years old she was giving piano lessons to increase the household's tiny income. Her mother, moreover, had separated from her father, and Victoire taught herself to read and write on her own. She learned by the same economical system to draw and to play the piano. Dissatisfied with her achievement so far, she determined to seek the advice of a qualified musician. Laboriously she hoarded the small cash put aside from what her pupils paid her. When she had saved enough she took the coach from Rouen for the three-day journey to Paris. In the capital she saw Louis Adam, teacher of the piano at the Conservatoire and father of the composer who wrote *Giselle*. He recognized her talent and offered to give her lessons. But she was too young to live alone in Paris, so it was agreed that every three months she would make the journey from Rouen to take a lesson. Full of admiration for her tenacity, Adam paid for her to have a piano at home so as to save her the expense of hiring one.

The strenuous Rouen-Paris arrangement had continued for some time when the nomadic virtuoso Nicolas Hüllmandel arrived in

Victoire's home town. In Paris, which he was forced to leave at the Revolution, he had established himself as a brilliant player of the piano, harpsichord and glass harmonica. His pupils had included Auber. He contributed the article on the harpsichord to Diderot's *Encyclopédie*, and in London, where he spent the last years of his life, he wrote two fat volumes combining musical theory with a teaching method for the piano. Like Adam, he was impressed by Victoire's ability, and his teaching helped to realize the considerable promise shown by the child musician.

Nothing more is known of Victoire's life until she married François Gounod in Rouen. The date was 1806. She was then twenty-six years old and her husband forty-seven. Her family did not, apparently, object to the disparity in age, and the couple removed to Paris. They set up house at No. 11 place Saint-André-des-Arts in the Latin Quarter. The building has since been demolished. A century or so before, Voltaire was baptized in an old church there. Twenty years later a near neighbour of Gounod's would have been Baudelaire.

François continued his agreeably aimless way of life. Marriage had not awakened him to ambition, nor had it inspired him to seek a career. His son was to tell how François, having entered a competition, was so struck by what he thought to be the quality of a friend's entry that he frankly told him so and destroyed his own, judging it unworthy to figure beside such excellent work. The curator of the Louvre, who admired François' talent, offered him a commission to make engravings of all the coins and medals in the museum. It would bring him an income of 10,000 francs a year, more than enough to keep a family in comfort. François turned it down. Ambitious ideas frightened him. He quailed at long-term projects. His health, he explained, was not equal to sustained effort. It was true that he lacked robustness.

He preferred to paint as the fancy took him. Pictures of the nobility came at an ambling pace from his studio. A portrait of the duc de Berry made a small sensation on account of its lifelike quality, and an engraving of a 'Mercury in Parian marble' was mentioned kindly. As soon as he had captured the features, the look, the attitude of the sitter, he tired of the work. Details like sleeves, jackets, shawls and dresses bored him. Then Victoire would readily take over the brush and dab in the wearisome buttons and insignia for him. It was Victoire who cleaned and prepared his palette. She watched over his work and made up for his vagueness with her own energy and decision. She adored him.

At the fall of Napoleon and the return of Louis XVIII François showed a rare initiative. The Bourbons had been the patrons of his family and had given them work and shelter at the Louvre. In 1814 he took steps to seek royal favour again. He was rewarded with an appointment as official artist to the duc de Berry and as drawing master to the pages of the King's Chamber. This second post was honorary until 1821, when François, having indicated that something more tangible would be appreciated, was granted a salary of 1,000 francs which rose next year to 1,200.

He was a gentle, contemplative man. François did not want to make a name for himself as an artist. Neither did he burn with zeal to guide the young. His greatest pleasure in life was to browse along the quays and there to pick up items that would add lustre to an art collection which was already substantial. It contained works by Rembrandt, Van Dyck and Chardin. Among others were sketches and drawings by Michelangelo, Jordaens, Poussin and Latour. There was nothing François enjoyed more than looking through his pictures and prints and medallions. The matching up of landscapes from different schools so that tone and style would blend happily on his wall provoked hours of delicious reflection. The sight and touch of medals dug up from the ruins at Paestum took him back again to his student days in Italy. And then, with a sigh, he would shut away these beautiful things and prepare for the long tramp out to Versailles where the King's pages awaited, in no great enthusiasm, their drawing lesson.

In 1807 a son had been born and christened Louis Urbain. He appeared to have inherited his mother's musical gift, for he had a good singing voice and took lessons on the 'cello. Eleven years later on 17 June 1818, another child was born to the Gounod family in the place Saint-André-des-Arts. It was a boy whom they called Charles François. Soon after his birth the family moved out to Versailles, where his father could be on the spot to give the pages their lessons without having to make the wearisome journey each time. They were given an official lodging in one of the large buildings that overlook the ornamental lake known as the Pièce d'eau des Suisses. In the distance, on the heights above Versailles, marched the woods of Satory.

Among the earliest memories of Charles, the second son, were the

lake and the woods. He also remembered many queer winding stair-
ways and a vast corridor running the length of the apartment which
seemed, in his childish imagination, to go on for ever. His father was,
for him, a quiet, bespectacled figure who sat reading, his legs crossed,
beside the fire. The figure wore thick flannel trousers, a short jacket
with white stripes, and on its head a cotton bonnet of the sort
favoured by Ingres. The small boy lay on the floor copying on his
slate the shapes of eyes, noses and mouths which his father had
drawn for him as a model.

François Gounod died in 1823 at the age of sixty-five. His widow
found herself left with two children to bring up. Urbain was fifteen
and Charles four. Once again, as in her childhood, Victoire Gounod
had to fend for herself. And once again her enterprise was equal to
the occasion. She quickly obtained tuition in lithography so that she
might continue the private drawing lessons with which her husband
had augmented his official income. The pupils, knowing her also to
be a musician, began to ask if she would give piano lessons to their
sisters. In time her piano teaching crowded out the art lessons, and
history repeated itself in the spectacle of the middle-aged widow
supporting her family by the means which, thirty years before, she
had as a child been driven to adopt. This income was increased
by a small allowance from her husband's successor in the royal
post and by the proceeds, not inconsiderable, from the sale of his art
collection.

Had Charles Gounod's father survived it is possible that the boy
would have become an artist. At a very early age he showed a talent
both for art and music. In later years he claimed to have imbibed
music with his mother's milk, for it was her custom to sing as she
fed him. Before he could talk he was able to distinguish between
major and minor keys, to sense intervals and to appreciate modulation. One day, hearing a beggar sing outside in a minor key, he enquired: 'Maman, why is he singing in such a weepy key of C ?'

The notes of music were soon as familiar to him as the words of
language. His brother, who was not so gifted, caused Charles' sensitive ear much pain by the wrong notes he scattered when practising
the 'cello. One day the proud mother invited the composer Jadin to
witness the child prodigy in action. Jadin, the author of songs then
fashionable, made him stand facing the wall in a corner of the room.
Then he played at the piano a succession of chords and modulations.
At each new modulation he would ask: 'What key am I in ?' Each

time the boy answered correctly. Jadin, Gounod recalled, was amazed, his mother triumphant.

In 1825, when Gounod was seven, his mother fell ill. The doctor, seeing his presence in the house as an added reason for the fatigue caused by giving music lessons all day, suggested he be taken each morning to a boarding school near at hand and then collected in time for dinner. The visiting music teacher there was a young singer called Gilbert Duprez. The thirteenth of twenty-two children born to a Parisian perfumer, Duprez was later to be a famous tenor and the star in many first performances of operas by Verdi, Halévy, Auber and Berlioz. His presence on stage was not imposing and he tended to exaggerate certain mannerisms, but the smoothness of his singing conquered all. He was still in his teens with a glorious career before him when he met the diminutive Gounod. Seeing the child could read music as easily as a book, he would lift him on to his knee and say to him, as the other pupils gathered round: 'Now then, little fellow, show them how it ought to be done.' And the little fellow did.

His mother, though duly proud of the boy's precociousness, did not favour the musical life for him. Knowing only too well the practical difficulties that lie in wait for whoever follows the arts, she preferred him to take up a solid professional career. That of notary, perhaps? There was always a demand for contracts and deeds and agreements to be drawn up. There were far fewer clients anxious to hear symphonies and quartets.

As the first serious step in his preparation for life, Gounod spent a year at a school in the rue de Vaugirard, which, besides having been the scene of his early education, also has the distinction of being the longest street in Paris. He went on to a school in the rue de l'Estrapade. Though the sinister name of the street recalls the harsher aspect of military discipline, Gounod's experience there was entirely happy. He left after two years' primary education with a certificate from his headmaster which read, 'This pupil's character is open, happy, lively sometimes to the point of friskiness, and a little restless, though generally excellent, all things considered. He is a pleasant child who will give satisfaction to his masters and who will become the pride and consolation of his mother.'

In October 1829, at the age of eleven, he entered, as a boarder, the Lycée Saint-Louis to which he had been awarded an exhibition. The school was congenial and the headmaster, a gentle abbé, gravely paternal. Gounod was not a bad pupil, though moods of flightiness

24

made him on occasion an unreliable one. Once, for committing a particularly headstrong offence, he was locked in a room on his own and condemned to bread and water until he had completed some vast imposition—a matter of hundreds of 'lines'. He was overcome with guilt at the thought of his mother. A condition of his being at the school was that Madame Gounod should pay three-quarters of the fee. Gradually, as a result of good conduct and satisfactory work, this was to be reduced until his education would no longer be a financial burden to her. He looked at the bread before him, earned by his mother's incessant labours, and he burst into tears. He thought of the Fates crying to Orestes, 'He has killed his mother!' and his mind filled with anguish.

It was natural that a classical allusion should have come to him at a moment of emotion, for Latin was his best subject. Few prize-days went by without his receiving an award or an honourable mention for Latin prose or verse. In his fourth year he also distinguished himself in Greek composition. By then the gentle ecclesiastic who ruled over the school when he entered it had been deposed by the Revolution of 1830. In his place there reigned a supporter of the new régime much given to putting the boys through military exercises in the yard. He strutted among them with his shoulders thrown back and head held high. His right hand lay between the buttons of his coat in the manner of Napoleon. His bearing was that of a drill instructor.

The neo-Napoleon was in turn displaced by another headmaster, this time a pedagogue of less rigorous habits. Events now occurred which were to decide once and for all the direction of Gounod's life. He was already in love with music. In the winter of 1831 he had done so well at his studies that, together with other good scholars, he was admitted to the school's annual Saint Charlemagne dinner and allowed two days' holiday at home. As a reward his mother promised him that he should go to hear Rossini's *Otello*. The stars were to include those famous singers Malibran, Rubini and Lablache. He was beside himself with joy and impatience.

On the evening of the opera he was so wrought up that he could not eat. His mother's threat that if he did not do justice to his dinner there would be no trip to the theatre was enough to make him bolt the food untasted. 'With such a threat,' he recalled, 'I'd have swallowed heroically anything anybody wanted me to!' He and his brother queued up for the cheap tickers which were all Madame Gounod could afford. It was bitterly cold and for two hours they shivered and froze. At last they entered the theatre. Gounod was seized with a sacred terror, 'as if at the approach of some imposing and fearsome mystery; at one and the same time I was lost in a confused and hitherto unknown emotion: desire and fear of what was about to happen in front of me.... There was a long wait before the performance began, but time seemed short; the auditorium, the chandelier, the grand surroundings, all dazzled me. In the end the ritual three taps were heard; the conductor raised his bow, a religious silence fell, and the overture began.'

His heart thudded as if it would burst. The evening passed in a delirium of excitement. When the curtain fell he walked home still dazed. The prose of everyday life no longer existed. It was replaced by the poetry of a world created from music. He later went to a performance of *Don Giovanni*. Mozart inspired emotions still more intense than had Rossini. The theatre became a temple where he heard a god speaking. Rossini had charmed and delighted the ear. Mozart revealed truth of expression and perfect beauty. The darkling chords and the ominous chromatic phrases that open the *Don Giovanni* overture struck a holy terror into his soul. His head fell on his mother's shoulder and he murmured ecstatically: 'Oh, Maman! what music! This is *really* music!'

What was the point of geography and history and all the other boring school subjects? In class, when he should have been writing out his lesson notes, he took to scribbling music. An angry master tore these furtive productions to pieces. Gounod protested. He was punished. No sooner had he purged his crime than he committed it again. More confinements followed, more batches of lines' were to be written, more bread and water was to be taken in resentful solitude.

Round about the age of sixteen he made up his mind. He sat down and wrote a long letter to his mother. There came a time, he declared, when a child, without neglecting the obedience he owed to his parents, began to think for himself about what his future should be. His inexperience prevented him from weighing up the merits of careers in general. Of one thing, however, he was certain: he himself had a very pronounced leaning to a career in the arts. He would not, he added, be so presumptuous as to infer that he was born to be an artist of some sort. He thought, nonetheless, that only in music would he find the happiness which he sought from life. 'For I can find nothing more impressive nor more moving than a beautiful piece of music. For me, music is such a sweet companion that a very great happiness would be denied me if I were prevented from experiencing it. How happy one is to understand that heavenly language! It is a treasure I would not exchange for many others, and it is a delight which will, I hope, fill every moment of my life.'

This unusual document, graced with classical allusion and written in the eloquent style of a prize-winning rhetoric student, so moved Madame Gounod that she asked the advice of her son's headmaster. He happened to be something of a musician himself.

'So, mon petit Charles,' said the headmaster, 'you want to be a musician?'

The boy agreed, nervous but determined.

'Pooh! being a musician isn't a profession!'

'So it's not a profession to be Mozart, Weber, Meyerbeer, Rossini . . . ?'

'You're being difficult!'

The headmaster tried another argument: 'Everybody can't be a Mozart. At your age Mozart had already given proof of genius. Show me what you can do. Then we'll see about it.'

He scribbled out the words of a Méhul aria and gave the piece of paper to Gounod. 'Go and set this to music. Write me some Méhul if you can. As for Mozart, there's time enough for him.'

It was easy for the boy to set words in the style of Méhul. Two hours later Gounod came back. His setting was complete with piano accompaniment.[1]

'Sing it to me!' was the order. Gounod did as he was told, and, at the end, looked timidly at his judge. Tears rolled down the headmaster's cheeks.

'It's beautiful, it's very beautiful, my child. . . . Be a musician then, since the devil forces you to it! It's impossible to fight against something like this.'

Faced now with the combined forces of the headmaster and her son, Madame Gounod bowed to circumstance and took Charles to see Anton Reicha, then teacher of composition at the Conservatoire. Reicha was a Czech who had settled in Paris and gained a reputation as theorist and teacher. He claimed that the study of algebra had enabled him to penetrate the mysteries of harmony. His 'Thirty-six fugues for piano based on a new system' aroused controversy. Other

[1] The manuscript survives in a private collection. It is dated 20 January 1835.

writers claimed that all he had done was to refurbish a method frequently used by seventeenth-century Italian composers. His opponents were incensed when he coolly described himself as having been responsible for restoring the art of fugue to an honoured position. Unsuccessful at his first attempt to enter the Académie des Beaux Arts, he addressed to the members of that body a dignified remonstrance which pointed out the absolute necessity of reserving places among their number for distinguished theorists. Persistence was eventually rewarded, and he in time ascended to academic honours on the death of Boieldieu. No one today is likely to perform his opera *Oubaldi, ou les Français en Égypte,* a topical work inspired by Napoleon's Egyptian adventure, nor is it likely that our age will thrill to the moving accents of *l'Ermite dans l'île de Formose.* Reicha owes his niche in history to the fact that he was the teacher of Berlioz, Franck and Liszt.

Before confiding her son to Reicha, Madame Gounod whispered to him: 'Make life hard for him, please. Go out of your way to show him the difficulties involved in music! If you can send him back to me hating music, I shall bless you!'

After a year of private lessons with Reicha, Madame Gounod inquired about her son's progress.

'Alas, Madam,' she was told, 'the best you can do is to resign yourself. This child is gifted, he knows what he wants and where he's going. Nothing puts him off, nothing discourages him. He now knows everything I can teach him—except that he doesn't know what he knows.'

All this time Gounod had been assiduously following lessons at the Lycée Saint-Louis. One day his prowess at Latin made him the hero of his schoolfellows. Their teacher had threatened to cancel the Easter holiday because one of them failed to own up to some prank or other. The culprit remained silent. Then Gounod had an idea. Their teacher was very partial to Latin verse. So the star pupil quickly composed an ode lamenting the sorrow of little birds shut up in a cage. In impeccable metre and well-chosen epithets, the verse evoked their regret at being deprived of the woods, the sun, the open air, and echoed their cry for freedom. The composition, anonymously delivered to the master's desk, was read by him with delighted amusement. Who had written it? Gounod? 'Gentlemen', said the master, 'I waive the punishment. You shall have your holiday. And thank Gounod, whose work has earned your deliverance.'

In 1835, soon after his seventeenth birthday, Gounod left school. His mother had accepted that music was the only career for him. He agreed, though, to sit the *baccalauréat* examination, and in the following year he passed it, having already done well in rhetoric. Later he was to regret not having studied on the science side. It would, he said, have enabled him to understand so many things which, as a humanist, he was only half able to grasp. But he was a young man in a hurry, and the glamour of music overshadowed everything else.

At this stage he had long since absorbed the influences and attitudes which helped to shape his character. The crucial early years which, according to some, have already completed their work of defining personality before the age of five, had made him what he was to be. He could not escape from the mould in which he was cast. The effect of heredity was clear. From his father, the product of a long line of craftsmen and silversmiths, he inherited a love for the arts in general, an appreciation of fine things and a keen visual sense. François Gounod passed on to him as well a temperament that was impatient of everything that did not respond to his immediate interests. With it there went a sensitiveness that inclined to morbidity and a softness of fibre that verged on the languid. A feminine element in his character made him react to life with extremes of emotion and to view everything in highly personal terms. From his strong-willed and practical mother, however, he received another artistic impulse which expressed itself in the genius for music. She also gave him, as a counterweight to the dreamier qualities of his father, a vein of hard determination that strengthened his purpose and often made him a surprisingly tough figure in the hectic rough and tumble of nineteenth-century French music.

It is significant that, as with his younger colleagues Massenet and Saint-Saëns, the most important person in Gounod's youth, one whose memory never left him and whose influence sustained him to the day of his death, was his mother. When he was nearly sixty he was to write, in the preface to his memoirs:

If I have been able to be, say, or do anything worthwhile in the course of my life, it is to my mother that I owe it; it is to her that I wish all the honour to be paid. She it was who fed me, brought me up and *formed* me: not in her image, alas! something that would have been only too beautiful; and what has been lacking is not her fault, but mine.

She lies beneath a gravestone as simple as her life had been.

May these recollections by a well-loved son leave upon her grave a wreath more durable than our short-lived 'everlasting' flowers [*immortelles d'un jour*], and may they ensure for her memory, beyond the limits of my own life, a respect which I would wish to have made eternal!

§II§

Rome and Palestrina

The Conservatoire at that time was the fiercely guarded domain of Cherubini. He had at last come into his own after years in the shadow of the neglect to which Napoleon's enmity consigned him. The tyrant liked neither the man nor his music, and enjoyed twitting him in front of others. Pained and discouraged, Cherubini retired from music for a while to console himself with painting and gardening. After Napoleon's fall the composer gradually rose to play a leading part in musical affairs. Largely due to the malicious and inventive wit of his recalcitrant pupil Berlioz, Cherubini has come down in history as a peppery old buffoon. Haydn and Beethoven, however, admired his musicianship, and today there is a growing respect for the romantic spirit which inhabits the solid classical structure of Cherubini's best works, and for the craftsmanship and gaiety which mark his operas from *les Deux journées* onwards to *Ali Baba, ou les quarante voleurs*.

When, in 1836, Madame Gounod and her son presented themselves at the Conservatoire, the boy brought with him some of the lesson books he had worked on with his teacher Reicha. Cherubini impatiently waved them aside. 'He'll have to begin again in a different style,' said the director of the Conservatoire, his Italian accent thickening as it always did when he delivered a judgement. 'I don't like Reicha's style. He's a German. The lad must follow the Italian method: I'll put him in my old pupil Halévy's class for counterpoint and fugue.'

Jacques Fromental Halévy was then thirty-seven. He belonged to that talented family which produced the writer Élie and the dramatist Ludovic, who collaborated on twenty or so Offenbach operettas and many plays, besides providing Bizet with the libretto for *Carmen*. In the year before Gounod entered the Conservatoire, Halévy had gained a brilliant success with *la Juive*. It launched him on a career which was to make him one of the busiest and most applauded composers of opera under the Second Empire. Although *la Juive* is the only work by which he is generally remembered, a string of elegant operas and ballets gave him popularity with audiences of the time. He was an amiable man of quick intelligence, who also wrote articles and memoires which make pleasant reading still. They were praised by no less a judge than Sainte-Beuve.

It is doubtful whether Gounod learned much from Halévy, charming and sympathetic though he was. His own theatrical affairs took up so much of his time that he had little to spare for his pupils. It was difficult for the hard-pressed musician to concentrate on teaching fugue while he was trying to think up a finale to his current opera. When he told his class to get on with some written work in lesson time, it was a heavensent opportunity for him to complete the orchestration of some long-overdue trio a theatre manager had been insisting on for weeks.

In the composition classes Gounod was taught by Henry Berton. At the age of nineteen Berton had written *les Promesses de mariage*, the first of close on fifty operas in which he relied for success on clever craftsmanship rather than inspiration. As a teacher he was fascinated by the problems of harmony and even produced what he called 'a genealogical tree of chords'. Upon this arboreal fancy he based a treatise on harmony. He subsequently wrote, in four remorseless volumes, a dictionary of chords, and he was partial, in the intervals between his more academic publications, to hearty vituperation against Rossini.

Berton's importance to Gounod's development lay in his warm advocacy of Mozart. As musical director of the Opéra Italien early that century, he had been responsible for the first performance in France of *The Marriage of Figaro*.

'Study Mozart,' Berton would keep repeating to Gounod. 'Study *The Marriage of Figaro*!'

'He was right,' Gounod commented later. 'It ought to be the musician's breviary. Mozart is to Palestrina and Bach what the New Testament is to the Old in the spirit of the Bible, one and indivisible.'

Berton died soon after and was succeeded by Jean Lesueur. Known at one time as the 'abbé' Lesueur, though he was never received into holy orders, he had been placed, at the age of sixteen, in charge of music at the cathedral of Séez. A little later he graduated to

1. Gounod's birthplace, 11 place Saint-André-des Arts, Paris, since demolished to make way for the rue Danton. (Photo: Stella Mayes Reed.)

2. Gounod's wife Anna (née Zimmermann) in 1859, seven years after her marriage. Portrait by Ingres. (Photo: Stella Mayes Reed.)

a similar post at Notre Dame in Paris, where he caused a sensation by introducing symphonic music into the services. This was the start of a career which was punctuated by libellous pamphlets and anonymous broadsides directed at his innovations. His departure from the post was engineered by a manoeuvre eminently worthy of the finesse with which ecclesiastical intrigue is traditionally conducted. He was then submerged beneath a stormy sea of calumny and defamation. The pamphlets written against him may be read today with profit and pleasure: profit, because they contain many a useful lesson in the art of invective, and pleasure because they are couched in the most graceful, though deadly, eighteenth-century style. His fortunes were restored when he attracted the favourable notice of Napoleon, and the battered survivor of many an ancien-régime scandal began the new century as a flourishing and envied figure. His grand opera *Ossian, ou les bardes,* which was based on that fake Gaelic legend which so enthralled the early Romantics, achieved a triumph. Napoleon gave him a snuff-box on which was engraved: '*L'Empereur des Français à l'auteur des Bardes*'. Even the fall of his patron did little to disturb the steady rate of Lesueur's progress. Throughout the different régimes that followed he prospered on an unbroken diet of honours and distinctions.

When Gounod knew Lesueur, he had the air of an ancient patriarch. Forty years of misfortune followed by another thirty of success had taught him all there was to know about human nature. His face was pale as wax, his manner grave and resigned. He treated his pupil with a fatherly tenderness. So many battles fought, so many insults endured, had only served to strengthen the convictions he defended so stoutly. Gounod was an eager recipient of his ideas for injecting church music with a colouring of theatrical excitement.

When Lesueur died his place was taken by Ferdinand Paer, the Italian composer whose ambition had led him to France. He was, perhaps, a better diplomatist than musician, for in his relations with Napoleon he showed himself to be such a polished courtier that the Emperor rewarded him with an income of 50,000 francs. For this he was ready to do any errands his master commanded. The restoration of the monarchy found him still scheming and soliciting with all his old zest the sources of patronage. He had written a *Barbier de Séville,* and when Rossini's version was announced he did his best to suppress it. But his practised gift of cabal was powerless, and as Berton's successor at the Opéra Italien he had the unspeakable chagrin of seeing his rival's opera overshadow his own effort completely—and, what is more, in a production for which he, Paer, was responsible.

The Italian influence at the Conservatoire was notably a strong one. For Cherubini, the school which descended from Palestrina was the beginning of all enlightenment. Paer supported him by his example and teaching: his operas followed the style of Cimarosa and Paisiello, and these were the models he proposed to his students. Halévy, the pupil of Cherubini, had begun his career at the Opéra Italien, and his later works showed the trace of his early apprenticeship. So the teachers Gounod worked with confirmed and strengthened the leaning he already had towards Italian music. In addition there was Berton holding up Mozart for his admiration and Lesueur urging the need to bring secular methods into church music. Just as Gounod's personal characteristics were clearly indicated early in life, so too were his musical affinities.

On the eve of his nineteenth birthday in 1837 Gounod made his first attempt to win the Prix de Rome. It was an honour that had eluded his father on four occasions. Perhaps because of this, Gounod had made up his mind to triumph, however much the effort cost him. He was awarded only the second prize for his cantata *Marie Stuart et Rizzio*. It was some consolation to him that in the same year his name appeared for the first time on the programme of a public concert. Admittedly it figured as 'Gourot', but the persistent inability of printers to get his name right was outweighed by the pleasure of hearing his Scherzo and an extract from *Marie Stuart et Rizzio* played before an audience.

Next year things went even worse for him. His Prix de Rome entry failed even to be placed. His mother, in order to cheer up her son and herself, took him on a short holiday to Switzerland. They wandered on mules at a gentle pace from Geneva by way of Chamonix, the Oberland and the lakes back to Basle. Each morning Madame Gounod, a hale fifty-eight-year-old, was up early to prepare everything for the day's travel before waking her son. He returned to Paris full of new enthusiasm for work and determined more than ever to conquer the Prix de Rome.

In October a service was held at the church of Saint-Roch on the anniversary of Lesueur's death. Among the composer's pupils who wrote music for the occasion was Gounod. The event was attended by Berlioz, who, then working as music critic for the *Revue et Gazette musicale*, told his readers: 'Especially noteworthy was an *Agnus* for three solo voices, with chorus, by M. Gounod, the youngest of Lesueur's pupils, which we find to be beautiful, very beautiful. Everything about it is novel and refined: the melodic line, the modulations and the harmony. M. Gounod has shown that much can be expected of him.' Although the two musicians did not yet know each other personally, Gounod was one of the few to appreciate the genius of Berlioz. The latter's *Roméo et Juliette* was being rehearsed one day in the hall of the Conservatoire. As soon as his lesson was finished, Gounod rushed off to hear 'that strange, passionate, convulsive music, which revealed to me such new and colourful horizons'. He was so struck by the grandeur of the finale that for days afterwards one of the phrases rang persistently in his head. A little while later he made the acquaintance of Berlioz.[1] Full of the excitement of *Roméo et Juliette*, Gounod played over at the piano the phrase that had burned itself into his mind.

Berlioz looked at him with amazement. 'Where the devil did you hit on that?' he asked.

'At one of your rehearsals.'

So prodigal of his inspirations was Berlioz that he could not believe his ears. He was then thirty-six, fifteen years older than Gounod and still regarded as something of a freak by the musical world in general. Young as he was, Gounod could see that Berlioz was doomed to be 'one of the famous victims of that painful privilege: being an exception! Exceptions must inevitably suffer, and, inevitably too, they must cause suffering. How can you expect the mob (the *profanum vulgus* that Horace detested) to recognize itself and to admit its inability to judge when confronted with that daring little David who has the nerve to give a flat denial in the face of ingrained habits and sovereign routine?' And with a shrewd knowledge of Berlioz' character, Gounod goes on to compare him with Alceste, the hero of Molière's *le Misanthrope*, whose rugged honesty and failure to compromise with the vices of society turn his life into misery. Berlioz, he says, was all of a piece: unable to make concessions, disgusted by the petty shifts of everyday existence, he was capricious and ill-tempered only because his acute sensibility had been worn raw by trials that are

[1] This must have been in 1839, before the 24 November, date of the first performance of Berlioz' *Roméo et Juliette*. Gounod, who was always vague about dates, speaks of it as being 'a few days after' the rehearsal. (Préface à la correspondance de Berlioz,' in *Mémoires d'un artiste* (Calmann-Lévy, 1896), p.338.)

the lot of a genius who is forced to see lesser men gain the rewards that should be his due. But, as Saint-Saëns, another of Berlioz' protégés, was to find, those who were admitted to his friendship treasured the essential sweetness of a kind and simple man. There is little doubt that Berlioz' *Roméo et Juliette* suggested to Gounod the opera that he himself was to write some twenty-five years later.

In 1839, the year of his twenty-first birthday, Gounod made his last attempt on the Grand Prix de Rome. This time he was successful, and on the 30 May a committee of judges awarded him the prize by twenty-three votes out of twenty-five. His cantata *Fernand* was based on a text written by a noble poetaster, senator and member of the Institut de France, who, as was the tradition with authors of Prix de Rome libretti, could boast of attainment in all fields save that of literary distinction. Another triumph that came Gounod's way in this period when it seemed that destiny had at last decided to recognize his struggling family was the performance in the church of Saint-Eustache of a mass he had been asked to compose. Though he was unable to afford the services of a professional copyist, his mother gladly took on the formidable task of writing out all the orchestral parts.

After the performance of the Mass a letter arrived at the flat in the rue de l'Éperon where Gounod and his mother then lived. 'Bravo, dear fellow whom I knew as a child!' it read. 'All honour to the *Gloria*, the *Credo*, and especially the *Sanctus*. It is beautiful and truly religious! Bravo and thank you. You have made me very happy.' The signature was that of Gounod's old headmaster at the Lycée Saint-Louis, the man who had first appreciated his musical gifts.

Madame Gounod could rightly be proud of her two sons. Charles, the younger, was now brilliantly launched on his musical career. His older brother Urbain was already a promising architect. Perhaps foreseeing Charles' success, Urbain had preferred not to enter for the Prix de Rome in the architectural section so as to avoid the possibility of depriving his mother of both her sons on their absence in Italy. He had entered for and won another prize, and at the annual ceremony in 1839 she enjoyed the experience of seeing Urbain and Charles receive their awards on the same day. Torn between feelings of joy at his success and sorrow at his departure, Madame Gounod said farewell to Charles on the 5 December as he set off on the journey to Rome.

From the rue de l'Éperon Gounod went to the rue Jean-Jacques

Rousseau where he joined two of his fellow laureates, Hector Lefuel the architect and the artist Vauthier. Their trunks were loaded on to the Marseille coach, and for the twentieth time Gounod felt nervously in his pocket to assure himself that his 600 francs' travelling allowance was intact. It was dark when the coach lumbered off at eight o'clock. They bumped over the cobblestones of the rue du Louvre, past lighted shop windows and through crowds of people swirling about the narrow streets. Paris was smaller in those days, and quite soon they were rolling along the main road to Marseille.

Their first stage was Lyon. After the horses had been changed and hot drinks taken, the travellers huddled together in the coach, their feet buried in straw thickly laid on the floor, for the air was bitter outside and the wind chill. They followed the Rhône down to Avignon and Arles, and then cut across to Marseille. At Marseille they transferred from the coach into a *vettura*, the old-fashioned cab which, to Gounod's regret, was soon to be superseded by the railway train: 'The *vettura*, which allowed you to stop, to look, and to admire in peace all the places through which—if not under which—the roaring locomotive now carries you like a common parcel and hurtles you through space with the fury of a meteor!' Thanks to the *vettura* he was able to enjoy at a leisurely rate the beauties of the Corniche as it wound along the coastline high above the sea's edge. At every point there were expansive views of the sea and the off-shore islands. Below, a thin white filament traced the spot where the waves came up to the beach. Above and beyond, the blue sea glittered in sharp sunlight. It was, he thought, a perfect introduction to the charms of Italy and to the picturesque route they were to follow by way of Monaco, Mentone, Pisa, Sienna, and Florence. On 27 January they came to journey's end.

Rome, he hoped, was to initiate him into, 'the grand, austere beauties of nature and art'. At first he was disappointed. As he looked out of his window at the soft outlines of the dome of Saint Peter's, he felt a wave of depression in his solitude. Despite the friendly companionship of twenty-two students of his own age, despite the gay reunions twice a day round the table in the familiar dining room hung with the portraits of earlier and illustrious *pensionnaires*, he could not overcome his melancholy. Where he had expected grandeur and majesty, he found squalor and confusion. Instead of ancient temples and stately monuments, he discovered the vulgarity and dirt of a provincial town.

It was some time before the true nature of Rome was revealed to him. He had been, he later realized, too young to understand at first sight that what he ingenuously took for coldness was austerity, that the seeming haughtiness of the atmosphere came from centuries of grave meditation, and that the deep serenity of the place concealed inexhaustible riches. Gradually his feelings of disappointment dropped away. He came to know the city better, and so began a love affair with Rome that lasted all his life. Once again the founders of the French Academy in Rome had been justified in their intention of exposing musicians and artists to the influence of an ancient culture. 'I made myself familiar with Rome,' said Gounod, 'and managed to emerge from the cocoon I'd been wrapped up in until then.'

Another reason for Gounod's awakening enjoyment was the presence of Ingres as director of the Villa Medici. Ingres was then sixty years old and the embattled defender of Classic principles against the Romantic ideas expressed by Delacroix. He was apt to be rough-tempered and violent in argument. Six years previously, angered by the reception Paris gave to one of his most ambitious pictures, he had decided to return to Italy, which he knew and loved. His appointment to the Villa Medici enabled him to live in a country he found sympathetic and, quite as important, to influence the young artists who came under his care. In Rome he had the opportunity of indoctrinating the best of the pupils being turned out by art schools—the best, that is, in academic terms—and could warn them against the dangerous example of the unspeakable Delacroix. 'Drawing is the probity of art,' he would argue. To Gounod, on one occasion, he remarked: 'There is no grace without strength.'

Ingres had known Gounod's father and admired his draughtsmanship. His first words as the young musician entered the Villa Medici were: 'So you're the one who's Gounod! Dieu! how like your father you are!'

François Gounod, declared Ingres in terms that warmed his son's heart, had been an artist of talent, a man of charming character and conversation. Cheered by this warm welcome, Gounod installed himself in one of the large single rooms allotted to students at the Villa Medici. Here, for the next two years, he was to work, read and sleep. Here he studied Goethe's *Faust* in a French translation. It was, he said, a favourite relaxation, and gradually the idea formed in his mind of setting it to music. He did not yet know what form it would take. Perhaps a cantata? Or an opera? He also read Lamartine and set a number of his poems. Among them were the famous *le Vallon* and *le Soir*. In ten years' time he was to use the second of these in the first act of his opera *Sapho*.

A great deal has been said about Ingres' taste for music. An amusing legend has grown up that he was prouder of his musical attainments than of his painting. Indeed, the phrase *le violon d'Ingres* has become the French idiom for a hobby. Even in Ingres' lifetime this little quirk was famous. Saint-Saëns, who as a boy had known Ingres quite well, remained sceptical. Ingres, he reported, always refused to play music with him. The only time Saint-Saëns ever saw the notorious violin was at the museum founded in the artist's honour. Gounod was more fortunate in his exploration of the legend. Ingres, he found, was passionately fond of music. Mozart was one of his idols. Had he not, one heroic evening, kept Gounod at the piano playing and singing *Don Giovanni* until Madame Ingres, drooping with sleep, insisted on shutting up the piano at two in the morning?

On Sunday evenings it was the custom for students to gather in Ingres' drawing-room. There they made music and the director of the Villa Medici propounded his enthusiasms: Mozart, Haydn, Beethoven and Gluck. His preference was for German music. Rossini? Well, admittedly *il Barbiere di Siviglia* was a masterpiece. Another exception he allowed was Cherubini. (At about this time he was painting Cherubini's portrait, in which Gounod modelled the hands for him. The composer of *Ali Baba* confronts posterity with the hands of *Faust*'s creator.) Gounod even persuaded him to appreciate Lully. When Ingres heard, for the first time, the scene of Charon and the Shades from *Alceste*, he cried in horror: 'It's awful! it's frightful! it's not music, it's iron!' Gounod tactfully let the storm blow itself out. A little later Ingres enquired, 'What about that scene from Lully: Charon and the Shades. I'd like to hear it again.' Gounod sang it to him once more. Soon it had become one of Ingres' favourite pieces. Was this, Gounod asked himself, the man whom the world saw as obstinate, intolerant and closed to argument? The Ingres he came to know was simple and sensitive. Humble towards the truly great, proud only in the face of stupidity, Ingres was loved by those who knew him well.

One day, returning from a stroll through Rome, Gounod met Ingres on the steps of the Villa Medici. The artist remarked an album under Gounod's arm. 'Do you draw?' he asked.

39

'Oh, Monsieur Ingres,' replied the musician, embarrassed, 'no . . . I mean . . . yes . . . I draw a bit . . . but . . . only a bit. . . .'

Ingres took the album. His eye fell upon a little figure of Saint Catherine which Gounod had just copied after a fresco attributed to Massaccio.

'You did this ?' he inquired.

'Yes.'

'All on your own ?'

'Yes.'

'Well! you know, you draw like your father!'

And then, gravely: 'You can make copies of pictures for me.'

It was an honour. Gounod spent many a lamplit evening at Ingres' side, his pencil tracing the outlines of pictures and engravings which he learned to know and intimately appreciate. At the same time Ingres would think aloud. He developed his theory of the need for grace complemented by strength: strength preserved grace from degenerating into affectation, and grace prevented strength from becoming mere brutality. Far from being despotic, as he was often so accused, Ingres, Gounod found, was a great admirer. His quick eye saw just how and why a work of art was to be admired. But, with prudence, he warned his pupils against imitating the characteristics which are individual to each master. It was precisely these characteristics which made the great painter what he was, and by their very nature they were incommunicable. Mere imitation, Ingres pointed out, led to exaggeration.

In all, Gounod made nearly a hundred copies for Ingres. So finely detailed were some of them that they were little more than an inch and a half high. 'If you like,' said Ingres, delighted, 'I can get you back to Rome with the Grand Prix for painting.' He drew a portrait of his young friend at the piano. Gounod looks out of the picture, his hands resting on the keyboard, fresh-faced, wide-eyed, romantically handsome. At the bottom is the inscription: '*Ingres à son jeune ami, M. Gounod. Rome, 1841.*'

It was, after all, music that Gounod had arrived in Rome to study, and not painting. Like others of his time, he found that the only place to hear religious music properly performed was in the Sistine Chapel. Entirely new for him was the sound of 'this severe, ascetic music, calm and horizontal as the line of the ocean, monotonous by virtue of its serenity, anti-sensuous, and yet so intense in its contemplativeness that it verges sometimes on ecstasy. . . .' He was troubled by its strangeness, not knowing whether he was attracted or repelled. After several more hearings he capitulated to its appeal.

The majestic surroundings played their part in shaping Gounod's reaction; 'Palestrina's music seems like a translation in song of Michelangelo, and I tend to think that the two masters are revealed to the understanding in a mutual light: the viewer develops the hearer and vice versa—so much so that after a time one is tempted to wonder whether the Sistine Chapel, both painting and music, is not the product of a single imagination.' As a musician who had also a keen painter's eye, Gounod saw Michelangelo and Palestrina as a perfect and sublime unity. They had the identical virtues of simplicity, humility in their choice of means, a total lack of interest in mere effect, and a disdain for the easy conquest.

For Gounod, hearing Palestrina was like reading Bossuet. As happened with the smooth and sonorous prose of the great preacher, 'nothing seems to strike you as you read on, and then, at the end of the road, you find yourself transported to marvellous heights; the words, faithful and submissive servants of the thought, have neither distracted nor held you up for their own sake, and you have arrived at the peak without jolt, diversion or artifice, led by a mysterious guide who has hidden his traces and concealed his secret from you. It is this absence of visible techniques, of worldly tricks, of vain ornamentation, which makes the greatest works utterly inimitable. To reach them you need nothing less than the same cast of mind and the same delights that brought about their creation.'

The theatres of Rome had little to offer a musician touched by the glories of Palestrina. Their repertory consisted entirely of operas by Donizetti, Bellini and Mercadante. Pleasant on occasion though these could be, Gounod conceded, they appeared to him like minor plants clinging to the robust tree trunk of Rossini. The singers were inferior to those he had heard in Paris. The productions were sometimes grotesque. He remembered a performance of *Norma* in which the Roman warriors preened themselves in jackets and fireman's helmets, their legs encased in butter-coloured nankeen breeches with cherry-red stripes. Long afterwards he savoured this memory of theatricals which proved that the art of Mr Vincent Crummles is international and is by no means confined to the invention of Dickens.

If the opera in Rome was to prove unrewarding, Gounod made up for it by studying Lully and Gluck in the quiet of his room at the Villa Medici. Mozart's *Don Giovanni* and Rossini's *Guillaume Tell*, were the other scores which he read and re-read throughout the summer of 1840. Soon he added to these idols a composer whose work had up to then been unfamiliar to him. After the revelation of Palestrina there came the revelation of Bach. The person responsible for introducing him to a new world of music was Fanny Hensel, the sister of Mendelssohn.

She was, Gounod said, 'an outstanding musician and a woman of superior intelligence, small, slender, but gifted with an energy which showed in her deep-set eyes and in her burning look.' Fanny had married the artist Wilhelm Hensel, and, with her husband, was staying in Rome. They were frequent guests at the Villa Medici and quickly struck up friendships with the students. 'Gounod', she wrote in her diary 'is passionately fond of music in a way I have rarely seen before.' He listened intently as she played, superbly and from memory, Bach fugues, concertos and sonatas, and new works by her brother. After the Italian music which had influenced so much of his early development the German composers were to have exhilarating effect on him.

His wild enthusiasm disconcerted Fanny Hensel. She found him 'passionate and romantic in the extreme. The revelation of German music to him is like a bomb falling on a house and it's possible that it may cause him serious damage . . . [it] disturbs him and sends him half-mad. In general, Gounod seems to me immature still. The only piece of music by him that I know is a Scherzo of little value, which he asks my permission to dedicate to me.'

He kept her up playing long into the night and demanded encore after encore of music which he already knew by heart. When he sought to thank her, he stammered and became incoherent. His emotion made him speechless. He kissed her hands in transports of maudlin delight. Her playing of a Beethoven sonata reduced him to such a state that he ended up screaming absurdities. His fellow-students, kindly but firmly, led him off to bed, shouting still.

These ecstasies were, perhaps, contagious, for three days later Fanny Hensel and the students went one evening to view the Colosseum by moonlight. On their return Gounod scrambled up into an acacia tree and pelted them with flowering twigs until, said the normally serious Fanny, they looked like the moving woods of Dunsinane. By the Piazza Colonna one of them started singing a Bach concerto. The rest took up the theme and marched across Rome in time to the rhythm, arriving home after one o'clock in the morning.

The music-making went on. Gounod would throw himself at the feet of the adored pianist and beg her to play an Adagio from a Beethoven sonata. His wish granted, he would embrace each member of the company and lavish upon their startled persons loud and smacking kisses. Despite the note of hysteria that inevitably crept in when Gounod was present, Fanny could not help liking him. The excessive flattery which Gounod showered on her was not unpleasing. He was to find, like Disraeli, that however much people murmur in protest when flattered, secretly they enjoy it. And Gounod, in true Disraelian fashion, laid it on with a trowel. He was not, in the heat of the moment, deliberately insincere. With all his heart he meant every word of the exaggerated praise that tumbled from his lips. Even when Fanny Hensel discounted the greater part of his admiring tributes, what remained was more than enough to gratify her woman's pride. She confided to her diary that 'I have known few people who can enjoy themselves so wholeheartedly or so thoroughly as he. . . .'

One aspect of Gounod disturbed her, and indeed his fellow students, more seriously than any other. She was worried by his acquaintance with Lacordaire, the Dominican friar and orator who had lately established himself in Rome. He was a disciple of Lamennais, the fiery priest whose aim was to rejuvenate the Catholic faith by a return to basic truths. Lamennais upset both the religious and secular authorities by proclaiming the need for complete submission to the Pope. From this, he argued, would emerge a liberal democracy which, throwing aside obsolete monarchical ideas, would flourish under the spiritual guidance of the Church. Having been condemned in two frigid encyclicals issued by a disapproving Pope, who was ungrateful enough not to appreciate the important role Lamennais proposed for him, the turbulent cleric left the Church. He joined the Republican party and divided his time between parliament, to which he was elected after the Revolution of 1848, and prison, to which he was periodically sent by uneasy governments. When he died he was buried in a pauper's grave. His polemical skill and literary graces attracted such writers as Hugo, Georges Sand and Sainte-Beuve. Perhaps his most influential follower was Lacordaire.

'Le Père Lacordaire' remained faithful to the Church when his mentor Lamennais broke with it. He had completed his novitiate just before Gounod arrived in Rome, and was now seeking recruits to his Brotherhood of Saint John the Evangelist. This group, which he intended to be the Italian branch of Paris headquarters already in existence, counted among its members a dozen or so artists and scions of important Roman families. Lacordaire sought youth for his evangelism, and the inmates of the Villa Medici were a fruitful source of material which he aspired to shape to the greater glory of God. Gounod was one of several who listened to the voice of the persuader and joyfully entered the fold. His friends, among them Fanny Hensel, feared the moment would come when he exchanged music for the Dominican's hood.

Another reason for Gounod's mystical turmoil was the presence in Rome at that time of a former schoolfriend called Charles Gay. He was about to enter holy orders and had arrived in Italy on a pilgrimage to see Lacordaire. On the feast of the Annunciation Gounod and his friend attended mass. They joined wholeheartedly in the service, and, for the first time, Gounod felt that he was in communion with the angels, with Christ, with God. Afterwards, in the vestry, tears of happiness ran down his face. He exchanged letters with Gay that discussed at length the unforgettable moment of divine reunion. One cloud alone shadowed Gay's contentment. Was not Madame Gounod, he sorrowfully enquired, still remote from Christian practice? Was it not a pity that she had yet to experience the ineffable joy her son had known?

The object of his pious solicitude was reluctant to improve her church-going habits. Instead, she feared that her impressionable son was being led astray. She urged him to be 'religious' but not 'Religious'. She recommended moderation, prudence, discretion. Like all artists, she warned him with a sigh, he was prone to 'enthusiasm', a word she invested with the pejorative sense it used to be given in the eighteenth century. If he chose to be a religious man with artistic interests, rather than an artist of a religious bent, then he was submitting himself—and she underlined the words vigorously—to an absolute power which would stifle his career and build up future sorrows. Though she did not doubt, she added hastily, that 'M. Lacordère' was a man of great talent and education.

Her elder son Urbain, while sharing his mother's taste for reformed spelling, was more positive in his exhortations. He deplored the manner in which 'your friend Guay' had won ascendance over his innocent brother. It was possible to be quite happy and worshipful, he sternly remarked, without constantly hanging about altars and hovering each minute over communion tables. The choice lay between art and family on the one side, and religion on the other.

44

It seems that in the end Gounod listened to the pleas of his family. He gave up the Brotherhood of Saint John the Evangelist. In return for this sacrifice his mother allowed him to 'convert' her. She went to church more often and improved her practice of Christianity to such an extent that Gay was able to tell her son that his prayer 'had ascended to God and come down again on your mother in a dew of grace and blessing.'

Once he had emerged from this religious crisis, Gounod left the blazing sun of Rome for Naples. His painter's vision absorbed 'the bay as blue as sapphire, framed in a girdle of mountains and islands where peaks and hill-sides take on at sunset that ever changing series of magical shades which defy the richest velvet and the most sparkling jewelry . . .' On Capri, where the violent heat of day drove him for coolness either indoors or into the sea, the starry nights bewitched him. The glittering of the stars made him think of an ocean with waves made of light as they vibrated in the endless spaces above. Often he spent hours sitting on a rock and listening to the silence of the phosphorescent dark. It was broken only by the occasional fall of a stone he threw into the sea, or by the mournful cry of a solitary bird that reminded him of that scene in *der Freischütz* where magic bullets are cast among the terrifying precipices of the Wolf's Glen. On Capri one evening he conceived the initial idea for the 'Walpurgis Night' in *Faust*. For Goethe's poem was always in his pocket, and the notes he made were growing steadily.

Yet however much Naples delighted him, however charmed he was by the museum and its wealth of Pompeian art, he was pleased to get back to Rome. Besieged by *facchini*, importuned by shopkeepers, hindered on his walks by coachmen anxious for a fare, he soon wearied of the constant state of high drama and argument in which the lively Neapolitans seemed to exist. Rome, with its solemn lines and placid contours, its silent ring of hills and gentle landscape, gave him, he said, the welcome feeling of an open-air cloister. His choice of word is significant.

From Paris came news of a harder world. He learned that while he was enjoying all the pleasures of an enchanted life, his mother had of necessity imposed on herself a laborious routine. Each morning at five o'clock she got up in time to greet her first piano pupil who arrived at six. Often she missed lunch so as to squeeze in an extra lesson, contenting herself with a scrap of bread and a glass of watered wine. She went on teaching until six, and after dinner she worked about the house. In addition she was a tireless supporter of charities, visiting the poor and making clothes for them. 'Your mother', a friend said to Gounod, 'is, for me, a miracle twice over; I don't know how she finds the time for all her activities, nor where she finds the money she gives to charity.'

Her correspondence was voluminous. Somehow she managed also to write long and detailed letters to her son in Rome. So, too, did Urbain, who was prodigal of good advice. 'I had great need of it', remarked Gounod shamefacedly, 'for, I must admit, wisdom has never been my good point. *Weakness* is very *strong* when reason isn't there to balance it. Alas! I profited little from it all. . . .'

Another jolt was administered in the September of 1841 by the composer Spontini. Students at the Villa Medici had periodically to send examples of their work back to Paris to show how they were progressing in their art. Gounod's *Te Deum* for unaccompanied voices came before the committee of the Académie des Beaux Arts, and Spontini drew up their report. It struck a ruthless and condemnatory note. Spontini was outraged that Gounod should have attempted to rival Palestrina in the oldest and most difficult of musical forms. Foreshadowing the criticism that Gounod's later religious works sometimes received, the pitiless judge described his *Te Deum* as utterly monotonous. In page upon page of angry reproof he slashed the thing to shreds and rejected the pathetic tatters with contempt. The *Te Deum* was bereft of melody, the fugues it contained were badly worked out, the technique was clumsy, accents were wrongly placed, the voices were handled ineptly, the score was filled from start to finish with inexcusable schoolboy mistakes. . . . The presumptuous student was even accused of an indecent partiality for octaves.

Nowhere in his published writings does Gounod refer to this thunderbolt. Its effect on his highly-strung character may, though, be easily imagined. His mother sadly recorded in a letter the 'unanimous' opinion of the committee. His old friend Ingres was beside himself with rage. He took it as a personal affront. In the spring of that year he had been succeeded at the Villa Medici by the artist Victor Schnetz, a pleasant man usually known as '*ce bon Monsieur Schnetz*'. Had Ingres still been there, it is not unlikely that Spontini would have received in turn a savaging from the hot-tempered artist. Gounod himself licked his wounds in silence.

By the October of 1841 he had completed his stay in Rome. A

last-minute appeal to the authorities enabled him to spend another six months there before going on to Germany as the regulations demanded. Reluctantly, in June 1842, he left what he called 'the Promised Land'. Rome had made its mark on him. He always, in the future, defended the practice of sending young musicians there. Its value was obvious so far as artists and sculptors were concerned. In Rome they would find a treasury of masterpieces in the arts they practised. Less clear, at first sight, were the advantages a musician could expect to enjoy. Apart from the music in the Sistine Chapel, Gounod found, Rome had little to teach a composer. This objection, however, related only to his art in its narrowest sense. The supreme benefit Rome offered was the opportunity to broaden aesthetic feeling to its greatest extent. There the musician was able to improve his acquaintance with art in the universal sense and to draw from it the strength he needed to be an artist and not a mere craftsman. If people were to question the value of Rome to a musician, said Gounod, one might also question the value of reading Homer, Virgil, Dante, Shakespeare, Molière and Pascal, none of whom had much to say about the technique of writing fugues or composing symphonies.

With just enough money in his pocket to get him to Vienna, he took his unwilling leave of the city that meant so much to him. 'So long as the road allowed, my gaze remained attached to the cupola of Saint Peter, the summit of Rome and centre of the world. Then the hills snatched it away from me completely. I fell into a deep reverie and wept like a child.'

❧ III ❧

Church or Theatre?

There was time for a brief call at Florence and a last glimpse of Michelangelo's *il Pensieroso* before Gounod arrived in Venice. It struck him as 'sad and happy, light and dark, pink and pale, flirtatious yet sinister. . . .' Venice, he decided, was an enchantress who attacked the senses and cast a spell on you immediately. Venice, he continued, extending the feminine metaphor with a knowledge of women somewhat unexpected in a young man of twenty-four, but no less shrewd for all that, was 'a pearl in a sewer'.

Then he went by steamboat to Trieste and took coach for Grätz, visiting on the way the grottoes of Adelberg which looked, with their stalactites, like underground cathedrals. At last he arrived in Vienna, a place where he had no friends and did not even speak the language. He cheered up a little on seeing *die Zauberflöte* on the opera bills, and the performance, the first he ever heard, delighted him. One of the orchestral players spoke French and introduced him to his family. Through this new friend Gounod made the acquaintance of Count Stockhammer, the influential president of the Vienna Philharmonic Society. Impressed by what he heard of the young man's talent, Stockhammer offered to arrange the performance of a mass Gounod had composed while in Rome. It was played on 8 September 1842, and so pleased Stockhammer that he asked his protégé to write a requiem. This was scheduled for November and left Gounod scarcely six weeks to prepare it. Fortunately he had with him the greater part of a requiem already written in Rome, and he was able to present his work in time and conduct it himself.

The *Requiem* was warmly applauded. The Viennese audience hailed its grandeur and originality of inspiration. Critics wrote with pleased surprise of daring but successful harmonies. They saw, for Gounod, a promising future. Later, the gratified composer noted in

3. Gounod in his late thirties (about 1855). (Photo: Stella Mayes Reed.)

4. The final trio, 'Alerte, alerte, ou vous êtes perdus', from *Faust*, Act V. Proof of the full score corrected by Gounod. (Bibliothèque de l'Opéra, Rés. A 622 C.) (Photo: Photo Pic, Paris.)

his manuscript score, above the Dies irae, 'Mendelssohn has done me the honour of writing to me that this piece might have been composed by Cherubini.' Perhaps, by now, the wound Spontini inflicted was healed.[1]

Soon afterwards Gounod fell ill with an abscess in the throat. While he convalesced he busied himself with yet another commission which the benevolent Stockhammer gave him. This was a choral mass eventually heard in the Carlskirche at Easter 1843. It had, wrote Gounod, jauntily ignoring the irascible shade of Spontini, been written more or less in the style of the Sistine Chapel music. Again he was successful, and critics wrote well of it.

His mother was relieved that Germany should have proved so welcoming. 'Since he's been in Vienna', she wrote to a friend, 'he has done a lot of work. He has found kindness and constant help there. If this is to his credit, it also shows us the German character in a favourable light because of the support it gives in launching a young artist. Charles appreciates his good luck and has decided to stay longer in this foreign land to carry on his advanced studies.'

At the end of April he went to Berlin where he planned an affectionate reunion with Fanny Hensel and her husband. Almost immediately he was ill again. This time it was a stomach complaint, which, like his earlier malady in Vienna, may well have been the first in that series of psychosomatic illnesses which were to punctuate his life. The excitement of new faces, of audiences applauding his music, of a social life in which he was constantly fêted, would have been enough to unsettle stronger nerves than his. Within a fortnight the Hensels' doctor had cured him. During that time he endeared himself more than ever to Fanny.

His musical judgement and acuteness of perception could not have been bettered, so Fanny's mother-in-law remarked. Yet his sensitivity was not limited to music alone. Although he knew little German, she was surprised at the speed and correctness with which he could seize the spirit of poetry in what was an unknown language for him. He acted as a stimulus, encouraging the Hensels by his enthusiasm to play and discuss music at even greater length than they would normally have done. They talked about his future. It was in the oratorio form, they told him, that the greatest potentiality for French music lay. He agreed, and said that he had already thought of

[1] Years later he was to use this Dies irae in *Faust*: it turns up as the melody to which Marguerite invokes divine forgiveness in Act V.

writing a *Judith*. He left them on 15 May, carrying in his pocket a letter of introduction to Mendelssohn in Leipzig.

The German composer soon found that his sister had not exaggerated in her accounts of the charm and talent which Gounod possessed. The twenty-five-year-old Frenchman, confronted with a musician who, though only nine years his senior, was a famous and established figure, responded to Mendelssohn's welcome. His host devoted four whole days to him, questioning him about his work and studies with a lively interest. After hearing Gounod play at the piano some of his latest pieces, he returned the compliment by assembling the Gewandhaus orchestra and giving him a special performance of the 'Scotch' Symphony. Then he took Gounod to the Thomaskirche, and there, on the organ which Bach himself had used, played to him for several hours.

The days spent with Mendelssohn brought Gounod's German visit to a happy climax. He carried away with him the memory of a great musician unspoiled by fame and ready to encourage beginners without envious fear of rivalry. In his baggage were packed scores which Mendelssohn had given him. Everything had gone better than he ever expected. After six days of travel and seventeen changes of coach he arrived in Paris. His brother Urbain was there to meet him. Together they made their way to the flat in the rue Vaneau where his mother now lived.

Madame Gounod hardly recognized her son. After three-and-a-half years' absence his face had changed. His several illnesses, the fatigue of the journey and the beard he had begun to sprout had altered the smooth features she once knew. But all that did not matter. He was back. And she was happy again.

In the same building lived Charles Gay, the friend whose religious influence over Gounod in Rome had caused such dismay to his mother. She was by now reconciled to him and even, encouraged by her son, took lessons in theology from him. Her new way of life overjoyed Gay. He saw her not only as a Christian but as one who had the generosity of a saint. Her few leisure moments were occupied in sewing clothes for the poor and writing canticles of a spiritual nature.

The house in the rue Vaneau positively exhaled an atmosphere of good works and meditation, for in another part of it there lived the abbé Dumarsais. Gounod had known him at the Lycée Saint-Louis. Now he was the local priest in charge of the Église des Missions étrangères lower down the street. While Gounod was still in Rome his mother had arranged with Dumarsais for her son to be appointed organist and musical director at the Église des Missions étrangères. This was her reason for setting up house in the rue Vaneau, where the rooms overlooked the gardens and where Charles would be near to his work. Gounod's condition for taking the post was that he should have absolute control over the choice of music to be played.

In November 1843, Gounod announced in a letter to Mendelssohn that he was starting on his new duties. He was to be paid a salary of 1,200 francs which rose over the years. The resources at the church were scanty. The organ was poor and limited in range. The choir consisted of two basses, a tenor and a boy. Yet in a way the conditions were ideal for a young man full of ideas and determination. He would be able to build up the sort of organization he wanted. He was free to put into practice all the theories he had formed over the past few years. Or so he thought.

His greatest ambition was to introduce the music of Bach and Palestrina, composers for whom few churchgoers of the time had any taste. Even Madame Gounod's maternal love balked at Palestrina. The music which her son adored she found 'cold as ice'. She glanced around her at a service where the austere progressions of the Italian master were numbing the congregation, and she saw expressions of infinite boredom which indicated that her opinion was widely shared. Among her neighbours was Berlioz. 'The years have given him the power of hiding what he really feels,' she commented drily. It seems that Palestrina had the same deadening effect on him as did Bach, whom he also disliked.

Gounod refused to budge. In his discussions with Gay about church music he received strong support for his ideas. What he had heard in the Sistine Chapel was to form the basis of a revival. It offered the opportunity of evolving a purer, truly religious form that would benefit from modern developments soberly applied. God, so Gay assured him, would take his hand and lead him toward this happy consummation.

Yet worshippers at the Église des Missions étrangères were slow to grasp the hand that was proffered to them. They missed the familiar, undemanding music which once accompanied their religious exercises. The serenity of Palestrina seemed colourless after the bright, facile melodies they knew and enjoyed. Hints were dropped to the abbé Dumarsais and observations were made. A certain coldness descended upon the faithful. The abbé spoke discreetly to his musical director. He was reminded, with some acerbity, of the terms of their agreement. If Gounod's kind of music did not suit parishioners, Gounod would leave. Which Gounod immediately did.

Half an hour later, the distressed abbé sent to Gounod's home and tried to pacify him. Let them, said Dumarsais, discuss the problem calmly. No, replied Gounod. His situation was clear: either he stayed on terms of complete independence or else he went for good. 'What a terrible man you are!' groaned Dumarsais. Gounod stayed. In time the parishioners came round to his way of thinking. Over the weeks and months that passed they were nourished on a healthy diet of Palestrina and Bach. In the end even Gounod's most determined opponents became his friends.

He was to spend five years as musical director at the church. It was one of the happiest periods of his life. Watched over by his mother and his brother Urbain he passed the days sheltered from the pressures of the secular world. The Église des Missions étrangères became a refuge where, for perhaps the only time in his existence, he was able to harmonize with complete success the dominant passions which absorbed him: music and religion. He lived in a mood of calm. No serpent troubled his Eden.

Only occasionally did Gounod venture into the profane outside world. He would go sometimes to a tavern in the rue Guénégaud, a little old street which joins the rue Mazarine on one side and, at the other, the venerable quai de Conti on the bank of the Seine. Down one length of it runs the grandiose façade of the Hotel des Monnaies, that early burst of Louis XVI's architectural glory. Once in the rue Guénégaud there had been a puppet theatre which offended the touchy Cyrano de Bergerac. Among its attractions was the monkey Fagotin, who, claimed the big-nosed knight, had been dressed up to look like him. Cyrano fought a duel with the luckless animal to avenge his honour and killed it. In Gounod's time 'le père Fricaud' offered dinners at a franc or so and a bottle of wine for seventy-five centimes. His tavern was frequented by artists such as Courbet and Gustave Doré, and by the poets Baudelaire and Théophile Gautier. It was here that Gounod made the acquaintance of the *chansonnier* Pierre Dupont.

Dupont had begun life as a silk-weaver before discovering his talent for popular verse. His 'Chant des ouvriers' was, said Baudelaire, 'the 'Marseillaise' of the people.' He wrote about the lives of the workers and the hard existence of peasants. When Gounod knew him he was a keen Republican whose political vision expressed itself in songs inspired by utopian socialism. He was also violently anti-Bonapartist, so much so that Louis-Napoleon sentenced him to seven years' deportation. He asked for, and was granted, a full pardon, carried out a brisk volte-face, and became the unofficial laureate of the Second Empire with songs glorifying the Crimean War. He was to die soon after the Franco-Prussian War, deserted by his Republican friends, poor and alone.

Since Dupont's musical gifts were untrained, Gounod helped by writing out the notation of his songs for him. This was a service also performed by Ernest Reyer, the friend of Berlioz and composer of Wagnerian operas that made a stir in their day. Like Reyer, Gounod was impressed by Dupont's talent. Equally attractive to him were the *chansonnier*'s mystico-political ideals. He found it pleasant to think that artists would come down from their ivory towers and stand shoulder to shoulder with the rest of humanity in the struggle for social equality. Dangerous notions were bandied about in the tavern in the rue Guénégaud. Madame Gounod found it necessary to remind her son of the horrors of Republicanism and to warn him against the 'advanced' ideas that certain hot-heads were propounding.

She worried, too, over the influence of Lacordaire. Dupont and Gounod were seeing much of him these days. They listened avidly to his sermons and studied them afterwards when they were printed in *l'Univers religieux*. The eloquence that had captivated Gounod in Rome was just as potent when he heard it at Notre Dame. Lacordaire's appeal was chiefly an emotional one. He argued that religious truth would become ossified and the faithful estranged if preachers were to be restricted to the narrow limits of age-old church services and ceremonial. Catholicism must come out into the open, must involve itself with the political, social and philosophical problems of the day. Lacordaire's ringing voice was heard speaking of democracy from the pulpit and discussing every topic that agitated secular controversy. He did not go to the extremes that had tempted Lamennais. His style lacked the profundity and elegance of his master. Yet what he said was enough to upset the traditionally minded clergy and to inspire idealistic young men such as Gounod, who, stirred by the warmth of his delivery, overlooked the inadequacy of his ideas.

Three years after he had been appointed musical director at the Église des Missions étrangères, Gounod felt what he later described 'as an inclination to take up the ecclesiastical life'. The atmosphere in which he had daily lived and the tumult of emotions Lacordaire set up in him now reached a point at which he could no longer resist the call of the Church. In 1846 the *Revue et Gazette musicale* even reported that he had taken holy orders. This item of news might have been suggested by Gounod's ambiguous epistolary habits. He invariably wrote to his correspondents on the official note-paper of the Église des Missions étrangères. This was headed by a monogram in the form of an oval. It enclosed a design representing a cross upon the letter M, beneath which were two hearts in flames crowned with thorns. A sword pierced one of the hearts, and a circle of thirteen stars framed the whole. To add the finishing touch, Gounod had adopted the priestly custom of drawing a cross at the top of the page. Thoughtfully, he signed himself 'abbé Ch. Gounod'.

In the summer of 1846 the 'abbé' Gounod went on holiday with his friends Gay and Dumarsais. Trouville was their choice that year, and here the would-be priest found another sign of what he took to be his vocation. He struck up acquaintance with an elderly gentleman who exhibited a misguided attachment to the Protestant faith. This member of a heretic persuasion was, despite his error, a man of intelligence and good will. Gounod conversed earnestly with him at the water's edge, tried to direct him into the true path, and dreamed of curing a soul that was grievously sick. While little boys ran about with shrimping nets and frivolous youth gambolled on the beach, the light of conviction descended upon the venerable Protestant. He resolved to abjure. Gounod proposed himself as god-father. The godson, who was more than twice the age of his twenty-eight-year-old sponsor, was received into the Catholic Church with rejoicing. The name of this lost lamb, one is pleased to record, was Wagner.

That autumn Gounod went on a retreat. Freed from his work at the Église des Missions étrangères, he was able to give himself up to solitary meditation and reading. He studied the Scriptures and annotated them with long reflective passages. The comparative history of religion was another of his subjects. The nature of prayer absorbed him.

Next year he holidayed again in Normandy. This time there was no erring Protestant to be rescued from the burning. When he came back to Paris he renewed an earlier friendship with his contemporary César Franck whom he had known at the Conservatoire. Only four years separated them, but Gounod's seniority was enough to make him the master and Franck the disciple. The timid and unworldly Franck, cloistered till then by his ambitious father and chained to a round of virtuoso concert tours, was about to escape, so it seemed, from paternal tyranny and looked forward to the illusion of freedom held out by his forthcoming marriage.

'Come and see me whenever you can', wrote Gounod. 'You know that my door is always open to you, and my heart even more so.'

For several months their association was close. Gounod talked with Franck about theology and the history of religion. He dilated on the links between music and Catholicism, a subject to which Franck himself had given much thought. Franck was a simple, straight-forward man. There is no doubt that for some time he found re-assurance in hearing the views expounded with such confidence by his friend. Gounod had read widely. His conversation was persuasive. Apt quotations sprang readily to his lips. It would have been difficult to resist the obvious good will that inspired him or the benevolence that lit up his handsome features.

The spell did not last. They drifted apart, and while Franck continued on the modestly obscure routine that bound him to the organ loft and teaching at the Conservatoire, Gounod was to launch on a sensational career in the theatre and to become an international figure. Later in the century the two composers were even to be rivals of a sort: they both wrote an oratorio with the title of *Rédemption*. Franck remained, as ever, respectful of his colleague's musical gifts and showed no jealousy of his glittering career. Gounod, it is said, became indifferent to him, and in the end his feelings were coloured by a contempt that shaded into dislike.

But at the time he knew Franck, Gounod's religious fervour was still at its height. In October 1847, the Archbishop of Paris gave him permission to follow lectures at the Carmelite Seminary of Saint-Sulpice. He entered its doors in the rue de Vaugirard fully prepared to devote the next three years to studies preparing him for the priesthood. At last the 'abbé' Gounod was justified in wearing a cassock. Willingly he submitted to the strict orders of the religious community whence he emerged once a week on Wednesday afternoons, the only time when there were no classes to be attended.

After five months of prayer and instruction the other side of Gounod's Janus-like personality revealed itself. Immersion in the

Scriptures and the daily round of ecclesiastical life failed to damp a thought that tormented him with persistence. In the midst of holy service, in the bleak solitude of his cell, often as he walked along the cloister, his concentration was disturbed by visions of another, garish world. The youthful memory of his first night at the opera came back to him. He saw, in his mind's eye, the red curtain which lifted to reveal enchantments he had never forgotten. He remembered the hazy footlights and the smell of greasepaint. He heard the sound of applause.

Suddenly he was depressed by the austerity of Saint-Sulpice. What earlier seemed a blessed retreat had become, in his new mood, a place of futility. He rejected it with the same eagerness as had at first impelled him to embrace it. Even the contented years at the Église des Missions étrangères appeared in retrospect as a waste of time. The beauties of Palestrina lost their attraction when he thought of the warmth, the colour, that the theatre offered.

That, assuredly, was where he ought to be. He had realized that only by way of the theatre could a composer achieve the reputation and rewards that were his due. As he later wrote:

The theatre is a place where every day you have the means and the opportunity of communicating with the public. It is available to the musician as a permanent, daily shop-window.

Religious and symphonic music belong, of course, to a higher order, in the matter of absolutes, than does music for the theatre; but the opportunities and methods of making one's name in them are rare and only reach an occasional audience, instead of the regular one that goes to the theatre. And then, what an infinite variety there is in the choice of subjects for a dramatic composer! What scope for fantasy, imagination, history! The theatre tempted me. I was then nearly thirty years old, and I was impatient to try my strength in this new battlefield.

The unsettled atmosphere of the time may also have encouraged him to break with his present existence. In February 1848, the monarchy of Louis-Philippe collapsed under pressures that strained an insecure régime to breaking point. There was, as usual, much talk at first of brotherhood and friendship inspired by the principles of 1789. And again, as usual, this developed with alacrity into murder and riot. By June there was vicious fighting in the streets. The starving and the unemployed rose up in bitterness. There were about twenty thousand of them and they were put down with savage fury.

Gounod left the rue de Vaugirard at about the time barricades were being set up in the streets. He put off his cassock for good. While France prepared for a new government and a new régime, he too set about getting ready for another phase in life.

❧ IV ❧

Pauline Viardot and *Sapho*

Up to now Gounod had been composing chiefly religious music. As musical director at the Église des Missions étrangères he wrote a great deal of music for daily use at services. Several masses, canticles and motets are known to have been written at this period, and in 1846 he had published the *Offices de la Semaine sainte*. Having decided to attempt opera, he now had the problem of finding a suitable libretto. Still more difficult was the task of convincing theatre managers that he, a church musician, was capable of writing for the stage.

His good looks and engaging manner soon won him friends. His social graces made him a favourite with hostesses and his obvious talent impressed professional musicians. One of these was the Belgian violinist François Seghers. He would have been a great virtuoso had he not suffered from a peculiar defect of temperament that made it impossible for him to play in public. The moment more than two or three were gathered together to hear him, his masterly style faltered, his beautiful tone evaporated, his fingers were overtaken by an uncontrollable palsy. Perhaps he had infected his wife with this disability, for it is a fact that she too, an admirable pianist and one of Liszt's most brilliant pupils, became instantly paralysed with fear whenever she had to play before an audience.

Seghers was passionately interested in new music. One of his ambitions was to give a series of recitals which would include the later Beethoven quartets, then considered unplayable and incomprehensible. Great excitement was generated within his circle of acquaintances. One of them spoke enthusiastically to his mother-in-law who sat embroidering peacefully in a corner. 'Don't get excited,' said the old lady, 'he won't give them.' She was right. He invited an audience of thirty to a trial concert. He took his place among the string players. When it was time to play, his hand slithered hopelessly over the instrument and the notes faded away. The project was abandoned.

But although Seghers could not himself play in public he was able to guide others. As a conductor he introduced to Paris the work of living composers who up to then had never enjoyed a hearing there. The august Société des Concerts du Conservatoire was interested only in dead musicians. Its audiences were select and its repertory was small. Mendelssohn was viewed as a daring revolutionary. It was some time before chamber music groups—among them, for example, the one in which Lalo played as second violin, and another expressly inaugurated to perform the late Beethoven quartets—helped to improve this state of affairs. Those enterprising rivals Colonne and Lamoureux did not start their popular orchestral concerts until more than twenty years later. In the meantime, music was represented for most people by the easy fare provided at the Opéra and the Opéra-Comique. Keen amateurs who did not have the privilege of attending Conservatoire concerts knew the symphonies of Haydn, Mozart and Beethoven through piano duets alone. Those who did not play the piano were unaware of them.

Seghers founded the Société Sainte-Cécile as a pioneer venture. His organization took its name from the old Salle Sainte-Cécile in the rue de la Chaussée-d'Antin. It was a big square hall where the acoustics, contrary to expectation, were ideal for sound. Seghers featured avant-garde composers like Schumann in his programmes. Even the members of his orchestra rebelled at the difficult modern scores he put in front of them. On occasion there were riots. Undaunted by hostility from his players and outraged murmurs from his audience, Seghers persisted with his attempt to secure a fair hearing for modern music. His concerts introduced the ultra-contemporary symphonies of Mendelssohn, the lesser-known works of Beethoven and the *Tannhäuser* overture. He was also to champion the cause of young French composers, of whom Gounod was one, by including their works in his programmes.

Seghers belonged to that 'advanced' circle of musicians which included Pauline Viardot, a close friend of his. The legendary Madame Viardot was the daughter of Manuel Garcia, one of the greatest tenors of his epoch. Her brother, also called Manuel, became a noted teacher, invented the laryngoscope, and taught for many years at the Royal Academy in London. There he died in 1906 at the age of a hundred-and-one. Her sister, Maria Malibran, had a short but memorable career during which she electrified the audiences of Europe with vocal powers unrivalled for splendour.

Pauline Viardot lacked beauty. She was, by conventional standards, ugly, but her ugliness was strangely attractive. Just as she turned to advantage the defects of her appearance and created an impression of desirability, so she was able to triumph over the flaws in her voice. She was a very great singer indeed. 'It was not a velvet or crystal voice,' remarked Saint-Saëns who knew her well, 'but a harsh one, rather, which some have compared to the pungent taste of a bitter orange. It was made for tragedy, epic verse, and was more superhuman than human. Light things, Spanish songs, Chopin mazurkas which she transcribed, were changed by her voice into the banter of a giant. She gave incomparable splendour to tragic measures and the severe strains of oratorio.'

She was also an intellectual who spoke and wrote fluently in Spanish, French, Italian, English and German. Her musicianship was so accomplished that she once impressed connoisseurs by singing to them a magnificent but unknown Mozart aria—which, she later confessed, she had written herself. No music was foreign to her, from Bach cantatas to the songs of Glinka which she performed in Russian. On Thursday evenings at her house in the rue de Douai she entertained a host of admirers. In the drawing-room hung Ary Scheffer's famous portrait of her. Next door, a few steps down, was a picture gallery which contained an organ. It was there that she sang arias from oratorios by Handel and Mendelssohn that Parisian audiences were unwilling to hear. Her taste for every kind of music was insatiable. So great was it, indeed, that at the end of her life she warned a young singer: 'Don't do as I did. I wanted to sing everything. I ruined my voice.'

One day Seghers arranged for Gounod to meet her. If anyone could help a talented young composer in search of a librettist and a theatre, then Pauline Viardot, at the height of her reputation, certainly could. They had met before, while Gounod was at the Villa Medici and Pauline and her new husband had passed through Rome on their honeymoon. Gounod then had appeared to be just like any other clever young student. Out of politeness, nine years later, she agreed to see him.

He went to her with memories of having heard her sister Malibran sing in the performance of *Otello* which, when he was twelve, had made such a shattering effect on him. His meeting with Pauline

Viardot, originally intended to last half an hour, was so successful that it stretched over two hours. Pauline's formidable intellect made her a difficult person to impress, but in the case of Gounod she was overwhelmed. His charm pleased her. What she called his 'genius' astonished her. She found in him nobility and distinction. He was, she thought, lofty but simple. They made music together for hours on end. Her new friend, she assured Georges Sand, belonged in the same sphere as Mozart.

Gounod was soon an intimate of the Viardot household. This consisted of Pauline, her husband Louis, and her lover Ivan Turgenev. Malicious tongues suggested that the triangle had become a square. Was Gounod, newly released from the cloister, Pauline's lover? Many people thought so. As a musician she spoke with Gounod a language that Turgenev did not know, and she shared experiences with him into which the novelist could not enter. Turgenev, perhaps, felt some of the unease he must previously have caused Pauline's husband. The two men were now united, whatever their other differences, in a piquant situation not unlike that of a Palais-Royal farce. In these circumstances fellow-feeling is intense. No evidence, however, exists to suggest that Pauline was Gounod's mistress, nor that she felt anything more for him than professional admiration and keen friendship.[1]

It was easy for Pauline to help her new protégé. In that same year of 1849 when Gounod met her she had just gained one of her most sensational triumphs. As Fidès in the first performance of *le Prophète* she had been, wrote an observer, 'the life and soul of the opera, which owed to her at least half of its great success.' Every door was open to her and theatre managers were ready to do her bidding. She spoke of Gounod to Nestor Roqueplan. This flamboyant figure was, in his time, director of the Théatre des Variétés and of the Opéra. His management of both theatres was brilliant and ruinous—for him. Like many of his theatrical colleagues ke knew little about music and was often mocked for his ignorance. Always teetering on the verge of bankruptcy, ever on the point of disaster, he somehow managed to keep going thanks to the generosity of friends who rarely failed him when catastrophe loomed. More important to him even than the extravagance of his lavish productions were the cut and colour of his dress, for he was an impenitent dandy: the only innovation he made

---

[1] Mrs Weldon, whom we shall meet later, was apt to discuss the mystery with some relish.

at the Opéra was to insist on the claque wearing black ties as a foil to the orchestral players, who wore white ones. 'My dream', he once said, 'is to die insolvent and in style.'

Meyerbeer was Roqueplan's idol. He would sign contracts with the composer without troubling to read them. Madame Viardot, as Meyerbeer's collaborator, shared, for Roqueplan, in his glory, and was prepared to grant her every favour. For Pauline's sake he agreed to commission an opera, as yet unwritten, by a totally unknown and untried composer. His sole condition was that it should be short, serious, and contain a role for Pauline Viardot.

Only a librettist remained to be found. Gounod remembered that as a child he had played in the Jardin du Luxembourg with Émile Augier. Since then Augier had become a famous dramatist, while he, Gounod....

'Go and see Augier,' Madame Viardot promptly replied, 'and tell him I agree to sing the leading role in your opera if he will write you the libretto.'

Once again the charm worked. 'Madame Viardot!' cried Augier. 'But of course! Right away.'

Augier is now little remembered except for *le Gendre de Monsieur Poirier*, a delightful social satire which stands out among his fertile production on account of its shrewd observation of character. He was known in his time as a Balzacian realist who purveyed a wholesome antidote to the excesses of Romanticism, an atheist lay preacher full of good intentions. Today an odour of mothballs envelops the dozens of moralizing plays with which he pleased the boulevard. He lived out at Nanteuil with his mistress, a former actress at the Palais-Royal. He was often to be seen outside his rustic retreat, shirt-sleeved and pushing a wheelbarrow, as he tended his little small-holding. Chosen for immortality and the Académie Française by a majority of one vote alone, he became a familiar guest at modish dinners, plump, pipe-smoking, the image of the men of substance he portrayed in his bourgeois comedies. Once he had been the lover of Rachel and of her sister as well. In old age, tortured by gout and deafness, a fading courtier desperate to keep in the swim, he haunted the great receptions where once he had been a popular guest.

The new opera was to be set in ancient Greece and the heroine was the poetess Sappho. By April 1850, Augier had completed the promised libretto. On the 3rd of that month Gounod signed a contract with Roqueplan for delivery of the score on the 30 September at the latest. This gave him six months to write the three-act work which was to be his début in the theatre.

Then his brother Urbain suddenly fell ill. Three days after Gounod signed the contract for *Sapho* Urbain died at the age of forty-three. His wife was distraught, his mother driven nearly out of her reason. He left a two-year-old son. Seven months later a second child was to be born. Gounod had to spend several weeks arranging for the family to be looked after and for Urbain's architectural practice to be wound up. It was impossible to work under these circumstances, yet already he had lost a precious month of the time allowed him to write his opera.

Pauline Viardot, who was then on a concert tour of Germany, took pity on his dilemma. She invited him and his mother to find the peace they needed in her country house at Courtavenel. There they stayed until September. Also in residence were Pauline's mother, her sister-in-law, and Turgenev. The Russian novelist, wrote Gounod, was 'a charming man . . . a close and excellent friend of the Viardot family.' Though Turgenev was the same age as the composer, his greater experience of the world and of the arts enabled him to play the part of mentor. He showed no apparent jealousy of the youth who had so quickly attained a privileged position with his mistress. Indeed, he was ready to comfort and encourage him when he had reached, as he thought, a dead end with the opera and despaired of ever finishing it. The letters Gounod wrote to friends from Courtavenel show that he admired and appreciated Turgenev.

In June Turgenev went home to Russia while Pauline Viardot travelled to London for more concerts. Gounod and his mother stayed on at Courtavenel. The family bereavement Gounod had recently experienced would, he thought, inspire him to write the tragic scenes of his opera with deeper feeling. By a freak of the imagination he was surprised to find that, on the contrary, it was the brighter passages which he wrote first and with ease. Was it, he wondered, due to a subconscious which, bent under the load of sorrow and mourning, felt an urgent need to react ?

He finished *Sapho* more quickly than he had expected. At the beginning of September Pauline Viardot came back from her wanderings. Gounod played the work to her, singing it in the veiled tones which made his voice so attractive. She was more than satisfied with what he had done and saw it as the justification of her faith in him. Within a few days she knew the score so well that she could accompany nearly all of it by heart at the piano. 'This', marvelled Gounod, 'was the most extraordinary musical tour de force I have ever witnessed, and one that gives the measure of this wonderful musician's astonishing abilities.'

Before the production of *Sapho* in April 1851, Gounod made a brief excursion to London for a concert of his music. It is probable that, once again, he owed this advancement in his career to the favour of Pauline Viardot. In 1850 the English critic Henry F. Chorley had visited Paris and, while there, met Gounod through Madame Viardot's introduction. From 1830 onwards Chorley had been music critic of *The Athenaeum*. He wrote many libretti, novels, dramas and poems, but it was his work for *The Athenaeum* that made him an important figure in London musical life. His admiration for Gounod dated from their first meeting, and he was to be a powerful advocate of his music. He noted in his diary: 'It was a great pleasure to me in Paris to add to my list of sensations Gounod, of whom the world will one day hear as *the* composer, or else H.F.C. is much mistaken.' Soon afterwards, at the concert in St Martin's Hall on the 5 January, Chorley acclaimed Gounod's début in England.

The programme included items from what later became the *Messe solennelle Sainte-Cécile*. Chorley wrote that he had never known such a successful beginning for an unknown composer. He was struck by the beauty and originality of the Sanctus. The Benedictus impressed him with its simplicity and exalted reminiscences of Gregorian chant. Most of all, a typical Victorian, he praised the religious fervour which kept the music on an exalted level and made it quite inappropriate by its nature for any profane subject. If, concluded Chorley, he did not perceive in these compositions a genius both true and novel, he would have to go back to school and relearn his critic's alphabet.

After this triumphant introduction to the country which was to figure so largely in his life, Gounod returned to Paris. *Sapho* was now in full rehearsal. The Opéra was not yet housed in that elaborate building which the architect Charles Garnier's riotous fantasy has since turned into an enduring landmark at the point where the boulevard des Capucines meets and mingles with the rue de la Paix and the avenue de l'Opéra. If the date of its start as a national institution is taken as 1669, when the librettist Pierre Perrin was granted letters patent to 'perform plays in verse and music, with dances and machines as practised in Italy,' then the Opéra may be said to have had fourteen different homes before at last settling-in at the 'Palais Garnier' for its official opening in 1875.

At the time of *Sapho* the Opéra was established in the rue le Peletier, not far from its present site. Intended only as a temporary refuge, the theatre in fact was used for the purpose during a period of fifty-two years, the longest time the ambulant Opéra had ever stayed in one place. Here were produced the later French operas of Rossini and the gorgeous spectaculars of Meyerbeer. The recent invention of gaslighting made opera productions famous for their scenic effects. In 1822, the year after the theatre opened in the rue le Peletier, audiences were excited by a colourful performance of *Aladin, ou la lampe merveilleuse,* an opera designed to exploit all the tricks that were possible with the new device. It was written by Nicolo Isouard, a Maltese composer settled in France. His long rivalry with Boieldieu provoked strenuous intrigues and bitter manoeuvrings on the part of their respective cliques. Worn out by these activities and, as his biographer darkly observes, by excesses which ruined his health, Isouard died at the age of forty-two. His unfinished *Aladin* was completed by other hands. The success of this posthumous opera might have consoled him, had he lived, for the election of the detested Boieldieu to the Académie des Beaux Arts, an event which caused him bitter disappointment.

Aladdin and his wonderful lamp inaugurated a tradition of splendour which opera-goers came to take for granted. Instead of the guttering tallow candles which only the agility of the attendants kept alight—their nimble ministrations were a subject for applause from the audience, who followed their evolutions with the intentness of a football crowd—it was gas that lit both stage and auditorium. The lamps suddenly shining by magic in the cloister during Meyerbeer's *Robert le Diable* brought sighs of admiration. Dawn broke with an evenness of graduation that owed its smooth flowering to switches turned by the firm hand of top-hatted stage managers. The mystery of the forest glade in *la Sylphide* was created by gauze veils muting the naked jets. This cunning trick was equally suited for evoking paradise, fairyland or the Elysian fields. Lightning flashed when resin was thrown on to a flaming torch. Castles burnt to the ground as stagehands brandished torches behind a transparent canvas and heaved chunks of moveable scenery to represent turrets crashing to earth. Such was the desire for realism that on several occasions the Opéra itself accidentally went up in flames.

Thunder rolled when the panting stage crew hammered sheets of iron and threw them clattering about in the wings. Hollow drums, vigorously turned by a handle, produced the moan of winds, and the gusts of the storm were imitated by the crumpling of taffeta. If rain was required, the effect was confined to the sound of small stones rattled violently together in a drum: earlier experiments with real water had only succeeded in drenching the audience. Snow was easier to counterfeit. A man perched high above the wings cast down handfuls of torn white paper, which, caught up by draughts back-stage, floated hazily before descending like the real thing.

All these shifts were necessary to create the tempests and torrents and cascades which patrons of the Opéra demanded for their money. The most popular effect, and one that drew cheers, was when the Devil or some other subterranean creature vanished through a trap-door. The singer carefully placed himself on the exact spot marked in chalk. At the precise moment he tapped with his foot. This was the signal for the stagehand beneath to pull a lever which opened the door. An assistant armed with a long tin pipe blew up sparks of flaming resin. Seconds later a plank slid quickly across to seal the hole. What the audience saw was the Devil going down to the flames of Hell. Success depended, of course, on speed and accurate timing, for if the trap-door failed to drop clear the singer was in danger from the plank that shot along almost simultaneously. History records only one performer who nearly met a distressing fate in this way. A curious fireman under the stage climbed on a chair the better to hear what was going on aloft. The trap-door opened, caught on the chair and stuck. The singer, a lady Devil, was marooned. She was saved from decapitation by the force of the machinery underneath. It smashed the chair to pieces and allowed her to find her way down to the stage Hell and not to the end which a fireman's careless curiosity had nearly ensured for her.

These elaborate mechanicals were not the only feature of life in the rue le Peletier which diverted Roqueplan's attention from the quality of the music he purveyed. Another topic which absorbed much of his time was the maintenance of an efficient claque to ensure that his luxurious productions were received in the favourable manner to which he hoped they would become accustomed. Since the time of Louis XV the claque had been an important feature of the Opéra. They were a fine body of men, respectably dressed and well disciplined, who took up their stations beneath the main chandelier.

Their leader had paid the theatre manager some 50,000 or 60,000 francs for the privilege of officiating. This money he recouped by selling complimentary tickets and by accepting contributions from performers anxious for the benefit of his professional assistance at their entrances and exits. Neither did prudent composers forget to include him among their expenses. He and his followers gave a play within a play, as it were, since their busy hands, setting up a thunder of applause amid an indifferent audience, combined with a lively manner to give a performance often better drilled and more convincing than what was seen on the stage. Sometimes their approach was different. When the management bore a grudge against a star singer or wanted, for some tactical reason, to make him end an engagement, the claque's tumultuous expressions of disapproval could be as impressive as their demonstrations of favour. The leader of the claque was a rich man. He kept a coach and pair and ran a country house as well as a place in town. He made even more money than the journalists who were rewarded substantially for their laudatory reviews of new productions.

This was the heady atmosphere into which Gounod, at the age of thirty-three, entered for the first time. Madame Viardot's great reputation probably saved him from the expensive and degrading precautions which little-known composers and even the famous Meyerbeer were forced to take. This was not the only difference which separated him and his work from the usual run of theatre composers at the time. With the exception of Italian opera—which anyway owed much of its success to brilliant singers—and isolated pieces like *Guillaume Tell* and a handful of passages from Meyerbeer, Halévy, Auber, Boieldieu and Ambroise Thomas, there was little of value in the permanent repertory. Even these names were represented by a small number of operas, the others comprising ready-made jobs run up by industrious journeymen. In the year of 1851 when *Sapho* was played there were five other new productions at the Opéra. One of these was *Pâquerette*, a ballet with scenario by Théophile Gautier and Saint-Léon. Another was the opera *le Démon de la nuit*. Both had music by Théodore Benoist, who is best remembered for having taught organ playing at the Conservatoire for over half a century. *Les Nations*, modestly described as an 'intermède', was the work of Théodore de Banville and of his counterpart in music Adolphe Adam, the composer of *Giselle*. Another ballet, *Vert-Vert*, was written in collaboration by Deldevez and Tolbecque, who later wisely changed their minds about their vocations and became respectively a conductor and a 'cellist. Finally there was *Zerline, ou la corbeille d'oranges*, a joint creation by the prolific team of Scribe and Auber. This was sheer vaudeville. The piece was notable for the début of Marietta Alboni who soon went on to higher things. In the meantime 'Achetez mes belles oranges!' became the hit-song of the week.

Amid this hotch-potch of picture-book effects and crude inspiration, *Sapho* stands out as work of a serious nature. In order to give his story dramatic interest, Augier combined the characters of Sappho the poetess and of another woman of the same name who, involved in a tragic love affair, threw herself into the sea. His plot gives us a Sappho whose rival for the love of Phaon is Glycera. The jealous Glycera, enraged by Phaon's preference for Sappho, plans to turn him against her. She threatens that unless Sappho gives him up, she will disclose to the authorities his implication in a plot to overthrow the tyrannical overlord Pittacus. At the same time she warns Phaon that he must leave the country because his secret is discovered. Phaon begs Sappho to accompany him, but she, silenced by Glycera's terrible threat, refuses. He sets off with the triumphant Glycera, leaving Sappho, maligned for her apparent fickleness, to kill herself.

Another distinction *Sapho* enjoyed was that it attracted the censor's attention. Unlike the usual entertainments at the Opéra, which flattered every official prejudice and avoided any opinion more controversial than a belief in happy endings, *Sapho* dealt, though incidentally, with political plot and the overthrow of authority. The short-lived Second Republic preferred its opera-goers to seek their pleasure in fairy glades and love potions. Louis-Napoléon had just become President, and in the year of *Sapho* he was bitterly opposed by a restive Parliament. Might not the lines calling on tyrants to tremble cause riots in the rue le Peletier? At the invitation of the police Augier obligingly changed them to something vague about Liberty, the austere goddess. Instead of a refrain urging the oppressed to brandish their chains, he wrote an appeal for aid from the revenging heavens to smash them. Subject to these changes the opera was allowed to be performed and the musical world was made safe for Louis-Napoléon's coup d'état some months later.

The audience at the first night of *Sapho* on the 16 April was surprised, and then, in general, pleased, by its novelty and freshness. It was quite different from the music to which they were used in the rue le Peletier. The press next day was not so favourable. Many of the critics were discomfited by the absence of familiar features. They felt uneasy in the presence of something new. Théophile Gautier, a reluctant journalist who used the services of the composer Ernest Reyer to 'ghost' the music criticisms that earned him a living and enabled him to write his poetry, complained at the absence of a ballet, though he gave the opera cautious praise. Another commentator, Adolphe Adam, who doubled the parts of critic and composer, shrewdly pointed out that *Sapho* was not a truly revolutionary piece but, rather, a work of restoration in so far as it harked back to Gluck. The 'new' elements in *Sapho* only appeared so because of the context in which it was placed.

Gluck, as Adam observed, is the mainspring of *Sapho*. His influence is particularly noticeable in the scene where the heroine— 'De la lyre et des vers je dispute la palme'—is greeted by the chorus as the muse of Lesbos when she enters a poetry competition. Her winning ode, 'Héro sur la tour solitaire', is another example of Gluck brought up to date, this time for the purpose of giving Madame Viardot a set-piece in which to show her talent. Memories of *Alceste* are also stirred by the poignancy of Phaon's 'J'arrive le premier au triste rendez-vous', which is a nostalgic lament for Sappho's lost love. Again, Sappho's 'O ma lyre immortelle' gives a tint of Gluck to her farewell of the world before throwing herself over the Leucadian cliff into the sea below.

The true originality of *Sapho* lies in the new spirit which shows itself throughout the opera. It owed nothing to Rossini, nor did it rely on the formulas which many of Gounod's contemporaries used. This emerges in the shepherd's song, 'Broutez le thym, broutez mes chèvres', in Act III, which the first-night audience greeted with shouts for an encore. Here are the unmistakable accents of *Mireille*, which was to appear thirteen years later. The tone is one of pastoral simplicity. It shines with a Hellenic radiance. By its very structure the opera lent itself to music of this nature. For once in the rue le Peletier, the stage crews, who normally worked miracles with elaborate machinery, stood idle. There were no earthquakes or tempests or burning palaces in *Sapho*. The drama was expressed solely in music that was dignified and restrained. When Sappho and Glycera battle to win Phaon, their Act II duet, 'Je veux que Phaon parte', resolves itself into a conflict of dark dramatic force. The clash of wills is translated by purely musical terms.

It is probable that this deceptively static quality and the lack of grand scenic effects robbed *Sapho* of the credit that was its due. There were, in all, seven performances of this *succès d'estime*, after which it vanished from the repertory. The opera surfaced briefly in the following January, having been brutally cut so that it might share the dignity of a double bill with *Vert-Vert*.

There existed, also, a faction violently hostile towards Madame Viardot and her husband. Her triumphs had brought her a number of enemies, the most eloquent of whom was Léon Escudier. He was a power in French musical life, the founder of a journal which he turned into an instrument of propaganda for Italian music. His publishing house represented Verdi's interests in Paris, and it was Escudier who organized the first French production of *Aïda*. 'Madame Viardot', wrote Escudier with his accustomed virulence, 'no longer sings. Every note that emerges from her intelligent voice is an ear-splitting shout. This singer, whom I once admired so much, is more or less dead to art. Her shattered vocal powers have lost their charm. They are but the shadow of a once beautiful picture.'

The rest of the pack followed Escudier's lead. They seized on the traces of wear that already showed in Pauline Viardot's singing and used them as an excuse for a wholesale attack. As early as the fourth performance of *Sapho* there were restive cries for it to be superseded by *Zerline, ou la corbeille d'oranges*. People were impatient to hear Alboni. *Sapho* was doing poorly at the box office, so *Zerline* was duly trundled forth. It lasted thirteen performances.

In July Gounod left Paris with the Viardots and travelled to London. The reason for their journey was a production of *Sapho* in Italian at Covent Garden. On the 9 August Michael Costa directed it there with a starry cast which included Pauline Viardot in her original part. With the exception of the loyal Chorley, critical opinion was unfavourable. English audiences found the opera dull and boring. Their ears were offended by the apparently long-drawn out modulations and understated effects. They thought the whole thing pretentious. Gounod wrote sadly to his mother: 'London isn't my sort of town.'

Many years later Gounod looked back at *Sapho* and was philosophical about it. He recognized its lack of stage sense, its ignorance of theatrical effect and its failure to exploit the resources of the orchestra. On the other hand, he detected in *Sapho* a genuine feeling for expression and a sure lyrical instinct. He saw the truth of that rough and ready rule that a work for the theatre usually gets the fate it deserves. The public's judgement, he admitted, was final. One could not expect an audience to react in any other way than through its emotions. In the meantime, he had experienced his first failure. And that, in the theatre, could in the long run be more useful than a first success.

V

The Reluctant Husband – *Ulysse* –
la Nonne sanglante

In his memoires Gounod tells an affecting story connected with the
first night of *Sapho*. According to this tender anecdote, he met Berlioz in the wings and perceived tears coursing down the lined features
of that emotional composer. Gounod then conducted him to his
mother, wishing to show her this lachrymose tribute as the best
review of his work she would ever see. 'Madame,' he reports Berlioz
as saying, 'I don't remember having felt such emotion in twenty
years.'

Like all artists, Gounod brought a strong creative element into his
everyday life. It was natural for him to embellish routine facts with a
more pleasing gloss and to mould them into a pattern that satisfied
his wish for artistic symmetry. The Berlioz story is all the more
delightful in that it is quite untrue. The basis of this flight of fancy is
contained in Berlioz' article on *Sapho*. Here he remarks that Sapho's
farewell, 'O ma lyre immortelle', which moved the audience as well,
'ended in masterly fashion a scene of melancholy grandeur that
caused me one of the keenest emotions I have felt for a long time.'

While Berlioz had reserves to make about some of the passages
in *Sapho*—he found them, odd to relate, too 'strong'—his praise in
general was unqualified. He saw a valuable talent in the young composer and a feeling for the noble and the exalted which deserved
encouragement all the more so in that the present musical age was,
in Berlioz' opinion, meanly corrupt and corrupting. This generous
review sealed a friendship between the two composers which dated
from Gounod's youth and his first hearing of *Roméo et Juliette*. Now
that the apprentice had begun to make good, the bond was strengthened by mutual appreciation.

Gounod was fascinated by the personality of his friend. He wrote:

There are two men, two beings in Berlioz. First, there is the child (both boy and girl) adorable in its charm, gentleness, tenderness, simple unconstraint—second, there is the grown character (man and woman), ardent, passionate, deep, a thinker and a dreamer, often carried away to the point of dizziness and just as often arguing to the point of splitting hairs. It is, I think, in this duality of make-up (if one may say so) that we must seek explanation of Berlioz' lack of success, *in general*, with what is called the *Public*. The Public doesn't *want* to be asked to work: it doesn't *seek* to understand: it wants to *feel*, and to *feel immediately*. . . . Now in Berlioz' [music] there is often a texture which the public finds difficult to grasp; it always wants to get back to *what it knows*: Berlioz has forgotten, or rather disdained, to check up on his music; it is gold which hasn't been coined and therefore is not in general circulation. . . .[1]

Although today Berlioz is regarded as one of the giants of his age, he was not at the time a very influential figure. In the eighteen-fifties he enjoyed more fame abroad than in France. His music was unpopular and the subject of cabals by jealous rivals. The articles he wrote, seasoned with a deadly wit and contempt for the second-rate, only added to the number of enemies his outlandish compositions had already earned for him. He was unable to do much that would further Gounod's career in a practical way, anxious though he was to help him. Here the support of François Seghers was more useful. In the early months of 1852 he played a number of Gounod's religious works at four of his Société Sainte-Cécile concerts. There was also a performance of *le Bourgeois gentilhomme* at the Comédie-Français for which Gounod arranged and adapted Lully's music. One of the numbers he wrote himself and substituted it for the original which the management, curiously, did not consider to be gay enough. The pastiche was so skilful that people were deceived and thought that a new piece by Lully had been discovered.

All these activities helped to make his name better known. He had lately renewed acquaintance with his former piano teacher at the Conservatoire, Pierre Zimmermann, who must have been impressed by the progress his former pupil was making—so much so that

[1] Bibliothèque de l'Opéra, Acq. 25209. Letter to Mme Charles Rhoné. Dimanche matin, 10 août. Baden Baden, 8h. [1862].

Gounod became engaged to his daughter Anna. Zimmermann was then in his late sixties and approaching the end of a very successful career in Parisian musical life. He was, appropriately, the son of a piano manufacturer, and the instruments which the father built the son was to play with supreme accomplishment. He also composed. One of his works, a three-act piece, was done at the Opéra-Comique. His many piano pieces include variations on the song 'S'il est vrai que d'etre deux', and, more bleakly, on 'Il est trop tard', though the brilliance of the writing made up for the regretful nature of the theme. Rondeaus, studies and quadrilles tripped in dozens from his ready brain. Just to show that there was something more to the piano than drawing-room entertainment, he produced a massive *Encyclopédie du pianiste* which included a weighty treatise on harmony and counterpoint.

Zimmermann excelled as a teacher. No less than fifty-two of his pupils won first prizes at the Conservatoire. This might suggest that he was a mere trainer of examination-fodder. The witness of his colleagues and pupils—who included Ambroise Thomas, Franck, Bizet, Massenet and Alkan—proves the contrary. He was loved for his good will and sympathetic manner. He was respected for his skill and wide knowledge. These qualities won him the devotion of his pupils. He had the gift of drawing the best out of the least promising student who came his way.

Opinion about his family was not so unanimous. He married a somewhat forbidding lady who it, seems, passed on to her daughters a number of unattractive features, not the least of which was a tendency to pettiness. Madame Zimmermann, it was said, had considerable trouble in finding husbands for her four daughters in spite of the handsome dowries they brought with them. When Gounod strayed innocently into their circle he was to prove easy meat for the shrewd Madame Zimmermann. Here was a young man of thirty-two, handsome, pliant and socially acceptable. True, he had no money, but he was launched on a promising career. She did not hold his priestly tendencies against him. He had clearly grown out of that youthful dream and was set for what should eventually be a lucrative position in the theatre. Her husband's professional estimate of Gounod's talent assured her that she would not be throwing away her Anna on a worthless failure. She was prepared to wait.

And so Gounod moved inevitably under the sway of the Zimmermanns. He frequented the household and enchanted every guest who came there with his affable ways. Sometimes he would sit at the piano and sing to his audience with the voice which, frail as it was, drew on fathomless reserves of charm. The ladies adored his expressive features, so eloquent of the admiration he felt for them, and his bright eyes, so full of subtle meanings. They felt that he really understood them. He would circulate among them distributing kisses and hugging them in the exuberance of his loving emotion. The men he embraced—his affection for humanity was universal— were not so overcome. But while they deplored his gushing manner and called him 'a philandering monk', they had to admit the force of his personality.

Gounod was used to the domination of women. Up to the time he met the Zimmermanns he had been guided by a strongwilled-mother. It was natural that in Madame Zimmermann he should recognize and submit to the familiar voice of command. After he had been frequenting her home for some time she noted that her daughter Anna was showing an interest in him. She took him aside and suggested that he make a decision either to marry Anna or to cease his visits. People might start talking. He went away and reflected. There was little he could offer a bride in the way of money or possessions. He wrote a letter explaining that under the circumstances he did not think he should aspire to Anna's hand. Not wishing to trust this important message to the post, he went to deliver it in person at the Zimmermann's house.

Madame Zimmermann herself opened the door. Before he could hand over the letter she exclaimed joyfully: 'Ah, my dear child, I was expecting your visit. Come and embrace your betrothed!' Slipping the undelivered letter into his pocket, he dared do nothing else but obey. Later on, he used ruefully to say: 'What a subject for a comic opera: *le Fiancé malgré lui!*'

However reluctant he may have been at first, he realized that his marriage was not such a bad idea after all. Anna's father was a man of wide professional acquaintance that would be useful to him in his career. The Zimmermanns, furthermore, owned property. These factors made up for the lack of romance. If there was some weakness in his character that usually made him bow to circumstances, then he might as well do so with good grace for the sake of a profitable match. Towards the end of April 1852, he married his Anna in the fashionable church of Auteuil. (The old one, that is, before it was replaced by the present building in 1877. It has always seemed just to miss the celebrity that comes from housing the bones of the famous. Voltaire's brother is buried there but not the writer himself. The father of Anatole France, though not his son, is also entombed in the grounds.)

There was one family in Paris which viewed with distress the Gounod marriage. The announcement of his engagement surprised Pauline Viardot, for Gounod had always poked fun at the Zimmermanns and their dreary daughters. Now, with a sweet solemnity, he insisted that Madame Viardot attend the wedding and promised to postpone it until the arrival of the baby she was expecting. In the days that followed she several times invited him and his prospective family-in-law to dinner. They failed to arrive. The next thing she heard was that the wedding would take place quietly. She was not invited.

She sent, nonetheless, a wedding present to which she added a bracelet for Anna Zimmermann. Next day Gounod returned it to her. He limply explained that as he was himself giving one to his bride, he thought it best to hand back the trinket. Louis Viardot wrote him a furious letter. Through a third party the Viardots learned that the Zimmermanns had received an anonymous note confirming the gossip about Gounod's relationship with Pauline. There were demands for apologies and threats of appeal to Gounod's father-in-law.

Throughout this unhappy episode Gounod whirled helplessly about like a leaf caught up in raging cross-winds. He swayed to the blasts of indignation that came from the Viardots, and he bent before the storm of anger that arose on the Zimmermann side. For there is no doubt that the Zimmermanns, despite an acquaintanceship with Pauline dating back many years, disliked her intensely. The obvious reason is that Anna was jealous of her. The feeling was shared by Madame Zimmermann. One account relates that when Pauline's gift of the bracelet arrived, Anna furiously declared that she did not accept gifts from her husband's mistress.[1] Faced with the prospect of endless family rows unless he did as he was told—for Anna had the same effect on her husband as did Mrs Proudie on hers—Gounod once more took the easy way out. In answer to protests from Louis Viardot he sought shelter behind vague excuses and regrets. He hoped, he added, that God would help him bear the affliction of

[1] Georgina Weldon: *My Orphanage and Gounod in England* (The Music and Art Association, 1882), p.96.

losing the valued friendship of the Viardots and their associates.

Pauline Viardot was deeply hurt. She had taken Gounod into her family, encouraged him to write his first opera and opened the doors of the theatre to him. No one could have been more helpful to a young musician. In her disillusionment she described him to Georges Sand as a Tartuffe. It was the hypocrisy of his action that shocked her most. Yet although Gounod the man aroused only contempt in her, she remained an admirer of his music. Her hope for him was that his genius would not be harmed by his present friends or by his own character.

So far as his career was concerned Gounod had done himself no harm. A brutal assessment of Madame Viardot's potentiality in this respect would have shown that she had served her purpose. The reception given to *Sapho* proved that she could not be counted on much longer as a patron. An ambitious composer would be unwise to link himself too closely with an opera star whose voice was not what it was and whose enemies were powerful. There was little room for gratitude in the jungle world of the theatre.

Very soon after his marriage Gounod received the reward for the step he had taken. His appointment as director of the Orphéon de la ville de Paris, in which his influential father-in-law must have had a hand, gave him at one stroke a well-paid permanent job and the opportunity for interesting musical work. The organization was founded in 1833 by Guillaume Boquillon Wilhem, a pioneer of choral singing in France and a friend of Béranger. Earlier, as head of musical education in primary schools, he had created a vigorous tradition of choral teaching for children which was approved by those anxious to see the working classes, whether they like it or not, enjoying the pleasures of harmless recreation. On his death in 1842 a benevolent government arranged for the work to continue, and by the time Gounod took up his appointment the system was well established. During the eight years in which he held the post he was to write many short choral works, and the experience he gained in handling massed vocal forces proved useful in oratorio work later. As part of his duties at this time he also perpetrated 'Vive l'Empereur!' the national anthem of the Second Empire.

Theatrically, too, his career was developing well. As early as the first night of *Sapho* he had been approached by the dramatist François Ponsard to write incidental music for the play *Ulysse*. This rather stuffy figure in the reaction against Romanticism occupies

77

today the same dim region as Émile Augier. The Goncourt brothers drew on their inexhaustible malice to describe his tragedies as resembling '*un camée antique . . . moderne!*' The witticism is cruel but apt in its reference to the cold spirit of neo-classicism which breathes faintly in his plays. *Lucrèce* gained an early success in which it was helped by the acting of Rachel. Many other pieces followed, including a comedy based, improbably, on an ode by Horace. Early in life Ponsard was cheered by students in the Latin Quarter, not because they admired the insipid merit of his dramas but because they approved his dislike of Louis-Napoléon's régime. Political attitudes have often excused bad art, and Ponsard was frequently to benefit in this way.

Another paradox is shown by the contrast between his work and his life. The verse of his plays is thin and bloodless. No air circulates around the flatly chiselled stances. His characters are frozen in heroic poses. Yet when Ponsard's mistress decided after a long liaison to marry someone else, the unhappy writer, who did not allow himself a line of unruly passion in his dramas, attempted to kill himself. A wretched old age was reserved for him. The man whose attacks on the corruption of the régime had won the plaudits of Left-wing students was obliged to accept doles from Louis-Napoléon, to beg with tears for a loan from Princess Mathilde, and to limp hopefully, in constant pain, among the suppliants who looked for favours from the great.

Ulysse recounts the familiar story of the hero's return to Ithaca and his onslaught on Penelope's suitors. By choosing this episode from Homer Ponsard gave himself a scenario which is neatly self-contained. Scenes of violence are, in the best classical tradition, kept off-stage, and a chorus is always at hand with smoothly scanned references to steaming altars and murder elsewhere than in the respectable precincts of the Comédie-Française. The verse throughout is, in the Tennysonian phrase, splendidly null.

While Gounod was writing the music for *Ulysse* he was assisted by a new friend, the seventeen-year-old Camille Saint-Saëns. Like Gounod, a child prodigy, Saint-Saëns was born to music. He had written his first composition while still an infant and made his début as a concert pianist at the age of eight. Mutual friends introduced him to Gounod who was astonished by his extraordinary command of musical techniques. Gounod was more than twice as old as his protégé, yet there were certain accomplishments in which the big-nosed lisping youth excelled his senior. Among them was playing the piano, an activity in which Gounod, when accompanying himself in his songs, was able to mask his lack of virtuoso powers. For other compositions it was a different matter, and Saint-Saëns was able to help out by playing at sight Gounod's inky manuscript.

Nearly every day while Gounod was working on *Ulysse* Saint-Saëns came at his invitation to play over the latest sections. 'Gounod was full of his subject,' Saint-Saëns recorded, 'and told me all about his aims, ideas and desires. His great ambition was to discover beautiful colour on the palette of the orchestra, and rather than take ready-made systems from the classics he sought at first hand the shades necessary to his brush by the study of tones and new combinations. "The resources of sonority", he once said to me, "are still largely unexplored."' With this in mind he prescribed, for the nymphs' chorus 'Déesse qui portes l'Égide', a glass-plated harmonica and a triangle to be beaten by a stick muffled in skin. This opening chorus, which is sung as Ulysse on his return approaches the nymphs' grotto, has the sort of delicate translucence that Gounod was anxious to achieve.

Sometimes in *Ulysee* there is a suggestion that the composer is thinking of the massed choirs of amateur schoolchildren for whom he was writing much at the time. The vocal parts are occasionally doubled in the orchestration with slavish fidelity, as if Gounod feared that his professional singers, like the boys and girls of the Orphéon, needed this type of insurance. What most alarms the unsuspecting ear is the irruption, in Act II, of a blatant waltz tune to which the swineherds' chorus invokes Bacchus. It has a lilt and swing that would make it more at home in the Opéra-Comique. This is all the more apparent in that the rest of the score is written with a sober elegance. The men's choruses are firm and virile. Those for the women have subtlety and grace of colour. One of the numbers, which blooms at the end into a delicious modulation. later knew success on its own as a song under the title of 'le Chant d'Euryclée'.

Considerable pains were taken over the production. The cast and the singers were distinguished, the scenery was lavish and the orchestra was large. At the first night the conductor was Offenbach, and we may imagine that he did full justice to the waltz mentioned above. Despite the generous efforts of the Comédie-Française, *Ulysse* met with indifference. Some of Ponsard's lines caused disapproving murmurs, and others, unconsciously bathetic, earned derisive laughter. Berlioz, who had studied the score in manuscript, thought highly of it and praised the way in which the music grew naturally in proportion to the drama of the piece. Other critics emphasized a noble, quasi-religious austerity. Some detected a follower of Gluck and Sacchini and looked forward to the emergence of Gounod as a genuinely French composer. But while the critics discussed the music for *Ulysse* with eager curiosity, the general public looked away. *Ulysse*, like *Sapho*, was too refined for the age, although a revival two years later brought it more of the success it deserved.

Only a few months later, by an ironic coincidence, the composer whose music was thought too lofty for the mob produced a trifle for which he has been damned ever since. On 10 April 1853, the conductor Jules Pasdeloup introduced at one of his concerts the 'Meditation sur le 1er prélude de Bach' which soon became known as 'Ave Maria'. Gounod referred to it as an *espièglerie*, or mischievous prank. It was his father-in-law who brought it into prominence. Hearing Gounod improvising one day in the family drawing-room, he found the theme charming and urged him to repeat it. Zimmermann wrote it down and had it played to Gounod on the violin accompanied by a chorus. The effect was attractive.

Soon afterwards things got out of hand. When Pasdeloup gave the 'Méditation' public currency, audiences which had been cold towards *Sapho* and *Ulysse* abruptly went mad for Gounod. It became the fashion for ladies to hear it with expressions of idyllic piety, and for gentlemen to listen with manly respect. No *soirée musicale* was complete without a rendering of the ubiquitous morsel. No drawing-room pianist or violinist could avoid requests for it. Gounod's little joke ballooned into a gigantic best-seller. Publishers rushed out arrangements for a wild variety of instruments and combinations. Soon the Méditation was being punched out by full orchestras complete with big drum.

Or was it only a little joke after all ? Naturally Gounod deplored the immense popular success of an unconsidered trifle and felt the annoyance of all artists when they see their important works ignored in favour of minor ones. He would have been less than human had he protested at the rewards in money and fame which suddenly came his way, even though he must have felt qualms over the disappointing fate of *Sapho* and *Ulysse*. The incident, however, points to yet another quality in his very mixed character. Like many people,

Gounod combined within himself several different personalities. There was the priest who yearned after mysticism and who was desperately aware of his own unworthiness. There was the admirer of Palestrina and Mozart who strove towards an ideal of purity in music. There were also the careerist who did not hesitate to desert Pauline Viardot, the hypocrite who justified his treachery with unctuous words, and the vulgarian who tampered with Bach. For, not content with laying hands on the first prelude in *Das Wohltemperierte Clavier*, he was, at the age of seventy-four, a year before his death, to produce a 'Second Ave Maria'.

Gounod's distinctive blend of piety and hypocrisy, of high-thinking and vulgarity, was one that increasingly puzzled the young Bizet, who already had won the older man's admiration for his precocious talent. Bizet took part at the organ in early performances of the 'Méditation' and was soon to do many odd jobs for Gounod. He made transcriptions of orchestral works, arranged the vocal scores of operas, and, with Saint-Saëns, was readily available to lend a hand in carrying out chores allocated by the busy composer. At the age of fourteen he heard *Sapho* and immediately recognized the superior talent that lay behind it. *Ulysse* confirmed the deep respect he felt for Gounod and at the same time increased his natural sympathy for him when he saw the cruel reception it had from indifferent audiences.

Naturally flattered by the respectful attitude of a young and gifted musician, Gounod did more than provide him with useful hack-work. (The earliest example of this was Bizet's vocal score of *Ulysse*.) He encouraged him with advice and gave helpful criticism of his early compositions. There were also personal circumstances that strengthened the friendship: each composer had been brought up by a devoted mother and each had an easy charm that made him attractive in society.

Bizet was then too young to appreciate the complexities of human nature. Enjoyment of his friend's company was sometimes clouded by a trace of malice or by a touch of deviousness on Gounod's part. As he grew older he was baffled by the unease that crept into his feelings for him. Some of this he attributed to Anna Gounod. The family's behaviour on occasion exasperated him, and he thought Gounod's wife, though well intentioned, to be a stupid woman who needed thoroughly snubbing from time to time. Gounod's willingness to be led by stronger, if coarser, personalities worried Bizet.

81

Eventually he could not help a certain disillusionment. Yet although he was later shocked by Gounod's weakness and even hurt by his apparent deceit, he could not help but pay tribute to his musicianship. Gounod's influence on his own work does not show itself in the earlier pieces alone.

The assistance of Bizet and Saint-Saëns was, at this time, very welcome to Gounod. He was a busy man. His work as director of the Orphéon involved him not only in writing music for his choirs to perform but also in conducting, administration, the supervision of rehearsals and organization. The pieces he composed ranged from the noisy 'Vive l'Empereur' to the schoolroom austerities of 'la Distribution des prix' and 'la Géographie'. The religious needs of his infant singers were provided for by 'le Catéchisme' and 'le Benedicite'. 'L'Écriture' and 'l'Arithmétique' led thankfully to 'la Récréation', though there was a hint of warning in 'le Temps qui fuit et s'envole'. The atmosphere of chalk and blackboard was lightened with the promise of 'les Vacances'. And then there were the arrangements of Lully, Handel and Rameau that guided his Orphéonistes up from the lowlands of pedagogical music.

The biggest piece he wrote for his children's choirs was the full-scale *Messe des orphéonistes*. The final rehearsal took place in the church of Saint Germain-l'Auxerrois before an audience that included the Prefect of the Seine and other notables. The first performance, on the 12 June 1853, was no less splendid. It is, in one way, more difficult to write for amateur musicians and to make them perform satisfactorily than it is to do so for professionals. On this occasion Gounod was praised for his dual achievement as composer and as conductor of the unaccompanied choirs.

On the 13 June, the day after the first performance of Gounod's Orphéon mass, his wife gave birth to a daughter. Not long afterwards the child died. In the autumn of the following year the family was bereaved again. Gounod's father-in-law, Pierre Zimmermann, had for some time been suffering from an illness which triumphed at last in his sixty-ninth year. The obituary notice Gounod wrote spoke of Zimmermann's tireless activity, his patient hard work and his respect for truth and beauty. He referred to the sociability and the charm of character which attracted to Zimmermann everyone of importance in musical life. Two days after Zimmermann's death on the 29 October he was buried at Auteuil. Outside observers would have said that with his departure the Zimmermann family had lost

its only bearable member. For his son-in-law there were compensa-
tions. The Gounods inherited the handsome country house out at
Saint-Cloud. It stood in the former parc de Montretout, near the
site of the château de Saint-Cloud which the brother of Louis XIV
had built for himself. Here died Henriette d'Angleterre, inspiring
Bossuet's anguished cry, '*Madame se meurt, Madame est morte!*' Here
too, in the nearby property, Gounod was to end his days. The house
was large and comfortable, with high-ceilinged rooms and massy
chandeliers. Tall windows looked out at trees and a neat garden, and
the greenery beyond vanished unscarred into the distance. Silence
was all around. From now on Gounod spent as much time as he
could here, composing undisturbed or reading in the extensive
library of books and music assembled by his scholarly father-in-law.

Despite a heavy programme of Orphéon work, he was able to get
away to Lyon and conduct the first performance of an oratorio called
l'Ange et Tobie. The little work pleased the Lyonnais, who, it appeared, were even more taken with the irrepressible 'Ave Maria'.
He returned to Paris and the busy routine of directing four Orphéon
concerts in a week, taking innumerable rehearsals and complaining
of amateur singers who were 'put to flight by the appearance of a
sharp or a flat'. He managed to train this unpromising material and
to give performances with a choir of eleven hundred *orphéonistes*.

At the same time he kept in touch with the theatre and never lost
hope. When a publisher offered to print the score of *Ulysse* he was
overjoyed. 'To be in print!!! *Saved* from oblivion!!!—Nothing can
convey an idea of my happiness,' he wrote, adding drily, 'The saviour
in question was M. Escudier who was generous enough to buy my
score from me . . . for nothing!' But then he thought of *Sapho*, who,
prophetically, had thrown herself into a sea whence no publisher
had attempted to fish her out. He accepted. Publication would help
his career and he must take a long-term view.

His earlier scruples were forgotten. *Sapho* and *Ulysse* taught him
a lesson. They had been composed with no other aim than that of
producing honest works of art. Of course, he hoped they would
further his ambition, but in writing them he had not stooped to
flatter the taste of the crowd. As a result these high-minded works
met with failure. The message was obvious: he must look for something more popular. In 1852 an opportunity presented itself. Roqueplan offered him a libretto called *la Nonne sanglante*, a title not fated
to charm but one that would perhaps create a thrill of agreeable

horror when seen on a theatre poster. The author of this saga of the bloody nun was Eugène Scribe. He received a down-payment of five thousand francs in addition to the royalties he might expect from his work. There was also a clause in his contract which must have originated in Roqueplan's ironic sense of humour: it guaranteed him a free seat for life on the nights when opera was played.

The generous terms given to Scribe were an indication of his importance in the theatre at the time. He was a one-man factory geared to the mass-production of plays. After studying the law half-heartedly, he wrote, at the age of nineteen, *le Prétendu sans le savoir ou l'occasion fait le larron*. Undeterred by its failure, he went on to turn out some four hundred plays and libretti, often in collaboration with a small army of hacks whom he drilled to produce the necessary raw material which his theatrical flair would then transform. He worked like a skilful watchmaker, contriving ingenious situations and bringing off clever effects with cynical ease. The stage technique he evolved was glossily efficient. He was not a cultured man. On election to the Académie Française he astonished learned members of that body when, on pleading that the theatre's mission was not to discuss politics, he uttered the memorable phrase: 'Do Molière's plays tell us about events during the century of Louis XIV? . . . Do they speak to us about the revocation of the Edict of Nantes?' In one sense he was only too correct, for Molière died in 1673 and the Edict was not revoked until 1685.

The collector of absurdities will find a rich field in the works of Eugène Scribe. A pearl like the following is by no means rare:

> *D'avoir pu le tuer vivant*
> *Je me glorifierai sans cesse !*[1]

Or the dramatist writes, and will not pause to correct: '*Quoiqu'il advienne ou quoiqu'il arrive.*'[2] At first these look like the symbols of acute verbigeration. Then one realizes that the haste in which he confected half a dozen plays a year for half a century is more probably the cause. *Adrienne Lecouvreur*, a biographical play about the actress, still shows one or two signs of life. His *le Verre d'eau*, a political comedy, retains its flavour as a mocking commentary on the ways of government. The libretti Scribe wrote for Meyerbeer, Halévy and Auber survive fitfully in relation to the varying fortunes of the com-

---

[1] 'I shall always glory in having been able to kill him alive!'
[2] 'Although it happens or whatever happens.'

posers with whom he worked. For *la Nonne sanglante* he co-opted the services of a fellow dramatist called Germain Delavigne, brother of that Casimir who made a precocious entry into the Académie Française at the tender age of thirty-two. The best-known of Casimir's plays was *les Enfants d'Édouard*, a drama about the children in the Tower which once moved sentimental audiences.

The libretto of *la Nonne sanglante* had already been offered to seven composers. For ten years it circulated from hand to hand, starting at the top with Verdi and Berlioz, then slipping down gently by way of Meyerbeer and Halévy until it reached the murky depths with Félicien David and Clapisson. Berlioz wrestled with the piece for more than five years until Scribe asked for it back. At last the vagabond libretto arrived in the eager but apprehensive hands of Gounod. He went, a little nervously, to see his friend Berlioz and to tell him how uneasy he felt at having accepted the libretto after it had been snatched away from him, Berlioz. The older man appeared generous and took pains to soothe Gounod's scruples. Yet Berlioz had already composed two acts, including the 'legend' of the bloody nun which he considered to be his best music.

There should have been a warning for Gounod in the libretto's nomadic history. So keen was he, though, to reach big audiences that he cheerfully accepted what he knew to be work of inferior quality. His literary taste was good. He appreciated words, their values and their beauties. *La Nonne sanglante* was a typical Scribe farrago. One sees Gounod manfully reading it through and gritting his teeth in determination. Ambition forced him to ignore both taste and refinement.

The source on which Scribe drew was a tainted one. Matthew Lewis' novel *The Monk* first appeared in 1796. The ingredients of magic, murder and torture soon turned this piece of trash into a best-seller. The author became known as 'Monk' Lewis and his novel was widely read by those who enjoyed the mixture of crudity and lasciviousness. A French translation appeared in 1840, and Scribe, ever alert to popular demand, pounced on it.

His version is set in eleventh-century Bohemia. Two warring noblemen, Luddorf and Moldav, agree to end the vendetta which has kept their families apart for years. The pact is sealed with Moldav proposing to marry off his daughter Agnès to Luddorf's eldest son Théobald. But Théobald's brother, Rodolphe, loves Agnès. His passion is returned. The two lovers decide to flee.

Rodolphe suggests they take advantage of the legend of the bloody nun whose ghost haunts Moldav's castle. Agnès will disguise herself in the spectre's white robes and appear at midnight. This will frighten everyone away, and in the confusion the lovers will make their escape. Rodolphe waits, the clock strikes, and the nun, a blood-stain soiling her long white veil, materializes beside him. He feels the chill of the grave upon him, for this is not Agnès disguised but the phantom itself. 'À moi! ! ! ' shrieks the apparition, and Rodolphe is borne off amid thunder and lightning. He is betrothed to her at a ghostly ceremony in the nether regions.

Returned to this world, Rodolphe learns that Théobald has died in battle and that his parents now agree to his marrying Agnès. Alas, that bloody nun shimmers in again and reminds him of the vows he took during the ceremony with her. Among them is an oath he swore to kill the man who deceived and then murdered her when she was alive. Worse still, she indicates as her murderer Rodolphe's own father, Luddorf. The plot now loops a few vertiginous loops, and it is enough to say that Agnès, horrified by Rodolphe's infernal oath, rejects him; that her family plan to assassinate him; and that Luddorf, stirred at last by the pangs of conscience, substitutes himself for his son and is duly liquidated by the avenging hand. The spectral nun, clanking daggers and graveside lanterns, then sums up the proceedings by chanting:

> *La vertu du coupable*
> *Est dans le repentir.*

This was the plot Gounod struggled with during the last weary months of 1853. While there was plenty of scope for Roqueplan's beloved effects—weird glimmers for the nun, thunder and lightning when she makes off with Rodolphe, creeping mists during the be-trothal ceremony—the musical opportunities were limited. Gounod was depressed by the unrewarding nature of the libretto and the emptiness of the characterization. In spite of the fantastic colouring of the action, he pointed out, the dramatic situation was poor. Scribe always replied to criticisms of his work by saying that he deliberately aimed at mediocrity since good poetry would detract from the music and hamper the composer's inspiration. The argument deserves credit at least for ingenuity.

After the usual delays inseparable from all theatrical enterprises, *la Nonne sanglante* appeared behind the footlights on the 18

October 1854. The critics were kind. Adolphe Adam declared that if Gounod had had a German name impossible to pronounce he would by now have become a great man. Théophile Gautier, or his ghost-writer (perhaps Reyer), decided that Gounod was a master. Berlioz sympathized with him in his battle to set an inferior libretto and mentioned, rather laconically, that *la Nonne sanglante* was an undoubted success. This was confirmed by takings at the box office. An excited stage-manager told Gounod that his opera was bringing an average of between 7 and 8,000 francs nightly. This compared favourably with Meyerbeer's block-busters which at the time averaged less. Moreover, at each performance Gounod collected a royalty of 250 francs. It seemed that at last he had found an audience.

But life in the theatre is never as simple as it may appear. After eleven performances of the opera Nestor Roqueplan resigned from his post. He left the management with debts of 900,000 francs. His successor was obviously a man of taste, for, declaring that so long as he was director of the theatre he would never put on such 'muck', he withdrew *la Nonne sanglante*. The opera was given a few perform-ances elsewhere and then vanished for ever. Its only monument was the vocal score prepared by Bizet. In the following year Gounod's mother-in-law, Madame Zimmermann, paid the cost of its publication.

Cautiously dedicated 'to my friend F. Halévy', *la Nonne sanglante* is an odd piece of work. One senses throughout the strain Gounod must have felt and the reluctance with which he handled the uncongenial task. Berlioz, perhaps like other composers who had glanced at the libretto, felt that the '*Légende de la nonne sanglante*' should be a highlight of the score. Gounod, too, thought it deserved prominence, and the tune he uses occurs in the brief overture. Rodolphe sings it after a duet with Agnès in which they lament his father's disapproval of their love. The legend has a pretty turn of phrase, but the springy rhythm so clashes with the lugubrious melody that the effect of eeriness is lost. Here Gounod, like the Fat Boy, is trying to make our flesh creep and does not succeed. This unconvincing essay in the macabre is immediately succeeded by a bouncy duet ('*adore*' rhymes with '*implore*' rhymes with '*aurore*') which looks as if it had strayed from an Offenbach operetta.

The composer was also guilty of including a pair of tinkling waltzes—one for the ballet and the other for a village wedding scene complete with jolly peasants. Better things are to be found in the

Wedding March and in Luddorf's Act V aria where the unhappy father laments his crime. Luddorf is an early example of what may be termed Gounod's Sarastro complex. So deep under Mozart's spell was he that he could not write a bass part without subconsciously invoking Sarastro and *die Zauberflöte*. This shows again in the Act I chorus, 'C'est Dieu qui nous appelle'. Gounod himself thought this to be one of the best passages in the opera.

Soon after the production of *la Nonne sanglante* he was singled out at a reception by Meyerbeer. The composer of *le Prophète* rushed up to him, shook him effusely by the hand, overwhelmed him with a torrent of compliments, and, in emotional tones, said to him: 'Ah, cher Maître, you must have been very frightened. Let me tell you that I—*who am but a humble worm*—am sometimes ill for a whole month after a first night!' For once Gounod, the master of blarney, was made speechless by this barbed remark—and that is why, perhaps, he took the trouble to deny that it had ever been made.

Twenty years later he was resigned to the failure of his first 'popular' work for the theatre. What he had attempted to do was to set the nineteenth-century equivalent of those modern horror films about vampires or Jack the Ripper or Frankenstein monsters, where the only criterion is the ingenuity of the devices used to thrill the groundlings. He realized that the subject was flawed from the start because the basic situation, fantastic and wholly improbably, lacked dramatic interest.

But he remained hopeful. Impressed by the initially favourable reaction to *la Nonne sanglante*, Scribe suggested another collaboration. Gounod went to see him and spoke of creating an opera that would this time win both artistic and financial success. Scribe had had by now the opportunity to scan reviews of their joint work. What he saw displeased him.

'Mon cher ami!' he said, angrily crumpling up the offending newspapers in his hand, 'I've had enough! I give you the finest, most dramatic, most effective libretto I've ever written, and now the critics tear it to pieces, say I've had my time and that it only remains for me to *retire*! Very well then. I *will*. So don't count on me.'

Gounod crept home, chastened and discomfited. Rejection by the most important librettist of the period seemed to have ruined his chances on the stage. Perhaps he should have stayed in the cloister and never ventured upon the treacherous path that led to the theatre. Soon afterwards his wife's sister died. Professional unsuccess and this reminder of mortality threw him into a studious melancholia. He strolled in the woods, reading and thinking of Saint Augustine. In translating the *Confessions* he found comfort, and he frequented with relief *The City of God*. He wrote in his notes: 'Pray always that my misfortunes and weaknesses of every description be changed into strength and enlightenment of the heart and understanding.'

VI

A Mass for Saint Cecilia –
le Médecin malgré lui

Ever torn between religion and music, Gounod soon afterwards deserted Saint Augustine for composing. In the last months of 1854 he wrote a Symphony in D. This, his first symphony, is a pleasant little work and shows no sign of the unhappiness he had lately experienced. After the disappointment of the theatre it was a relief for him to write music that had no other aim than his own satisfaction. Unhampered by the tyranny of a foolish libretto or by the demands of an improbable plot, he was free to compose just as he pleased.

The andante has a slyly contrived little fugue and there is a scherzo of Haydnesque vivacity. Most noticeable is the influence of Schumann, who was then very much the property of 'advanced' musicians. Though disconcerted by this tribute to the modern German school of composers, those who heard the first performance in 1855 liked the work. Encouraged by the welcome, Gounod wrote a successor to it.

The second Symphony, which is in E flat, pays a respectful nod to Haydn with an extended slow introduction. The allegro agitato of the first movement testifies again to the influence of Schumann, though here it is an influence filtered through a Gallic sensibility. The writing for woodwind is crisp and cool. Scoring is light. Though not a miniature—the symphony takes over half an hour in performance—the proportions are slender. People enjoyed it when it was given by Pasdeloup at one of the concerts at which he was cautiously introducing French music to Parisian audiences.

The concert hall, though less spectacular than the theatre, helped to restore Gounod's confidence after the failure of *la Nonne sang-*

lante. He also began to make a name with his songs. One day in 1855 he met the well-known singer Anatole Lionnet. Their meeting took place in the Escudier brothers' music shop. (Léon Escudier, it will be remembered, was businessman as well as music critic. Although a member of the anti-Viardot faction, he had obviously by now forgiven Gounod his association with her.) Lionnet was taken into the back-room to see Gounod.

'I went in', Lionnet recalled, 'and I saw, sitting at the piano, a man of about thirty-five [thirty-seven] with a full, neatly cut black beard. His distinguished features impressed me straight away. His eyes were lively and shone with subtlety and wit. The forehead, wide and receding, showed the deep thinking of a man of genius. In addition to these attractive qualities there reigned over his face, so wonderfully expressive and intensely vital, such a feeling of graciousness, of benevolence, that I felt captivated and overcome with an instinctive liking for him as keen as it was sudden.'

The famous charm having done its work, Gounod asked Lionnet to hear one of his songs. He played 'Venise', a setting of Musset's poem. It is a typical example of his method. A brief introduction sketches the quiet flow of water, and then a rhythmic accompaniment, slow and regular as the lapping waves, depicts evening in Venice, the clouded moon and the stillness of the lagoons. The words are discreetly supported by the music, no more, and at every turn the melodic line enhances the literary values of the poem.

Lionnet was a professional musician and so his remarks on Gounod's singing are of special value. He recalled: '. . . what impressed and charmed me as much as the song was the wonderful artistry with which Gounod sang. . . . He had a tone and a style that were all his own, a generous way of phrasing that made him one of the most moving singers I'd ever heard.'

With a hint of bitterness Gounod observed that publishers were reluctant to bring out his songs. While acknowledging the artistic worth of the music, all those he had so far approached argued that it was too difficult for average singers to warrant the expense of engraving. As if to prove them wrong, Gounod launched into 'Mon habit', a setting of the poem by Béranger, author of light verse and witty *chansons* that live today because of their genial simplicity. 'Mon habit' is in some ways the poor man's version of Diderot's 'Regrets sur ma vieille robe de chambre'. The poet speaks of his old, worn suit. They've been together for ten years now, and he hopes that his garment will, as he does, resist the passing of time like a philosopher. The suit has been through so much with him and has known all his ups and downs. He pleads, 'Let's not drift apart, old friend.' The music Gounod wrote for the poem reflects its gentle humour. He mixes, in just the right proportions, sentimentality and rueful comedy.

Lionnet was enthusiastic. He took 'Mon habit' and sang it that very evening at a dinner party. Next day he called on Jacques Heugel, who for many years had run the important publishing house that bears his name and had founded the music magazine *le Ménestrel*. Heugel raised the usual objections, 'Mon habit' was too difficult, it was above the heads of the general public, it wouldn't sell. Lionnet persisted. He promised to include it in his concerts and to sing it everywhere he went. At last, and only on condition that he kept his promise, Heugel agreed to pay a hundred francs for the song. Lionnet reported the news to Gounod. It was the first time he had ever earned money for a song. He exclaimed, happy as a child: 'With Heugel publishing me I'm well and truly launched!'

Dedicated 'to my friend Anatole Lionnet', 'Mon habit' quickly became popular. A similar piece, 'Deux vieux amis', a duet written soon afterwards for Lionnet and his brother, confirmed the earlier success. Together with the 'Ave Maria' which Heugel also published, these little works did more for Gounod's reputation than either *Sapho*, *Ulysse* or *la Nonne sanglante*.

In other spheres, too, his fame was increasing. While the bread-and-butter duties of the Orphéon continued—massed concerts a thousand-strong, choral functions in Notre-Dame, tours of the provinces—he was preparing for the performance of his first big religious work. Isolated numbers from the *Messe solennelle Sainte-Cécile* had already been heard and praised. On the 29 November 1855, it was given in full at the church of Saint-Eustache. Astonishment at the novelty of the style soon turned into admiration. There were critics who saluted Gounod as a master of religious music.

The *Messe* sounds better to modern ears than do the later grandiose oratorios such as *Redemption* and *Mors et vita*. Some of it dates back to Gounod's time in Italy. The characteristics which, in old age, were to become tedious mannerisms, appear as signs of a fresh individuality. The ideas are not yet ossified into a mechanical system and the approach has not had time to degenerate into a threadbare formula. Except for a 'Domine salvam'—where Gounod, following the custom of the day, set prayers for Napoléon III, for the Army (punctuated by flippant trumpet fanfares) and for the Nation—the work as a whole avoids the triviality which so often was to mar his later work in this field.

The opening 'Kyrie' shows the adroit student of Palestrina at work. It flows with a purity that was new for the time. A somewhat unthinkingly robust 'Laudamus te' is compensated for by an affecting soprano solo. Then comes a swaggering 'Credo' that reminds us of the nineteenth-century audience's liking for an operatic spice to its religious music. The 'Sanctus' returns to a more intimate style, one that is yearning and reflective. The 'Agnus dei' softens into a moving tenderness. As in his songs, Gounod emphasizes the vocal interest. It is the voice which receives his closest attention, and not the orchestra with its temptingly big resources. He writes for the voice cleanly and simply, giving to the sopranos in particular an inviting warmth and, at the same time, a remoteness appropriate to the mystery of the text.

The *Messe solennelle Sainte-Cécile* was the work of a man still youthful in spirit but already in full control of his style. It avoided the well-trodden paths followed by other composers of the time and gave audiences the experience of hearing something new in technique and inspiration. Among the musicians to be impressed was Berlioz. Soon after hearing it, he wrote in a letter, 'Apart from Saint-Saëns, another fine composer who is nineteen years old, and Gounod, who has just written a very beautiful Mass, I can see nothing but short-lived insects hovering over this stinking morass we call Paris.'

Although his career was not developing quite in the way he would have liked, Gounod now was a celebrity. In the New Year honours list of 1856 he was awarded the cross of Chevalier in the Légion d'honneur. This was not a sign that the government had magically acquired the ability to appreciate his *Messe solennelle Sainte-Cécile*. It meant, simply, that the composer of 'Vive l'Empereur!' was looked on with favour in official circles.

As much as possible these days he sought refuge in the tranquillity of his home at Saint-Cloud. It was not often that he could get there since the demands of Paris took up his time increasingly. Invitations to dinner, to meetings, to banquets, to receptions, piled up on his table. Ruefully he quoted Moliere: '*Qui se donne à la cour se dérobe à son art. . . .*' Visitors called unannounced to ask for his assistance. Reporters lay in wait outside the house. He was interrupted in his work by pianists, singers, violinists and poets who thought he could help them. The inventors of new teaching methods pestered him for his views. Founders of magazines harassed him with requests for support and the prestige of his name. There were also the letters from admirers and the pleas for photographs which the fans thrust under his nose to be signed, and the albums to be inscribed.

Another ordeal was invited when he put forward his candidature for the Académie des Beaux Arts. Not quite so celebrated as that other section of the Institut, the Académie Française, it still represents national recognition for the composer who is lucky enough to be elected. The five departments cater for painters, sculptors, architects, engravers and musicians. There are six places reserved for composers. When Adolphe Adam died in 1856 Gounod was one of the candidates for the vacancy. The others included Louis Niedermeyer, the Swiss composer who had given up writing opera for teaching and established a school which numbered Fauré and Messager among its pupils. Another candidate was Aimé Leborne, composer of an opera written in collaboration with Rossini's mischievous friend Carafa. Auguste Panseron, who also presented himself on this occasion, compiled textbooks on singing which are still sometimes used today. François Bazin had to his credit ten comic operas and a solid professional career which was to be much embellished with official honours. The list of hopefuls continued with the names of Antione Elwart, a tireless author of pedagogical works; Adolphe Vogl, who owed his brief celebrity to a patriotic song written for the July Revolution in 1830, and Boieldieu, the best known of them all, with a series of some thirty operas ranging in subject from Little Red Riding Hood and the Exiles of Kamtschatka to *le Calife de Bagdad* and *la Dame blanche*.

The two remaining candidates were linked, if in no other way, by several coincidences. Félicien David had been a missionary in Egypt and returned to France with a brand of anodine exoticism in music. Deserting his early enthusiasm for the social and political philosophies of the comte de Saint-Simon, he exploited the vein of orientalism with an operatic version of Tom Moore's *Lalla-Roukh*. The final candidate was Berlioz. David was to succeed him both at the Institut and as librarian at the Conservatoire.

It is the unenviable task of the candidate to visit each member of the Académie and to explain the reasons why he should be elected. There may be as many as thirty-nine Academicians to be wooed. The round of visits must be carried out, the diplomatic letters must be written and support must be canvassed with discretion. The musician finds himself soliciting painters, discussing opera with architects and explaining counterpoint to sculptors. Some of Gounod's artist friends already belonged to the Institut and he could rely on their vote. With other members he had to exert all his powers of charm and persuasion.

At the first ballot on the 21 June, three of the candidates obtained no votes at all. Berlioz gained most and was followed by Panseron with Gounod and Niedermeyer trailing behind. Panseron, who made a useful sideline out of correcting and refurbishing amateurs' songs, had already suffered from the mordant wit of a Berlioz newspaper article in which he was mocked as 'the doctor of secret songs'. Throughout the four ballots that were necessary to achieve an absolute majority, the tenacious 'doctor' clung in the wake of Berlioz while the other candidates moved up and down in terms of support like figures in a share quotation list. Finally Berlioz emerged triumphant. 'Here I am, at last a respectable person!' he gleefully declared.

Only a short while before, on the 8 June, Gounod had left the house to direct a concert. It was the day of an important annual function given by the Orphéon. On his return he found that his wife had produced a son. They decided to call him Jean. 'The arrival of this child, which I had so much longed for,' wrote Gounod, 'was a joy and a great occasion for both of us. . . .' Failure at the Institut was overlooked in pleasure at the birth of his son. In any case, he could always try again for the Académie des Beaux Arts.

Later in the year his paternal feelings were stirred again by the success of his protégé Bizet. Offenbach had organized a competition as a means of publicizing his theatre and to spread his ideas of what an opéra-comique should be. The contestants were given a libretto called *le Docteur Miracle* which was to be judged by a committee including Gounod and Halévy. The prize was divided between Bizet and Charles Lecocq, the crippled musician who later wrote those charming operettas *le Petit Duc* and *la Fille de Madame Augot*, though longing all the while for distinction in 'serious' music. Lecocq maintained afterwards that had it not been for Halévy's determined support of Bizet, he would have had the prize all to himself. It may also be supposed that Gounod was another strong partisan of Bizet.

Gounod himself had been working on an opera to be called *Ivan le Terrible*. From his study came the sound of his fragile voice singing: 'Die! die! die, O unfaithful Tsarina—And let us throw her remains to the wind!' as he laboured to find music for the verses given him by an absurd libretto. Eventually he gave up trying to set this ungrateful work. Some of the music was salvaged for use in later operas. The march in *la Reine de Saba* began life as a chorus intoned by conspirators against the Tsarina as they lurked balefully in the shadows. Another passage was the source of 'Le jour se lève' in *Mireille*, and *Faust*, too, was to benefit from the wreckage of *Ivan le Terrible*. A few years afterwards Bizet took it over, though he had little more luck with it than had Gounod.

The year ended disastrously. On the 8 October Berlioz reported to Léon Escudier: 'You probably know about the new misfortune that has struck the Zimmermann family. Poor Gounod has gone mad. He's now in Dr Blanche's clinic. His reason is despaired of.' The strain incurred by his attempt on the Institut had obviously upset a nervous system which was erratic at the best of times.

One Tuesday evening in October he decided to go riding at Saint-Cloud. After caracoling in front of the house to amuse his infant son Jean, he galloped away over the fields. When he returned and came in for dinner his face was deathly white. He burst into tears and rushed up to his room. There he was found lying on the floor in a dead faint. On reviving he clamoured to go back to Paris. He was convinced that his mother, who was ill at the time, had taken a turn for the worse. Once in Paris he went straight to bed and fell into delirium.

For two days he moaned and shrieked. 'Peace! peace!' he was heard to shout over and over again, his eyes starting from their sockets. It was as if, at the age of thirty-nine, he had already reached the end of the road and could struggle no longer. On the Friday he quietened and could sip a little sugared milk. He was, he said, quite well and eager to start work once more. He remembered, with complete lucidness, the family praying at his bedside, the anxious regard of his brothers-in-law, and the friends who came to watch from the threshold.

The family sent him for a fortnight to Dr Blanche's famous clinic. This was in the rue Berton at Passy, today one of the few areas of Paris to keep in places the rustic atmosphere of earlier days. Balzac's

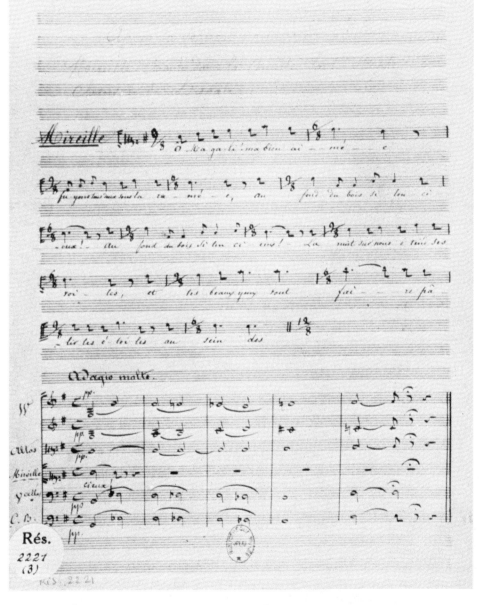

5. 'Ô Magali! ma bien aimée', from *Mireille*, Act III. Manuscript. (Bibliothèque de l'Opéra, Rés. 2 221 (3)). (Photo: Photo Pic, Paris.)

6. Georgina Weldon at the age of 20 in 1857. From a painting by J. R. Parsons after the portrait by G. F. Watts. (Photo: Stella Mayes Reed.)

old house is not far away. Standing in its garden among trees and ivy-grown walls, one can forget for a time the granitic blocks of flats that tower above. The effect is as if a nineteenth-century country villa had been suddenly put down in the heart of metropolitan Paris, and had been endowed by some magical hand with a restful setting of greenery and well tended paths. In Gounod's time the district was countrified still, and here Dr Blanche set up his clinic in the pure air on the heights of Passy. Three years before Gounod's arrival Dr Blanche had nursed the unfortunate Gérard de Nerval. Some time later Maupassant was to die insane under his care. The doctor had a weakness for literary men at the end of their tether.

Gounod's fate was happier than either Nerval's or Maupassant's. On the 18 October he was already back home in Saint-Cloud and at work again. His thoughts were of *Faust*, the poem which had haunted him ever since he read Goethe's masterpiece at the age of twenty. At various times in his career *Faust* rose to the surface. In 1850 he chanced to see a dramatic version of the story by Michel Carré. It was called *Faust et Marguerite* and contained the elements he was to use in his opera. He was still not yet certain of the musical shape his work should follow. Then, in 1855, he was introduced to Jules Barbier by Émile Augier, his collaborator on *Sapho*. Gounod sang 'Mon habit' and Barbier was immediately attracted to him. 'There are', said Barbier, 'no singers to equal him, even among tenors who earn 7,000 francs a minute!'

Among the few surprises which the hamlet of Châtenay-Malabry has to offer is a plaque attached to the house at 129 rue Anatole France, where Barbier used to live. Returning from a visit to Chateaubriand's old home at la Vallée-aux-loups, the traveller passes by this trim little villa with a handsome garden where Barbier planned some of the dozens of plays and libretti he wrote with tireless fertility. Despite his choice of country retreat, he was a confirmed boulevardier. He constructed libretti for Meyerbeer, for Ambroise Thomas, for Bizet, for Offenbach and for Saint-Saëns. 'M. Barbier', wrote an admirer, 'is an eminently Parisian personality. Everybody is acquainted with his tall stature, his handsome person, and the delicate fair features with the clear blue eyes that sparkle so brilliantly in animated conversation.' One sees it all.

When Barbier confided to Gounod that he would like to adapt *Faust* as an opera, their friendship—and Gounod's fate—were sealed. Barbier had already approached Meyerbeer with the suggestion. The composer, a German who knew the true measure of Goethe's poem, reacted with horror. *Faust* was, for him, a holy object not to be touched by impious hands. He had, in any case, had his fill of presenting a devilish tempter in music when he wrote *Robert le diable*. Gounod's enthusiasm for the idea revived Barbier's ambition. He spoke with his friend Michel Carré whose *Faust et Marguerite* had interested Gounod. From it he took the 'Chanson du Roi de Thulé' which he incorporated in his own libretto. Carré later wrote the 'Chanson du veau d'or'. The libretto that emerged was chiefly the work of Barbier.

The Opéra turned it down. There was, said the management, little opportunity for 'spectacle'. Léon Carvalho, director of the Théatre-Lyrique, was more receptive. In later years he was to claim a large part in the responsibility for unleashing *Faust* on the world. According to his account, he one day reproached Gounod for not offering him a new work.

'I could ask for nothing better,' replied Gounod, 'but what? Find me a subject.'

'Well, write *Faust* for me,' Carvalho is said to have answered.

Carvalho goes on: 'After thirty-five years I can still see the joy and astonishment that shone in his eyes. "*Faust*!" he cried, "I've had it in me for years!"'

This romantic tale is in keeping with Carvalho's habit of embroidering reality. Fact was not enough for him. Neither could he resist tinkering with the operas he produced. He once drove Saint-Saëns nearly mad by constantly suggesting changes in one of his operas. First he wanted to switch the leading role from that of dancer to singer. Then he thought it would be a good idea to bring wild animals on to the stage. Another inspiration was to cut out all the music save that for the leading lady and chorus, and to have the rest of the opera played by actors. When Carvalho heard that the rival Opéra was incorporating a water scene in a production of Ambroise Thomas' *Hamlet*, he wanted to arrange an episode where Saint-Saëns' heroine would dive to the bottom of a river. Saint-Saëns was not alone in the feelings of exasperation which Carvalho induced. Bizet, Wagner, Berlioz, in fact all the composers who had dealings with him, were at one time or another irritated by Carvalho's mania. Not even established works were safe from his attention. He could not keep his hands off anything.

This well-known habit may have resulted from Carvalho's

repressed creative ambitions. After training at the Conservatoire he had been taken on as a singer at the Opéra-Comique. When it transpired that his voice was not good enough he left and took up a career as impresario. Yet if his disappointed hopes made him an inveterate meddler with other people's work, they also gave him a genuine sympathy for the composers whom he engaged. He treated them with a benevolence and a charm which helped to make up for the atrocities he inflicted on their operas.

Carvalho was a native of Mauritius. The exotic climate in which he was born suggests a reason why his behaviour was larger than life and why his eyes saw things in more dazzling colours than did the inhabitants of Northern climates. The dinners he gave were lavish. The wine he served had been sent to Mauritius and back again to Paris, because, he swore, it was improved by the ocean trip. At Dieppe he had a seaside home and a garden where he proudly showed visitors the trees and the flowers he had planted. His wife, who added his name to hers and became Madame Miolan-Carvalho, was a famous soprano of the time. She made a reputation in the featherweight music of such as Hérold, Clapisson and Massé—the sort of music which her husband, to tell the truth, really preferred—though later she was to specialize in Mozart opera.

No sooner had Carvalho agreed to put on *Faust* than another impresario told him he was about to produce a play on the same subject almost immediately. The work, added his rival pointedly, would also include music. Carvalho decided to postpone his production for a year and asked Gounod to write something else. The composer spent a week or so digesting this cruel disappointment. At a later meeting with Carvalho the impresario again urged him to choose another subject.

'I've no heart for anything,' replied Gounod miserably. 'I'm like a lover separated from the woman he loves and unable to think of anyone else.'

'Well,' said Carvalho shrewdly, 'change the atmosphere and write a comedy. Take a Molière play.'

Molière's name was the spark Gounod needed. At once his enthusiasm returned. He quickly agreed on *le Médecin malgré lui*. Barbier and Carré produced a libretto, and within five months the *opéra-comique* was composed.

Le Médecin malgré lui belongs to the same year of 1666 as *le Misanthrope*. Both were written at a period when Molière was the target for intrigues mounted by clerics whom he had outraged with *Tartuffe*. Soon afterwards *Don Juan* met a similar fate. At the same time Molière began to suffer from the illness that in seven years was to kill him. He started to cough up blood. As an accomplished actor he needed all his craft when on stage to disguise his malady. Yet in the midst of all these worries and harassments he was able to write his greatest farce.

The character of Sganarelle, the woodcutter who has a leading part in *le Médecin malgré lui*, figures in six of Molière's plays. His first appearance is in *le Cocu imaginaire*, his last in *le Médecin malgré lui*. Sganarelle was perhaps Molière's favourite role and the one for which the forty-four-year-old actor put on his make-up with most eagerness. Ill at ease in playing gentlemen and aristocrats, Molière as Sganarelle the drunk, the libertine, the bully, created storms of laughter. It was laughter pure and simple, a laughter that sprang, like farce, from a basic ruthlessness.

In *le Médecin malgré lui* he mocked with a keener satire than ever before the medical profession which he, frail of constitution and rarely in the best of health, had good cause to distrust. Doctors were among his favourite butts. He ridiculed their unwillingness to accept new ideas, their annoyance with patients whose illnesses refused to follow the established rules, and their self-enrichment at the expense of human credulity. Sganarelle masquerades as a doctor and attends Lucinde, the daughter of Géronte. When he has given his diagnosis—an impressive oration tricked out with dog Latin and fluent nonsense—Géronte intervenes to remark, in his puzzled way, that he had always believed the heart to be on the left side of the body and the liver on the right. Yes, replies Sganarelle blandly, that's how things used to be . . . '*Mais nous avons changé tout cela*', for doctors use new methods these days.

The plot Molière threw together was, as often the case with a busy actor-manager, a rag-bag of incidents borrowed from traditional stories, jokes he had heard from friends and even scenes from his own earlier plays. But the speed of the action and the lively dialogue make up for this. Most important of all—and this is the reason why Molière survives as a great dramatist—his portrayal of men and women is as true today as it was at the time he wrote. The human types he showed are eternal. With unusual modesty and great wisdom, Barbier and Carré made few alterations in the text of *le Médecin malgré lui*. Whole stretches of Molière's dialogue are left untouched, and arias follow very closely the original words he used. *Le Médecin malgré lui* is, as a result, the best libretto Gounod ever worked on.

The overture, consisting of melodies which occur later in the work, opens on a pompous maestoso introduction with a strong flavour of Lully. Then the clarinet plays one of those comically conspiratorial tunes of the type Rossini favoured. The atmosphere is one of airy high spirits, and while there are occasional pauses for more reflective interludes, usually provided by the woodwind, the overture as a whole pursues its way in a vein of extrovert cheerfulness.

Sganarelle and his wife Martine are discovered quarrelling. She reproaches him with his drunkenness and his shameful inability to provide for the family. 'I've four poor little children on my hands,' she complains. 'Drop them on the ground, then', he brutally replies. Each of her protests is greeted by him with an equally cavalier retort. He, for his part, bemoans his ill-luck: for six years he worked in the service of a doctor and picked up a lot of his technique, and now he's reduced to living with this shrew. There aren't many wood-cutters about who, like him, can talk learnedly and boast a knowledge of medicine! He gives Martine a vigorous beating. When a kindly neighbour intervenes, however, husband and wife both turn on him. It's none of his business to poke his nose into other people's affairs. As Sganarelle observes, such little incidents are necessary in friendship, and a good beating only serves to warm up affection between those who love each other.

Martine quietly swears vengeance on him in a charming little aria of rustic simplicity. He, meanwhile, guzzles from his bottle:

> *Qu'ils sont doux, qu'ils sont doux, qu'ils sont doux,*
>   *bouteille jolie*
> *Qu'ils sont doux, qu'ils sont doux, vos petits*
>   *glou-gloux, vos petits glou-gloux.*

This song, which Molière intended Lully to set, is, with its neat use of descending chromaticism, an inspired piece of comic invention.

When Géronte's servant passes through the wood looking for a doctor, Martine realizes that her opportunity has come. Géronte's daughter Lucinde has been stricken dumb and her father is anxious to cure her. Martine points out Sganarelle. He is, she says, a brilliant doctor though very eccentric. The only way to put him in the mood for exercising his genius is to beat him soundly. Sganarelle, fuddled with drink, is heartily beaten until, in self-defence, he promises to attend Lucinde.

In a serenade which owes something to Leporello's example in *Don Giovanni*, the young Léandre introduces himself as the lover of Lucinde. He is handsome, though penniless, and therefore the object of her father's disapproval. In order to avoid being married off to the wealthy suitor Géronte has chosen for Lucinde, she has decided to feign dumbness. Enter Sganarelle wearing robes of doctoral splendour: a pointed hat and sweeping black cloak. The bizarre medico is more interested in the prominent charms of Jacqueline, one of Géronte's domestic staff. Might he not test out the quality of her milk? Perhaps he might bleed her a little or give her a soothing clyster? Reluctantly he withdraws his wandering hand and addresses himself to the problem of Lucinde.

The sextet that follows contains his diagnosis of the illness. It is obvious, he declares, that Lucinde's pulse shows the rhythm associated with dumbness. Géronte is much impressed. How clever of Sganarelle to define the affliction so speedily! (A horn in the orchestra imitates the beat of the pulse.) Furthermore, Sganarelle learnedly explains, the dumbness is caused by the action of the tongue being hampered. Hearing that Géronte does not understand Latin, Sganarelle embarks on a nonsensical tirade in that language sustained by a subservient tremelo from the orchestra. While he protests his contempt for money, he discreetly accepts the weighty bag slipped into his hand. The sextet, which is one of the best written numbers in the opera, ends with general praise for his astonishing skill.

'Vive la médecine!' chants Sganarelle at the opening of Act III. It's a wonderful profession because, whether your patient lives or dies, you get paid all the same. You just can't go wrong! Sganarelle's fame spreads. All the people in the neighbourhood flock to ask his advice and fill his purse. Another opportunity for turning a dubious penny comes his way when Léandre asks for his assistance in overcoming Géronte's opposition to him as Lucinde's suitor. Money changes hands. Léandre dresses up as an apothecary and Sganarelle lets him into the great secret of medicine: success depends on the inevitable discretion of the dead, because no corpse yet has ever been heard to complain of the doctor who killed him.

Léandre enters Géronte's house. In his supposed professional capacity he takes Lucinde's pulse and seizes the chance to discuss tactics with her. Suddenly, to Géronte's delighted astonishment, she speaks out loud and clear. What a clever doctor Sganarelle is! But what she says is not what Géronte would like to hear. In the course of a vivacious quintet she overwhelms her spluttering father with a torrent of words and insists she will marry no one but Léandre. The dam has burst and Géronte can only interject the occasional syllable as she bears irresistibly on. Despairingly he appeals to Sganarelle: make her dumb again!

Time is getting on and Molière must bring his third act to some sort of conclusion. So Lucinde elopes with Léandre and Sganarelle is threatened with the noose for having connived at her abduction. The last scene is quickly polished off with one of those devices Molière brazenly relied on when he was in a hurry to finish his play. Léandre's rich uncle providentially dies and leaves him all his wealth. Géronte relents and agrees to the marriage. Sganarelle is saved from the scaffold. The woodcutter forgives his wife the trick she has played on him but warns her that she must treat him, the 'doctor', with respect in future, and must remember that 'a doctor's anger is more to be feared than you'd think'. Molière, whose gibes at the fraternity had inspired their fury, knew what he was talking about.

Gounod's score shows a humour which accords perfectly with the nature of the play. This is what Bernard Shaw referred to when, in speaking of the English version, he mentioned 'the irresistible flavour of Molière' that clings to it. Though the farce is broad it demands what Shaw termed 'skill and delicacy' in performance. Where tenderness is required—as in Léandre's serenade or in his '*fabliau*'—Gounod is equal to the call with '*une chanson lénifiante, émolliente, édulcorée*', as specified by Sganarelle. If jollity is needed— as in the chorus

> *Nous faisons tous*
> *Ce que nous savons faire–*

he is ready with tunes that have the nonchalance of a Rossini and the force of a Verdi. The orchestration is full of ingenious details such as the horn notes which occur during Sganarelle's pulse-taking and the sly bassoon phrase that underlines his words, '*Votre fille en aura besoin*', when he introduces Léandre the 'apothecary' to Géronte. It is not surprising that *le Médecin malgré lui* was a favourite with

Diaghilev. One would give much to hear the recitatives he commissioned from Erik Satie for the 1924 revival he staged at Monte
Carlo with dances by Nijinska and scenery by Benois.

Before this delectable opéra-comique could appear on the stage of
the Théâtre-Lyrique there were, unbelievably, problems of censorship to overcome. Although the Comédie-Française had allowed one
of its leading actors to coach the singers in the Molière tradition,
there was a strong feeling that Gounod and his musicians were
trespassing on a preserve rightly the fief of that venerable institution.
The censorship let it be known that the liberties of language taken by
Molière would be out of place on the stage of the Théâtre-Lyrique.
So the authorities, who had detected threats of revolution in *Sapho*,
decided that the farce which was played regularly at the Comédie-
Française should not be allowed to sully the ears of music lovers or to
corrupt them with its low buffoonery. Fortunately Gounod could
rely on the support of Princess Mathilde. This indomitable female,
niece of the first Napoléon, cousin to the third, and an insatiable
collector of celebrities both literary and artistic, had lately included
Gounod in her bag. Her influence brushed aside the jealous protests
of the Comédie-Française and the clumsy attempt at censorship. She
was rewarded by the dedication of the work.

Le Médecin malgré lui appeared at the Théâtre-Lyrique on the
15 January 1858. The date was the anniversary of Molière's birthday,
and after the curtain fell on the last act a pleasant little ceremony took
place. Madame Miolan-Carvalho, draped in the robes of a Muse,
sang an invocation to Molière for which the music was taken from
Sapho. Surrounded by the cast of *le Médecin*, she then crowned with
a laurel wreath the bust of the playwright. Although she had not
taken part in the production she was not the sort of woman to miss a
chance of being associated with success.

For a success *le Médecin malgré lui* most certainly was. 'My work
was very well received by the audience,' Gounod wrote to Bizet, who,
on studying the score, had described it as the most charming piece of
its kind since Grétry. Berlioz singled out for praise Gounod's
discretion in echoing Lully, Molière's contemporary, and so
providing music that matched the words of the play. For once the
press was unanimously in favour of a stage work by Gounod.

At last he was established in the theatre. The audience had laughed
where he wanted them to and applauded as he had wished. At the end
he had been summoned by their cheers and walked on to the stage to

receive an ovation. A publisher offered 4,000 francs for the score. Although a third of this went to his collaborators, Gounod was thrilled to have earned his first real money on the stage. *Le Médecin malgré lui* continued to draw large audiences for the rest of the year. During the hundred consecutive performances it received, Sganarelle's comic drinking song, 'Qu'ils sont doux', was invariably encored. Other numbers that won a special popularity included the Trio where Sganarelle is beaten, the 'consultation' Sextet, Léandre's melancholy Fabliau, Sganarelle's consultation with the peasants, and his duet with Jacqueline. Revivals have shown that the taste of modern audiences agrees with that of opera-goers who filled the Théâtre-Lyrique throughout the year of 1858.

On the very day after the triumph of *le Médecin malgré lui* his mother died. The pleasure of his success was, he wrote, poisoned by this incident. She was seventy-seven. For two years she had been completely blind. Her death occurred after months of illness. She was the most important person in his life. He owed everything to her. The cruellest thing of all was that she had been denied at the very last moment the joy of seeing her hopes realized.

Madame Gounod knew, moreover, where his true talent lay. When he was only in his twenties she discerned his gift for comedy. Of course, she told him, he would be able to distinguish himself with serious work. On the other hand, she hoped that he would achieve recognition for his ability to write music that was both comic and tasteful. *Le Médecin malgré lui* proved how shrewd she was in judging the aptitudes of her clever but wayward son.

With the death of his mother Gounod lost his most powerful support. For close on forty years she had guided his steps and defended him against the harsh world. She understood him as no one else did. She alone could fully appreciate the conflicts within his personality that drove him to unworthy acts while cherishing the highest aspirations. Now he was on his own. Had she survived a little longer she would, perhaps, have been able to preserve him from the disastrous path he took after the success of *Faust*.

VII

Faust – Philémon et Baucis – la Colombe

The rival version of *Faust*, which inspired Carvalho to postpone the launch of Gounod's opera, was, wrote the disappointed composer, 'a heavy and luxuriously produced melodrama with a tawdry brilliance as violent and short-lived as fireworks that leave nothing after them but the acrid smell that takes you by the throat....' It ran, nonetheless, for at least six months and even had the distinction of being parodied in a burlesque under the name of *Faux Faust*. With Fausts proliferating all around him Carvalho at last decided, in spite of the circumstances, to go ahead with his own production. He planned to open at the end of 1858. In the event, it was not until Spring of the following year that Gounod's opera was heard.

The reason for this hitch was to be found in the last-minute crises and delays peculiar to the theatre. Madame Carvalho, who was to sing the part of Marguerite, shared with her husband the taste for altering the operas he put on. While her industrious spouse exhausted his ingenuity in rewriting plots and changing scenes, the no less determined wife wrought havoc with the music. Her bad taste was monumental, her will implacable. She lived in an atmosphere of adulation created by the fans who worshipped her undoubted talent as a singer. This, she believed, gave her the right to titivate music written by composers who had not made sufficient allowance for her genius. She loaded their melodic lines with arabesques and trills. No aria was safe from her greedy hands. Regardless of the dramatic context she gilded and gelded with majestic unconcern the music put before her. Everything must be adapted to show off the beauty of her voice. Mozart was tidied up to provide her with encores. Lesser composers found the notes they had written overlaid with a crust of bejewelled inanity. Each alteration was sanctioned by the unanswerable comment: 'Variante de Mme Carvalho'.

The singer chosen to play Faust opposite Mme Carvalho's Marguerite was not so difficult to handle. Hector Gruyer, who later suppressed the overtone of cheese that clung to his name by adopting the pseudonym of Guardi, had studied under Bizet's father and was a close friend of Bizet himself. To Bizet, then working at the Villa Medici as a Prix de Rome student, Gounod wrote: 'My *Faust* rehearsals are in full swing. Guardi is, as you know, a good and worthy fellow, full of the superior qualities that go to make up an artist. He is, above all, completely free of vanity; and since he modestly reckons himself not up to much, he is in the best frame of mind to become something very considerable. . . . As for me, I can't tell you whether my score is good. I'm so up to my ears in it that I'm a very bad judge. Nothing seems to have an effect on me any more. I'm saturated in music. Performance is very much hampered at the moment by production problems. People can think only of their arms, their legs, and nobody sings or tries out phrases any more. The orchestra saws away . . . it will all come right at the final rehearsals and at the first night. Everyone seems very satisfied. I hope to God they're not wrong! The sets will be splendid.' Though Bizet was doubtful in private about Gounod's choice of subject—still only twenty, he was shrewed enough to sense that his mentor's instinct had betrayed him—he fervently hoped for the success of *Faust*.

At the last minute Guardi became hoarse and was temporarily replaced by another singer. Still more complicated were the alterations that had to be made in the original score. It was much longer than the final performing version. At least one whole scene was dropped. Another excision sacrificed a duet between Marguerite and Valentin at the beginning of the Kermesse. Carvalho argued that it was dramatically inappropriate at this point. After a day or two of sulks Gounod agreed. The famous Soldiers' Chorus was added as an afterthought. One evening when Gounod was entertaining Carvalho to dinner at his home, a guest asked the musician to sing them a chorus from the stillborn *Ivan le Terrible*. The melody was originally an Orphéon male voice chorus entitled 'le Vin des Gaulois'. Gounod went to the piano and launched into that vigorous tune. Everyone advised him to use it in place of an aria he had written for Valentin. Gounod's old friend Ingres was present and insisted: 'Don't hesitate. Put in the Chorus.'

The Minister of Fine Arts, who had been so concerned over the moral effect of *le Médecin malgré lui*, was just as disturbed about

Faust. This time, it appeared, the church scene was likely to cause a diplomatic incident. An emissary arrived to announce: 'We are on very bad terms with the Vatican, if I dare explain myself thus.' The Minister let it be understood that in the interests of diplomatic harmony the scene must be taken out—and *Faust* robbed of much of its point.

Here Gounod's social connections were of value. He had a particular friend in Monseigneur de Ségur, the Papal nuncio. The nuncio, though blind, had attended many rehearsals of *Faust*. It was Gounod's custom to guide him to a box where he could sit and listen to the music in comfort. One day Gounod suggested that Carvalho ask Monseigneur de Ségur point-blank whether the church scene was likely to offend Papal susceptibilities. 'Ah, Monsieur Carvalho,' replied the nuncio, 'I wish theatres were filled with scenes like this. Suppress the church scene? Who on earth is asking you to do so?' No more was heard from the Minister of Fine Arts.

On the 19 March 1859, *Faust* made its long-awaited appearance. The first-night audience was not what gossip columnists would have described as 'brilliant'. It did not abound in the rich financiers or the high-class prostitutes or the noblemen whose attendance was necessary for a première to qualify as fashionable. It was made up of much less spectacular folk—musicians like Berlioz and Auber, painters like Delacroix, and intellectuals curious to see how Gounod, the new hope of French music, had treated a subject already the excuse for boulevard melodrama and burlesque.

Faust is now so much a part of musical legend that it is difficult to imagine how it sounded to people who heard it for the first time. The opera is like a part of the furniture. The average music lover is always half-conscious of it, if only to refer to it with an embarrassed smile. The immense popularity *Faust* was to obtain and the neglect into which it has fallen today are both undeserved. While *Faust* may contain some of Gounod's best music, it offers equally clear examples of his limitations.

Gounod's version will always seem an impertinence when compared with the original poem. The spirit of philosophical enquiry and profound symbolism is replaced by a single episode treated within a slick operatic convention. The Germans were right to perform the opera under the title of *Margarethe*, for she is the star. The result is basically a simple love story flavoured with demoniac elements for picturesque effect—more credibly, perhaps, than in *la Nonne sanglante*, but no less artificially. When set beside Goethe the libretto cannot help recalling an 'image d'Épinal', one of those naïve pictures done by country artists who celebrated, in primary colours and quaint perspectives, the glories of Napoléon.

Yet the 'image d'Épinal' has its value. Collectors prize originals as enjoyable types of primitive painting. The conception of *Faust* is likewise crude and simplistic. Its 'prettiness', by contrast with Goethe's lofty work, has earned it in England the nickname of 'Daisy Faust'. Gounod's achievement nonetheless was to make his opera an important date in French musical history.

The first section of the prelude is one of the best things in the score. Often lost amid the shufflings of an audience settling down and exchanging last-minute chat before the curtain rises, this tightly structured piece is well concentrated. The austerity of the four-part writing and the rigorous manner in which the thought is developed show that Gounod had profited from his study of Bach. From the point of view of the drama, too, the prelude is successful: the harmonies which occur as each part steadily unrolls create the feeling of mystery, of world-weariness, that the philosopher Faust experienced.

Unfortunately this noble episode collapses into a nondescript tune which represents the other side of Gounod—the facile melodist who could not resist an easy idea. Next come a dozen or so bars introducing Faust's monologue which recapture the mystical spirit evoked in the prelude, only to degenerate, once again, into a conventional and hearty 'romance'. Things brighten up with the entry of Méphistophélès. Slithering violin phrases depict his ingratiating manner and a series of brief, hopping thirds create the impression of irony. Despite the poverty of the libretto Gounod manages to convey something of the clash between the devil and the disillusioned scholar. With the vision of Marguerite at her spinning wheel— violins representing the hum of the machine while a solo horn plays the theme of the love duet in Act III—he is on safer ground.

The Kermesse which opens the second act brings colour and gaiety to its evocation of a village fair. Méphistophélès' 'Ronde du veau d'or' gives the bass who sings it a good excuse for diabolo-comic by-play. The 'Choral des épées', where the cast raise their swords in the form of the cross against Méphistophélès, happily avoids turning into an overblown Meyerbeerian production number. The most striking feature of this act is perhaps the famous waltz that brings it to an end. The well-known tune is light, graceful and pleasantly unaffected. Two characteristics lift it into a class of its own. The first of these occurs when, by an enchanting modulation into F sharp, the theme suddenly enters on a whole new realm of tenderness and beauty. The other consists of the Andantino where Faust meets Marguerite for the first time:

> *Ne permettrez-vous pas, ma belle demoiselle,*
> *Qu'on vous offre le bras pour faire le chemin?*

The music to which Faust sings this greeting is neither Italian nor German. It is purely French and purely Gounod. It is languorous and free in rhythm. The tone is informal, almost spoken. When Marguerite replies

> *Non, Monsieur, je n⌣ suis demoiselle, ni belle,*
> *Et je n'ai pas besoin qu'on me donne la main,*

Gounod writes a phrase which, in its flexibility, prophesies the technique of Massenet and, eventually, of Debussy. He is here being completely original.

Though somewhat spoilt by Siebel's trivial aria, the third act improves with Faust's cavatina, 'Salut, demeure chaste et pure'. The purity of the vocal line is Gounod's own. As in the Andantino mentioned above, he gives the natural curve of the phrase an exquisite proportion. The style has something conversational about it and a movement which, though free, is moulded to perfection. The orchestral writing is delicate and lucid. It is the music of love and innocence.

Marguerite's 'Chanson du Roi de Thulé' skilfully employs the formula of the old *chanson* and, at the same time, breaks it up with episodes touchingly hesitant in which she wonders about the attractive young man whom she has just met. '*Il avait bonne grâce, à ce qu'il m'a semblé*', she muses before returning to the main theme of the delightfully archaic song Gounod has given her. She leaves her spinning-wheel and takes up the jewel box Méphistophélès has left to tempt her. The 'Air des bijoux' which follows was dictated by Madame Carvalho's influence. Admittedly the incident is to be found in Goethe, but the librettist's decision to build it up into a principal number must have been encouraged by the prima donna's insistence on what are now known as 'show stoppers'. The result is a glittering waltz song, brilliant of its kind and craftsmanlike in manner, which gave Madame Carvalho the opportunity she wanted.

Then Marguerite's neighbour Dame Marthe trots busily on to the scene accompanied by a humorous figure on the violins. The quartet that follows gives a vivid portrayal of each character: Méphistophélès and Marthe on the one side, Faust and Marguerite on the other. To the chattering of the ancient gossip, the devil replies in music that points up his mocking sarcasm. The comic nature of these exchanges is contrasted with the tenderness of what passes between Faust and Marguerite. The tone which Gounod had found in the Andantino of the waltz in Act II and in 'Salut demeure chaste et pure' is realized again. The final love duet sets the crown on his achievement. The troubled emotion that besets Faust and Marguerite is translated by supple phrases and quick modulations which express every rise and fall, every hesitation and shade of feeling. The duet reaches its highest point with 'O nuit d'amour, ciel radieux!' in music of a concision and clarity which represents Gounod at his finest.

Act IV comes well below the earlier level of inspiration. It contains the Soldiers' Chorus which recalls, only too abruptly, the shining faces of boys and girls marching up to the rostrum to receive their prizes at speech day. This is the Gounod of the Orphéon, the purveyor of music for scholastic occasions. Another disappointment is 'Marguerite au rouet', which invites an unflattering comparison with Schubert. On a quite different plane is Méphistophélès' Serenade, another set-piece which mingles buffoonery with the ironic spirit in well-judged proportions. In the church scene, where Marguerite attemps to seek forgiveness, Gounod shows a sense of theatre which is sometimes lacking elsewhere. The contrast between the rich harmonies of the organ and the faltering voice of Marguerite is cleverly managed. There is a sustained intensity throughout this scene which makes wholly credible the dramatic conflict between Méphistophélès' jeers and Marguerite's repentance.

Act V opens with the 'Nuit de Walpurgis'. In an attempt to make Faust forget Marguerite, Méphistophélès takes him to the desolate region where the souls of the dead wander eternally through the landscape. As the example of *la Nonne sanglante* showed, Gounod was not a very convincing dealer in horror, and the music he provides for this episode is altogether too neat and tidy. The ballet was only added ten years later in 1869, when *Faust* was played for the first time at the Opéra. (The Opéra production also included recitatives, for the original work was performed with spoken dialogue.)

Still anxious to efface the remembrance of Marguerite, the Devil summons up beauties from the past—Cleopatra, Helen of Troy, and a group of famous courtesans. They dance to music which, though not as inspired as some of the best passages in *Faust*, is certainly far better than most of what was being turned out for operas of the time. The style has an airy grace tinged with melancholy. When played by a Beecham its gossamer qualities can be fully enjoyed. And the music is, as critics sometimes tend to forget, very danceable.

The prison scene which concludes the opera is ingeniously put together. Among the themes which reappear and which are worked in to good dramatic effect are several from the majestic introduction, together with a snatch of the waltz song from Act II and the motif '*Ne permettrez-vous pas, ma belle demoiselle*' of the original meeting between Faust and Marguerite. These wistful shreds, enclosed within the solemn framework of the scene, have a rare poignancy. The final trio leads with a blaze of harps into Marguerite's 'Anges purs, anges radieux' and is sent on its way by the inescapable heavenly choir. 'Anges purs', originally a part of Gounod's youthful *Requiem*, has that facile swing he often adopted. Instead of developing it, he simply repeats it in different keys, each time screwing up the tension. Though the trick seems crude when studied in cold blood, on the stage it brings down the curtain with an exciting flourish.

Faust was by no means an unqualified triumph. During its first year it ran for fifty-nine performances, a figure which was respectable though not sensational in view of its later success. The critics were undecided in their reactions. The most enthusiastic and informed was Berlioz. Good-naturedly suppressing the envy he might have felt when he remembered the fate of his own *Damnation de Faust*, he gave praise to many aspects of Gounod's work. The prelude he declared to be the work of a skilled harmonist. It is interesting that he immediately detected the superiority of Marguerite's 'Non, Monsieur, je ne suis demoiselle, ni belle' and of Faust's 'Salut, demeure chaste et pure'. The latter, he enthused, deserved twenty times more applause than it had received on the night: 'Caviar to the general,' he remarked sardonically. As for the Soldiers' Chorus, Berlioz added in an article that ranks among his wittiest, it was 'pudding to the general'! Marguerite's aria at the spinning wheel left him cold, but he thought highly of the 'Chanson du Roi de Thulé', of the quartet in Act III, and of the church scene.

à ma chère amie Georgina Weldon.
Ch. Gounod

7. Gounod at the age of 57 when he met Georgina Weldon. (Photo: Stella Mayes Reed.)

Geronimo (seated, right) and some of her singing pupils in

Other musicians shared Berlioz's opinion. At seven or eight consecutive performances Madame Carvalho detected the presence of Meyerbeer in his usual seat. Ill and failing in health, Meyerbeer died five years later. In the meantime his admiration for the new music urged him to as many hearings as possible. If professionals appreciated *Faust*, however, the general public was still reluctant. Publishers were hesitant about taking it up, and only after much canvassing was Gounod able to persuade one to bring out the score. This was Antoine de Choudens, until then a publisher in a small way of business. Under the contract he signed with Gounod the composer received 6,666 francs, 66 centimes, a figure whose eccentric precision is accounted for by the share which fell to Barbier and Carré.

This sum represented an outright purchase of all rights to *Faust* in France and Belgium. Choudens was authorized to print and sell it in every form of arrangement without further payment. 'M. de Choudens was poor and so was I,' Gounod commented drily. 'And poor people don't insist.' The immense revenues that the sheet music of *Faust* eventually earned all went to Choudens and helped to make his firm and himself more than prosperous. He was a plain businessman with not much interest in the music he published so long as it made a profit. *Faust* meant little to him except as a valuable property. Whenever his small children misbehaved he would threaten as a punishment to take them to see it.

Worse still for Gounod, he made very little out of the English rights. The London publisher neglected to secure the copyright, with the result that both composer and librettists were deprived of royalties from the British Isles or from the colonies. The German situation was only slightly better. For the sum of a thousand francs, which had again to be shared with Barbier and Carré, the publishers secured in perpetuity all the rights to *Faust* in that country. It is not surprising that for the rest of his life Gounod regarded publishers with the darkest suspicion and was apt, like H. G. Wells in similar circumstances, to treat them as fair game for every sort of manoeuvre.

Faust gradually began to win a reputation. A performance in Strasbourg, for which Gounod added the recitatives, opened the long tours of the French provinces which were to follow. Theatres in Belgium and Germany put *Faust* in the repertory and played before enthusiastic audiences. (An Augsburg newspaper even claimed that Gounod was Flemish. This non-French ancestry, argued the writer, was the reason for the 'Germanic' nature of his music.) The opera travelled on to Stockholm and Milan. In 1863 its Victorian fame began with a Covent Garden performance of *Faust e Margherita*. Soon afterwards Méphistophélès was being encored in Saint Petersburg and Barcelona. By 1864 he was singing with a New York accent.

The historical importance of *Faust* is that it sounded a new note in French music. The conventional pomposities of the grand opera which then dominated the stage were superseded by a more intimate and poetic approach. The fashion Gounod set was one of conversational exchange rather than declamation. The people in *Faust* sang naturally. They were familiar in their actions. They did not strike flamboyant attitudes. The difference between *Faust* and its predecessors was the difference between Gerald du Maurier and Henry Irving.

As for Gounod himself, *Faust* is the opera in which he fully reveals his talents for the first time. At his best when he expresses simplicity of feeling, he yet contrives, even at his most 'brilliant', to suggest foreboding under the surface glitter of trills and roulades. With 'Ne permettrez-vous pas, ma belle demoiselle', he brings French music back to its proper tradition. True feeling takes over from rant and proportion is restored. He controls the play of emotion with a subtle touch. The music suggests perpetual nuance. It advances and retreats in line with the varying moods of a sensitive, almost feminine mind. Listening one day to the scene where Marguerite dreams at nightfall by the window, Gounod remarked: 'Can't you feel a woman's hair coiling itself round your neck?'

There was danger in the triumph of *Faust*. Its overwhelming success led him to emphasize in his later work those very elements that are weakest: the showy and the grandiose. He was to misunderstand the nature of his real talent and to force it into a mould that did not suit him.

In the same year that *Faust* made its début Gounod was writing an opera which, though not a major work, is certainly a delightful and, generally speaking, more characteristic one. *Philémon et Baucis* was taken from La Fontaine who in turn had skimmed it from Ovid. In La Fontaine's version two gods descend on earth to test men's piety. They arrive at a village where no one will give them shelter for the night. Only Philémon, an old peasant living with his wife, offers them hospitality in his poverty-stricken home. As usual La Fontaine adduces a polished moral:

Ni l'or ni la grandeur ne nous rendent heureux;
Ces deux divinités n'accordent à vos voeux
Que des biens peu certains, qu'un plaisir peu tranquille;
Des soucis dévorants c'est l'éternal asile . . .

The gods disclose their identity and warn Philémon and Baucis to seek safety on the mountain. The couple do so, and when they look back they see that the inhospitable village has been drowned in a mighty flood. As a sign of godly favour they are made priest and priestess . . . before being turned into trees: '*Baucis devient tilleul, Philémon devient chêne.*'

Philémon et Baucis opens with a gentle bucolic prelude. The duet 'Du repos voici l'heure' presents the elderly Philémon and Baucis getting ready for bed. They are resigned to the havoc age has worked on them both: the days of singing and dancing are long ago passed, the pleasures of youth are gone, but in their declining years they still have their love for each other. Their words are set to a skittish Allegretto which ends in smiling acceptance of their lot.

A Rossinian storm announces the arrival of Jupiter and Vulcan. The trio they sing with Philémon when he invites them to stay under his roof demonstrates the mastery of vocal writing Gounod had already shown in the *Faust* quartet. This is followed by Vulcan's comic lament, 'Aux bruits des lourds marteaux', where he confesses that, black and misshapen, he is ill at ease anywhere outside the smoky forge. As, in his sooty bass, he deplores the awkward figure he cuts in polite society, the music imitates the steady beat of the blacksmith's hammer. After a brisk ariette from Jupiter, who tries to console him for his unhappy married life—the gods, as we know, underwent strangely human experiences of the conjugal state—Baucis has a 'mélodrame' in which she remarks that the encroachments of the years have not left her ungrateful for the happy times of his youth. These spoken words are accompanied by an orchestral andantino of wistful tenderness: a hint foreshadowing Bizet's music for *l'Arlésienne*?

Baucis' aria, 'Ah! si je redevenais belle', where she reasons that if she regained her youthful beauty Philémon would love her all the more, has the freedom that had been such a novelty in *Faust*. A perky quartettino, 'Prenez place à la table', sets the two gods in their places ready for Baucis' humble fare. No sooner have they started than Jupiter astonishes the elderly couple by turning water into wine. As

Philémon and Baucis fall into a bewitching slumber he promises that when they awake they will find their reward.

In Act II Gounod's librettists, the old firm of Barbier and Carré, depart from the original story. Philémon and Baucis wake up to find themselves reborn at the age of twenty. Their wretched hovel has been turned into a magnificent palace. Marvelling at the result of his own magic, Jupiter resolves, in 'Vénus même n'est plus belle', to seduce Baucis, who is now a young girl of ravishing beauty. She is divided between her loyalty to Philémon and the pleasure of having conquered a god. But she concludes that this dangerous emotion is far less worth while than the affectionate companionship of old age. She begs Jupiter to restore her wrinkles and white hair. Jupiter, disgruntled, refuses to try to please her any more. He leaves her to live her old love all over again with Philémon.

The second act has its moments. These include the charming modulations of Baucis' 'Philémon m'aimerait encore', the attractive naïveté of her duet with Philémon when they realize that they owe their newly recaptured youth to Jupiter, and the humour of the trio in which Vulcan, clumsily trying to do his best for everyone, only succeeds in pleasing nobody. On the whole, though, the previous act is better inspired.

Philémon et Baucis had originally been commissioned for performance at Baden-Baden. When Carvalho heard extracts from it he immediately wanted it for his own Théâtre-Lyrique. The impresario in Baden-Baden graciously withdrew on the understanding that Gounod would write him another opera as a replacement and *Philémon et Baucis* was duly premièred in Paris on the 18 February 1860. In its original three-act version the piece was not a success. Its first run lasted for only thirteen performances.

'The work, I think, was not without value' observed Gounod 'or at least that is what I have heard people say. However, it did not make money. That is the only touchstone in the theatre, and I have always held the opinion that when the abandoned composer is faced with poor receipts, there is nothing for him to say.' Gounod's unfavourable opinion of publishers was accentuated by the fate of *Philémon et Baucis*. Choudens had offered 10,000 francs for the score with the prudent stipulation that the full sum should be paid only when the opera reached its twenty-fifth performance. This it did not do, so that in the end Gounod and his librettists were left with only 5,000 francs to share between them. The guardian angel that watches over publishers ensured, on the other hand, that the score sold well. Choudens recovered his original outlay, and unlike his composer, gained a satisfactory return on the investment.

Although the public was little impressed by *Philémon et Baucis* the critics were favourable. Berlioz, for one, enjoyed it. 'The work by MM. Barbier and Carré was a complete success', he wrote. 'M. Gounod was luckier still, and his score seems to us one of the most graceful he has written.' Despite these warm remarks, the opera had disappeared by April. Soon afterwards Carvalho gave up the Théâtre-Lyrique. His wife, whose 'miracles of vocalization' in *Philemon et Baucis* had dazed at least one critic, departed for an engagement in London. It was not until 1876 that the opera entered the repertory of the Opéra-Comique, where the definitive two-act version was to hold the stage up to the nineteen-forties.

To keep the promise made to the Baden-Baden impresario Gounod wrote another little opéra-comique called *la Colombe*. The subject again came from La Fontaine by way of the Barbier/Carré production line, where it received a number of retouches. *Le Faucon*, as La Fontaine christened his story, was closely modelled on Boccaccio. A falcon being perhaps too fierce a bird for opera-goers, the librettists replaced it with the gentler dove. The impoverished Horace falls in love with Sylvie, a rich woman. He rashly invites her to dinner. His despairing cook hunts through the garden for something to offer their guest. There are no chickens left since they have long ago been immortalized in broth. Horace tells her to kill his pet dove and serve it up. The party dines off the bird. At the end of the meal Sylvie is deeply touched when her lover confesses that, out of devotion to her, he has had the cherished creature murdered for the pot. Moved by this proof of adoration, she agrees to marry him. Whereupon the cook reveals that the dove is alive and well—what they ate was a neighbour's parrot that happened to fly in at the window. It was, she adds, half-dead anyway. So her master wins Sylvie without sacrificing the bird. Cook is pleased too, because henceforward, Sylvie being well-off, there will always be something in the larder to eat.

The main theme of the overture to *la Colombe* is introduced by the 'cello. This nonchalant little tune gives a hint of the light-heartedness that follows. Yet even in such a small work as this, Gounod is too refined a craftsman to produce routine stuff. The quartet in Act I where the guest arrives and everyone bustles about laying the table—

ragged cloth best side upwards, odd glasses, forks lacking prongs—sparkles with comedy. When the cook feeds the dove there is just enough true feeling in the ballad she sings to preserve it from mere flippancy. The household is, indeed, a democratic one for the butler melodiously reproves his master's infatuation and the cook takes it upon herself to deplore the arrival of Sylvie. Why, she asks, was the house, though poor, so tranquil a place? Because up to now few women had ever set foot in it.

La Colombe, feather-light though it was, received a very enthusiastic welcome at Baden-Baden. One account reported that such warm applause had never before been heard in the theatre. Madame Carvalho, who took the part of Sylvie, was called many times in front of the curtain. Gounod came in for ovations. Afterwards, in the wings, aristocratic ladies rushed up to shake his hand. Such attentions were not unacceptable. Then, later in the evening, the orchestra marched by torchlight to his hotel and serenaded him. He replied with suave thanks—was it not a privilege to be applauded in the land that had given birth to the world's greatest composers?—and punch vas offered all round.

The verdict of Baden-Baden's fashionable audiences was not endorsed in Paris. The slight charms of *la Colombe*, which had furnished a pleasing interlude in the more serious pursuits of gambling and flirtation, failed to awake much response among less holiday-minded Parisians. After its first performance at Baden-Baden on the 6 August at the height of the 1860 summer season the little opera took six years to reach the capital. Even then it only played twenty-nine times at the Opéra-Comique. Nearly half a century was to pass before Diaghilev rescued it from obscurity and presented it, refurbished by Benois, to a Monte Carlo audience which, like the one at Baden-Baden, found light opera a pleasant way of killing time between sessions at the casino. In any case, when Gounod returned to Paris after the triumph of *la Colombe*, he found the musical world agitated by events more disturbing than the fate of a pet dove. For Wagner was settled there and was about to discharge *Tannhäuser* at the heads of stunned opera-goers.

𝕾VIII𝕰

The Queen of Sheba – Return to Rome – Provence

Wagner settled in Paris towards the end of 1859. He took a house near the Champs-Élysées and spent a lot of money decorating it. Within a year the local authority demolished it in the cause of street improvements. This was typical of the many setbacks he was to encounter in Paris. The three concerts of his music which he gave were met with furious hostility by the press. For much of this he had Meyerbeer to thank.

Through Berlioz, Gounod was introduced to him. 'An irresistible charmer', was the German's verdict. Gounod tried to persuade him not to have *Tannhäuser* put on at the Opéra. Knowing only too well what the public's attitude to new music was like, he urged Wagner to perform it at first in concerts. His advice was ignored and the three performances at the Opéra, all of which he attended, proved chaotic. Members of the Jockey Club were annoyed by the absence of a ballet and demonstrated noisily. Others who had looked forward to a harmless evening's entertainment were confused and irritated by the new style of opera. A number of spectators joined in the whistles and catcalls simply because they disliked Germans.

Gounod was among the musicians—others included Saint-Saëns, Auber and Rossini—who were farsighted enough to appreciate Wagner's music. 'God give me a failure like that!' Gounod observed when he spoke of the *Tannhäuser* fiasco. Friends who were with him slyly remarked that he must be pleased by Wagner's misfortune and the downfall of a rival. 'Let's not be mistaken,' Gounod replied. 'You call this a failure. I call it a riot, which is something very different. Let's meet again ten years from now before the same work and the same man. You'll take off your hat to them both. A matter like this cannot be judged in an evening.'

Wagner found Gounod pleasant enough. But his music would not do. It lacked depth, said Wagner, and the melodies were affected. *Faust*, of course, was unforgiveable. It was a 'theatrical parody of our German *Faust*', and the hero and Méphistophélès were like two students from the Latin Quarter chasing a bit of skirt. Gounod had talent, Wagner admitted, but his temperament lacked the breadth needed for tragic subjects. In future he should choose his libretti with more care.

The performance of *Tannhäuser* had been commanded, not without prompting from influential Wagnerians, by the Empress Eugénie. It may have been this flirtation with the musical art that soon afterwards inspired her to suggest collaborating on a ballet with Gounod. For in October 1860, the composer was invited to stay with the royal family at Compiègne. In the grandiose château built by Louis XV and richly ornamented by Napoléon I, Gounod admired the room that had been put at his disposal: it was embellished, by a tactful Imperial order, with scenes from *Faust*.

The court was then in mourning for the King of Portugal. To Madame Gounod, who had not been invited, her husband wrote urgently for black trousers. These, with an austere waistcoat, he judged, would make for an admirably sepulchral effect. Early on in his visit he spent over an hour with the Empress. Suddenly she proposed that they write a ballet together. He looked at her, speechless.

'I'm not joking,' she went on.

Gounod recovered himself enough to play the courtier. A sovereign's word, he assured her, was worth all the official treaties imaginable.

'Then it's understood,' said the Empress, placing her hand in Gounod's.

At lunch she spoke of it again. Then Gounod played the piano to her. 'Just imagine,' Gounod reported to his wife, 'Her Majesty literally *dissolved into tears*. I played for nearly three-quarters of an hour and they kept saying: "More, more." I thought I'd never be able to satisfy my listeners' appetite.'

While the Emperor rode on horseback the Empress and Gounod drove in a carriage through the oaks and beeches of the forest. They got out and walked a little, the Empress apologizing prettily for her tears. In the evening Gounod sang for them and treated them to 'Mon vieil habit'. 'You sing', said Eugénie, 'with such beautiful "expressiveness".' The Prince Imperial was brought in and Gounod accompanied him in 'Au clair de la lune' and 'Marlborough s'en va-t-en guerre'. When the composer sang an extract from *Faust* the Imperial tears ran again.

Once more they went for a drive in the forest. The Empress repeated her comments on the ballet they were to write together. At the end of his visit Gounod left Compiègne flattered by her ambition and impressed by a lachrymosity which rivalled even his ability to shed tears of ready emotion. Nothing came of the Imperial whim. Instead of the ballet Eugénie proposed, his next work took the shape of *la Reine de Saba*. With it, unfortunately, he sacrificed the good will he had gained at Compiègne.

Believing himself now to be firmly established in the theatre, Gounod resigned from the Orphéon which had sustained him through the early days of his career. His ambition was to create the grand operas for which he felt his talent ideally suited. The first of these was *la Reine de Saba*. It originated in the story *Histoire de la reine du matin* by the arch-romantic Gérard de Nerval who had preceded Gounod in Dr Blanche's clinic. This exotic personage wrote prose as beautiful as his habits were eccentric. It was his custom to take a pet lobster for a walk in the street, having first attached to it a lead of gaily coloured ribbon in order to prevent it from running away. At the age of forty-seven he committed suicide by hanging himself from a lamp-post in the sinister rue de la Vieille Lanterne.

Nerval's imaginative variations on the theme of Balkis, Queen of Sheba, gave Barbier and Carré the framework of their opera. In this version of the encounter between the Queen of Sheba and Solomon as told in Chapter X of the first Book of Kings, the hero is an architect-cum-engineer-cum-foreman called Adoniram. He is in charge of the massive building programme that Solomon has put in hand to glorify his reign. Balkis arrives on her State visit. Though mildly impressed by Solomon's magnificence, she falls in love with Adoniram. Solomon, however, has also conceived a passion for her. Adoniram and Balkis plan to elope together. Before they can do this a trio of disgruntled workmen murder Adoniram. Balkis concludes that Solomon has plotted the killing and resists his embraces long enough to put a sleeping draught in his wine. While he falls asleep she makes her escape.

The plot is curiously lopsided. Act I ends superbly with the arrival of the Queen of Sheba and her splendid retinue. The march and fanfares which greet her foreshadow those of *Aïda* ten years later. (They consist of material left over from *Ivan le Terrible*.) The conclusion of Act II is provided by a spectacular scene in which a furnace blows up. Solomon and the Queen attend the casting of Adoniram's masterpiece. But his enemies have sabotaged the mould. Amid smoke and explosions a tide of molten brass floods out. Beams crack. The giant furnace crumbles into ruin. It would be difficult to cap such a spectacle in the same opera, and the emotional temperature of the remaining three acts declines in proportion. What follows is simple anti-climax which is made still more incongruous by the feeble triangular love interest between Adoniram, Balkis and Solomon.

Hampered already by a clumsy plot, Gounod was unable to achieve the grand manner that might have saved him. The most successful passages in *la Reine de Saba* include the sweet and particularly Gounodian chorus of Sheban women at the beginning of Act III, 'Déjà l'aube matinale', which gives way to an equally attractive chorus, 'Que Dieu vous accompagne'. Another item of the same cut is Balkis' 'Plus grand, dans son obscurité', where the feminine delicacy of the tune expresses her feelings for Adoniram. One may also applaud Adoniram's 'Faiblesse de la race humaine', an aria of some nobility. On the whole, though, the opera is stilted and uneasy. There is an impression of strain about it that contrasts with the spontaneous nature of Gounod's best work. He was, in *la Reine de Saba*, attempting a style completely foreign to him. There was little room for his true gift to declare itself in this type of opera.[1]

Six weeks of anxiety preceded the first performance. Gounod was the target for complaint from singers who felt their talents were not being recognized, from dancers who wanted to alter the music—the ballet, in particular, is a depressing affair and includes the inevitable waltz—and from stage-crews who grumbled at the complications of the set. Even the conductor took no notice of Gounod's directions. At last the desperate composer appealed to Count Walewski. This influential acquaintance, who owed his important place in the Emperor's government to the useful chance that he was one of the first Napoléon's bastards, heard Gounod sympathetically.

'It seems to me', said Gounod, 'that the conductor is nothing more than the driver of the coach engaged by the composer. He

[1] The 1970 revival at Toulouse confirmed that the inspiration of *la Reine de Saba* was limited to intermittent flickers.

should stop at every request or quicken the pace according to the fare's orders. Otherwise the composer is entitled to get out and complete the journey on foot.'

'On foot!' replied Walewski. 'People already complain that composers don't do the journey fast enough. Stay in your coach, M. Gounod, and I will try to make the driver see reason.' The conductor paid heed to the voice of authority and Walewski's reward was the dedication of *la Reine de Saba*.

The opera was eventually heard on the 28 February 1862. It began at a quarter past eight and the exhausted audience was unable to leave until twenty minutes after midnight. The Emperor and Empress were there. Louis-Napoléon did not like what he saw and heard. He was offended by an opera which showed a queen preferring a humble workman to a king. The rebellious workmen who killed Adoniram were, he felt, showing dangerous socialist tendencies which undermined the relationship between master and man. There was, in the architectural digressions of the plot, a nasty hint of that masonic cult which the Emperor detested. In short, all the favour Gounod had earned at Compiègne was thrown to the winds.

Toadying journalists carefully echoed the Imperial displeasure. Music critics who had noted Gounod's unfashionable praise of Wagner claimed to find 'deplorable' traces of that composer in the score. Even Berlioz, who had been a strong supporter up to now, was unable to approve of *la Reine de Saba*. 'There is nothing in the score, absolutely nothing,' he confided to a friend. 'How can one support something which has neither bone nor muscle?' Another critic summed up the general opinion: '*Faust* was Gounod's Austerlitz. *La Reine de Saba* will be his Waterloo.'

Although the opera did well initially at the box office, it only survived fifteen performances. In Europe it had a rather happier fate. A few years afterwards it turned up at the Crystal Palace in a version known as *Irene*. The work had been made fit for Victorian ears by turning Adoniram into the cosily named Muriel, an ambivalent change by modern standards but one that apparently caused no surprise at the time. The Queen of Sheba became Irene and Solomon was transmuted into a Turkish sultan.

The loyal Bizet, who arranged the vocal score and as usual carried out the odd jobs associated with a Gounod production, was hot in defence of the opera. When someone observed that *la Reine de Saba* had deserved to flop, he assailed the detractor with furious language and challenged him to a duel. Gounod calmed them both down, though not without taking a sad pleasure in Bizet's generous action. The outlook was bleak. He could not help envying the triumph then being enjoyed by another opera for which Carré had written the libretto. 'Tell Carré', he remarked in a letter to Choudens, 'that I congratulate him this time on falling into hands which haven't, like mine, the bad luck of murdering everything they touch. If he'd given *la Reine* to Meyerbeer people would have found the drama and the music excellent and they'd both have had a terrific success. I think that one of these fine days I'll do as Barbier did, buy a carrot field and devote myself to the peace of the country. How touching that would be!'

Still shrouded in gloom by the collapse of *la Reine de Saba*, he had fresh cause for sadness in the death of Halévy, which occurred a few weeks later. Gounod was fond of his old master, liking the man and respecting the artist. He wrote to him at Nice, where Halévy had gone for the sake of his health. 'I didn't want to let you know my impressions after the first performance of *la Reine de Saba*: they were too sad and couldn't have failed to grieve your friendly feeling for me.' Halévy died on the 17 March, and the *De profundis* sung at his funeral contained a section set by Gounod. The occasion, wrote an obituarist, was in a way 'a public bereavement'. Yet despite the great popularity Halévy enjoyed during his lifetime, it was not long before *la Juive*, *l'Éclair*, and *la Reine de Chypre* joined him in the grave.

Gounod continued to lament his Queen of Sheba. In Baden the following year to see the production of *Béatrice et Bénédict* by his old friend Berlioz, he met an acquaintance who was surprised to see him there. 'Yes,' replied Gounod, 'a death in the family has sent me on my travels.' 'You've lost a relative?' 'Yes, a woman I loved very much: *la Reine de Saba*.'

Only a month after the disastrous première he was off to Italy. With his son Jean, now six years old, and his wife Anna, he left Paris for Rome. Accompanying them on the journey were a couple of family friends. Such a trip was, of all things, the one best calculated to cheer him up. 'So many memories! and what memories,' he exulted.

At Marseille, before going on board, they lunched to the strains of the soldiers' march in *Faust* played by a brass band. That popular tune had quickly made its way into the repertory of café orchestras and military bands. They left the heavy rains of Marseille behind and at two o'clock one afternoon they entered Rome, where the name of the first church to be glimpsed was reverently noted down. The Capitol and the baths of Caracalla lay quiet and serene under a blue sky. By night, Gounod thought, the columns of the Forum stood out in the dusk like ghosts. An owl screeched over the Coliseum in moonlight and torches flittered mysteriously along the upper vaults. Again and again he went back to Saint Peter to hear the music of Palestrina, '. . . that persistent and wonderful network of voices, those harmonic vibrations in the upper registers, that almost visionary sound of the greatest Christian temple in existence, all of which carries the soul beyond reality and uplifts it in exaltation.'

He returned to the Villa Medici and wandered through the gardens he'd known as a youth. In the drawing-room, among the cyclamens, the distinguished former student heard extracts from *Faust*. One day, in the Pantheon, he was shown his father's name scratched on a pillar. At Albano a guitar was bought and he sang to his fellow-travellers the shepherd's song from *Sapho*.

The days were spent in a flurry of visits and excursions to the places that had captivated him when he first saw them years ago. He was to love them all his life. The main party broke up, and with his family Gounod was left to explore Naples and Capri again. 'I feel that leaving Italy will be a great sorrow for me', he wrote, 'in spite of everything that binds me to Paris and calls me back there with so many links: I feel that this land of Rome and Naples is my true, my only country. It is here that I would have wished to live until the end of my days. My real instincts do not belong to the place where my home is.'

On his forty-fourth birthday, to the friend he affectionately called 'mon Bizet', he wrote: 'I've seen Rome with the feelings of a desperate man, of a lover who has to depart. I should never have left the place . . .'

Throughout June he travelled slowly back to Paris by way of Florence, Venice, Milan and Switzerland. The guitar accompanied him and he amused himself with his new-found skill at performing on the instrument. He sketched a lot and composed not at all. By the middle of July he was home and reluctantly considering projects for new operas. While in Italy he had toyed with the idea of setting *le Cid*. This he soon rejected, leaving Massenet twenty years later to add his own version of Corneille to the twenty-six operas already inspired by the Spanish national hero. For a time he also thought of returning to the source of *Faust* and extracting a *Mignon* from Goethe's *Wilhelm Meister*. Barbier and Carré had a libretto ready and waiting. Then he changed his mind again. Four years later it was Ambroise Thomas who was to triumph with the subject.

Gounod stayed in Paris long enough to see a successful revival of *Faust*. Since any excuse for a trip to Italy was enough, he hurried to Milan for the first performance of the opera at La Scala. Then he went to Darmstadt and conducted *la Reine de Saba*. Despite the ovations and the laurels that decked the rostrum, the work owed its good reception more to a brilliant production than to its musical value. Schumann joined the audience and, in his diary, echoed the general opinion that the score was of no great consequence.

Comforted a little by the apparent revival of his ailing *Reine de Saba*, Gounod was ready to consider the next suggestion from his librettists. Michel Carré now proposed a *Mireille* based on Mistral's poem. The basis of the story appealed to Gounod: a tragic love affair, a young and beautiful heroine, and a setting in the Provence which reminded him so poignantly of Italy.

Mirèio was written in the Provençal language. For true Provençal is a language and not just a dialect. The earliest tongue born of Latin, it reached perfection in the eleventh century, only to be, in Sainte-Beuve's words, 'brutally crushed in its flowering and drowned, as it were, in the blood of those who nurtured it' during the Albigensian wars of the century that followed. Provençal then deteriorated, for social and political reasons, into a humble patois. Six centuries afterwards Frédéric Mistral restored Provençal to its place of honour with *Mirèio*. He had made of Provençal, said Lamartine, 'a language classic in images and harmony that delight the ear and the imagination.'

Mirèio came out in 1859. It was Mistral's first big work and it brought him an immediate reputation. Some of this was due to Lamartine's warm praise, though even without the support his authority gave it the poem would eventually have made its own successful way. Mistral was born just outside the little Provençal town of Maillane where he spent most of his life. After taking, with not much enthusiasm, a law degree, he returned home to help on his father's farm. He was the son of a second marriage, and when his father died the other sons dismissed him from the family *mas*. He then set up house with his aged mother in the 'Maison du Lézard'. There they lived peacefully for many years. In 1854, with a group of six other local poets, he founded the movement known as *le Félibrige*. Its aim was to revive the Provençal language. Soon afterwards the publication of *Mirèio* gave a practical example of the beauties of Provençal when a genuine poet used it. Mistral became something of a legend. Admirers of his poetry travelled long distances to see his little house. He wrote many more poems, all of them in a language he had made into a perfect instrument for poetic expression. At the late age of forty-six he entered on a commonsense marriage with a lady who was prepared to share his fame. The award of the Nobel Prize for literature confirmed the wisdom she had shown in choosing her husband. She lived on for some time after his death in 1914, carefully preserving the home which is now the Museon Mistral and playing her part of 'noble veuve', some thought, with a shade too much of perfection.

The narrative content of *Mirèio* is the least important of the elements which comprise the poem. Mirèio, daughter of the wealthy farmer Ramon, loves the basket-weaver Vincent, son of the humble Ambroise. Ramon strongly opposes the relationship and seeks a rich husband for his daughter. She has other suitors as well: Ourrias the herdsman, Veran the horse breeder, and Alari the shepherd. Like the bulls he tames and brands, Ourrias is a fierce and powerful creature. He fights Vincent, and, when defeated, wounds him with the trident he uses for driving the bulls. On his way back to the Camargue he crosses the Rhône. His boat sinks and he is punished for his crime with drowning: for it is the day of the year (St Médard's eve) when the ghosts of all those drowned in the river rise up in search of good deeds which, when enough are collected together, will admit them to Paradise. Having heard of Vincent's misadventure, Mirèio goes on foot to the mediaeval church of Saintes-Maries-de-la-Mer hoping to invoke divine assistance. To get there she has to walk over the arid plain known as the Crau, a vast expanse of stone and pebble. After covering seventy miles under the glancing hot sun she reaches the sanctuary. There, exhausted and smitten with sunstroke, she dies surrounded by her repentant father and sorrowing Vincent.

What matters in this extended lyric poem is not the story but the rich tapestry of Provençal traditions, beliefs and customs that Mistral unfolds. Few are the lines where he does not refer to some fact of

Provençal life. He is not so much interested in his characters as in the folk costumes they wear, the things they believe, the way they farm the land, the faiths and symbols that weave the texture of their existence. This is not to suggest that *Mirèio* amounts to little else than a jumble of folklore. It is much more. The very spirit of Provence is captured in Mistral's sweet singing verse. When he writes about the wild horses of the Camargue or the nomad shepherds leading their flocks over the Crau he does so in tones that are a rare blend of realism and poetry. He had read and appreciated Virgil and Homer, whose memory remained with him. The timelessness of *Mirèio* reflects the antiquity of Provence:

> *Cante uno chato de Prouvènço.*
> *Dins lis amour de sa jouvenços*[1]

In February of 1863 a series of courtly exchanges took place between Mistral and Gounod. The poet readily authorized librettist and composer to base their opera on *Mirèio*. 'I'm delighted you like my little girl,' wrote Mistral, 'but up to now you've only met her in my poetry. Come to Arles, to Avignon, to Saint-Rémy, come and see her on Sundays when she walks out from Vespers. . . .'

The composer accepted Mistral's invitation. He needed little urging to get away from the bustle and distraction of Paris. Early in March he came to Lyon, where a concert performance of *la Reine de Saba* was to be given on the 7th. He also heard a performance of Verdi's *Ernani* during his stay there. It disappointed him. 'I think it's execrable,' he wrote. 'The only thing (in my eyes at least) to be found in the music is what is exterior to it, in other words the voices of the singers. As for the quality of feeling, form, character and conception inherent in the text itself, it's worthless. It's organ grinder's stuff.'[2]

---

[1] 'A girl of Provence I sing. / In the loves of her youth . . .'

[2] According to Henri Busser it was Gounod who had interceded with Hugo to obtain permission for Verdi's use of his play, as in the case of *Rigoletto* (*le Roi s'amuse*), on the occasion of the Paris production. He is said to have done a similar service in persuading Dumas *fils* to let Verdi base *la Traviata* on *la Dame aux camélias*. Gounod also arranged the Paris Opéra's commission of *Don Carlos*, Verdi having earlier been of help in organizing the first Rome production of *Faust*. Busser adds that at the Paris rehearsals of *la Traviata* Gounod suggested a repeat on the strings of the '*grande phrase si belle, si expressive*' from the Act I prelude at the moment when Rodolpho and Violetta part. He obviously liked this opera better than *Ernani*.

From Lyon he drive on to Maillane and a warm welcome by Mistral. Next day they went to the village of Baux, a place of ghostly ruin with little more than eighty inhabitants. Once a rich and powerful castle town, it huddles now forlornly on a headland above a rocky cliff. The strangeness of the site and the immensity of the view it commands make it unique in France. The place figures, of course, in *Mirèio*. Standing on the heights Gounod was able to see the desert expanse of the Crau stretching far away to the Mediterranean.

'I'm delighted with Mistral,' Gounod wrote. 'God has given him a lot: he's worthy, simple, handsome, sensitive, generous; and as a poet you know only too well what he is! His style expresses the man himself completely. He is pure and primitive, though gifted with charming manners that sophistication would assuredly never have equalled. He suits me very well indeed and I've the good fortune to suit him a little.'

Gounod put up at a hotel in the nearby town of Saint-Rémy, which, if not prehistoric in origin like Baux, dates back well over twenty centuries to the period when it was founded by Greek colonists from Marseille. He signed himself 'Monsieur Pépin' in the register of the Hôtel Ville-Verte, which today carries a plaque recording that he composed *Mireille* there. 'Pépin le Bref', he explained, 'because he didn't talk much.' Even so his incognito was quickly revealed as such and the local church was crowded with people to hear him play the organ at Easter services.

A piano was sent over from Nîmes and he settled to work on his opera. His letters home were full of the serenity and happiness he was enjoying: 'How well I understand Mistral staying in this paradise of country life and refusing to exchange the riches of peace for the poverty and wretchedness of excitement! My window is open; the sky is azure; I can hear only the cooing of pigeons in the yard: all else is cloistered silence. Six weeks of quiet meditation like this and *Mireille* will be in the bag. The place is pure and beautiful like Italy: it's the Italy of France and I did well to settle here.'

Within a week he had written important sections of the opera. Mireille's cavatina in Act IV, 'Heureux petit berger', came to him while he sat beside a little stream. Birds sang, the trunks of the trees glistened in the sun, and thick swaying grass carpeted the river-bed like 'velvet under diamonds'. Once again he had found the Theocritan tone of *Sapho*, that simple and timeless vein of melody exalting the freedom of the shepherd alone except for his flock under the blue sky.

Most of the time he deserted his piano and wandered outdoors, notebook in hand, savouring the sights and perfumes of the country-side. Sometimes, in the endless silence of the Provençal landscape, he held his breath the better to hear 'the mysterious concert of those thousands of little creatures that people earth and air. Their un-interrupted humming trembles on the ear just as the atmosphere trembles to the eye on a hot day.' He went to the church of Saintes-Maries-de-la-Mer, from whose terrace the dying Mireille looked her last at the sea beyond, and he took Communion, sensing that his faith was renewed by contact with the humble villagers who for centuries had worshipped inside its twelfth-century walls.

The only discordant note in this rhapsody of contentment was a brief encounter with Madame Carvalho. After singing at the opera house in Marseille she told Gounod that she would like to see him on her way back to Paris. The train stopped for a few minutes at Tarascon. Gounod obediently awaited her on the platform. He began to tell her of the progress he'd made, of how happy he was, of how inspiration was flowing easily. . . . The haughty prima donna popped her head out of the carriage window and cut him short, '*Surtout, n'est-ce pas, faites brillant, très brillant, brillant!*', while from the depths of the compartment her husband piped up: 'And tell him even that won't be enough!'

Poor Gounod, crestfallen, replied that *Mireille* would only be 'brilliant'—that is, written with the maximum show enabling Madame Carvalho to display her flashy gifts—insofar as he was himself 'brilliant'. The window shot up and the wretched woman, having issued instructions as she would to her butler, whistled off to Paris. The episode rankled. 'I don't think, for example, that Mir-eille's sorrows—and she had quite a few—need be so "brilliant" as all that,' Gounod complained in a letter, 'and this is the place to say: all that glitters is not gold. The sky is orange, lilac and blue!' The beauty of Provence, Mistral's lovely poem, the drama, the character-ization and the music all meant nothing to Madame Carvalho, provided there was 'brilliance' enough for her to shine.

The annoyance caused by her intrusion soon faded. 'I would get up before dawn,' Gounod said, 'and stroll along shady paths listening to the songs of the birds God created, happy and delighted to find myself in this scented Eden. From time to time I'd meet on my way some languorous-eyed Provençal charmer who'd throw me a "Bonjour, Monsieur", with a smile . . . I was literally drunk with happiness; musical ideas sprang to my mind like a flight of butterflies, and all I had to do was to stretch out my hand to catch them.'

Under such conditions *Mireille* was quickly written. By the end of the month he had completed the larger part of it and was free to welcome his family to Saint-Rémy. He lingered on there to see the great annual pilgrimage at the church of Saintes-Maries-de-la-Mer, when the holy relics are solemnly lowered on a rope decorated with flowers, and then, in an atmosphere taut with emotion, as reverently drawn up again.

On the 26 May the people of Saint-Rémy arranged a banquet in his honour. Mistral offered a toast in Provençal:

Gentlemen, the master musician who came to share the sun with us for a morning or so is about to leave. The valley of Saint-Clerc is saddened. Alas, the crickets and warblers will hardly console it for the novel chords it has heard.

In honour of Gounod, friends, let's drink a toast that God may keep him long at his music desk. May each glass ring harmoniously in Gounod's honour, that lucid musician who has made the murmurs of Provence ring.

Then Gounod sat at a dusty old harmonium and played over the score of *Mireille*. 'You came into the world to discover Provence,' said Mistral. 'You've succeeded in your opera.'

Three days later Gounod and his family were back in Paris. There he was dragooned by his publisher Choudens and the impresario Carvalho into a journey to London for the first Covent Garden performance of *Faust*. This production had been arranged by 'Colonel' Mapleson, an entrepreneur of sprightly resource. Alone of English impresarios at the time he had sensed the possibilities of *Faust*. By contriving a 'paper' house at the first three performances and only allowing two stalls actually to be sold for money, he stimulated intense public curiosity. As a result, a paying audience filled the theatre at all remaining performances and *Faust* was launched on its very successful English career as the source of countless '*bouquets de mélodies*', 'pot-pourris', 'reminiscences', 'transcriptions', and arrangements for every type of instrument. The wholesome and acceptable nature of the work was proclaimed by a thoughful preacher who told his flock at the Montpottinger Unitarian Chapel:

'The interests of religion and morality are never compromised but are substantially promoted by such a work as Gounod's *Faust*.'

The composer was paid a fee of a hundred pounds for supervising the production. He helpfully arrived in London just before seven o'clock on the evening of 11 June, the date fixed for the première. All the hard work had already been done by Luigi Arditi, the conductor. Gounod fully approved. Before the opening act finished he turned to Choudens, who sat beside him in the stalls, and remarked: 'Praise be to God! *This* is my *Faust*!'

Madame Carvalho sang her original part of Marguerite. Gounod could have been forgiven a malicious pleasure in the comment by *The Times* that she walked the stage 'with the placid composure and muscular rigidity of a somnambulist.' The brusque meeting at Tarascon was avenged.

While in London he stayed at 62 Avenue Road near Regent's Park. One Sunday he went to St Paul's and noted that it offered 'the finest musical service in Christendom.' Most of the time, though, he was paraded about the city and used, he grumbled, as 'a walking advertisement poster' by Choudens who was anxious to display his merchandise. The more performances of *Faust* there were the more copies of the music Choudens sold, and naturally he sought to gain the maximum amount of publicity. In a bitter chapter of his autobiography Gounod presents himself as an innocent who believed that Choudens did all this through personal devotion and a pure love of art. Looking back, he compared his own lack of business sense with the acumen of a Verdi who could demand, and receive, 40,000 or 50,000 francs for directing the production of one of his operas in Paris. While it is true that Gounod paints too dark a picture, it must be admitted that he was justified in his artist's annoyance that a shrewder commercial mind should be picking up the finest plums.

He was outraged, furthermore, to learn that he would receive only a pittance from the hundreds of performances *Faust* was to have in England. When Frederick Gye, a rival theatre manager, sued Mapleson over performing rights to the work, it emerged from legal discussion that, in fact, no one had an exclusive lien on them. A technicality arising from failure to register the opera correctly deprived Gounod of the rewards he was entitled to expect.

It was all, as Mapleson remarked with a poker face, 'painful enough for M. Gounod.' The unlucky composer decided, as on his earlier visit, that London would never be 'his' city. As if to confirm this, on his return to Paris he suffered a breakdown. After putting the finishing touches to *Mireille* he was obliged to take a rest cure. And once again Dr Blanche welcomed his musical guest at the establishment on the health-giving heights of Passy.

₪ IX ₪

Mireille – Roméo et Juliette

While Gounod recuperated at Passy in the autumn of 1863 his friend Bizet's opera *les Pêcheurs de perles* had its first performance at the Théâtre-Lyrique. Although it failed to draw big audiences this youthful masterpiece by a composer not yet twenty-five years old was recognized by discerning musicians as proof of his original talent. Gounod was delighted at his protégé's artistic success. A first work, he told him, was a duel; a second was a battle and a third was victory.

In September his wife gave birth to a daughter whom they named Jeanne. His old friend Charles Gay wrote to congratulate him. The birth of this child, he suggested to Gounod, was the first reward of his having dedicated himself anew to God earlier in the year. The experience in the church of Saintes-Maries-de-la-Mer had probably stimulated in Gounod another wave of religious feeling.

Throughout the coming months he was to need all the fortitude religion could offer, since by October rehearsals of *Mireille* had been put in hand. Madame Carvalho was exigent as ever. It was her insistence that forced Gounod to write for her, as Mireille, the 'brilliant' waltz 'O légère hirondelle', a tinselled appeal to the sensibility which has been quietly dropped from modern revivals of the opera. There were six months of argument, rewriting, shortening here and lengthening there, before Gounod was released from his hard labour. At one point he threatened to take *Mireille* away from Carvalho, who, true to form, had been as tiresome as his wife in attempts to revamp the work. Only his old friendship and long association with the impresario prevented Gounod at the last minute from taking this step. A moment even came when legal summonses flew back and forth between composer and prima donna.

Just before the unveiling of *Mireille* Gounod directed a private performance of it in his house. The accompaniment, on piano and harmonium, was provided by Saint-Saëns and Bizet. The singers included Gounod himself and the vicomtesse de Grandval, a young lady who added to her noble quarterings the distinction of having composed oratorios, operas, operettas and symphonic works. She studied as a private pupil with Saint-Saëns, who, at that time working hard but unsuccessfully to establish himself in the theatre, must have observed with astonished envy her achievement in having stage-works produced one after another at the Opéra-Comique and other important places. They are all, like their aristocratic author, forgotten today.

This private performance went well and the guests predicted another success for Gounod. The first night of *Mireille*, which took place on the 19 March 1864, was, however, only a muted triumph. The opening act was tolerably successful, but the rest of the work did not appeal. The simple tale of peasant love was too colourless for Parisians. There could be nothing romantic, it was decided, about the sentimental problems of such lower class folk as basket weavers and herdsmen. An opera that ended in the death of the heroine was a mistake.

Despite Gounod's protests *Mireille* was taken off after its tenth performance. If he wanted to see it put on again, explained Carvalho and his inexorable wife, he must conform to what the public wanted. Cut the five acts to three! Let Mireille stay alive! Put in a happy ending! All these things Gounod did. The heroine miraculously recovered in time for a last duet and the prospect of marriage to Vincent. Spoken dialogue took the place of recitative and many hasty cuts were made. The score was touched up throughout with the addition of vocalizes for Madame Carvalho. No wonder Saint-Saëns was later to exclaim in puzzlement: 'When I've seen *Mireille* on the stage I've never been able to recapture the first impression of a complete and finished work that so charmed me when Gounod played it to me at the piano.'

Gounod has been much abused for so meekly submitting to the will of the Carvalhos. It is sometimes overlooked that an atmosphere of back-stage panic does not encourage art for art's sake. So Gounod, as a working man of the theatre, did what experienced people advised. The version he produced was the one that ran for many hundreds of performances and later revivals. Not until 1939 was the original restored and played at the Opéra-Comique with the aid of detective work by Gounod's pupil Henri Busser and the support of Reynaldo Hahn.[1] Since even the score used at the 1864 performances had been vitiated by the Carvalhos' tamperings, the Hahn-Busser production was the true first performance. It had taken nearly seventy-five years to put Gounod's conception into effect.

Admirers of Mistral have often been reluctant to give credit to Gounod. Their unfavourable opinion was probably influenced by the clumsy changes in the plot which the composer had had to accept. The original version should have done something to pacify them when allowance is made for the exigencies of the stage and the fact that Carré as poet stands to Mistral in the relationship of journeyman to genius. It was, besides, thanks to Gounod that *Mireille*, in the days when opera was a living and popular form, spread Mistral's fame much more quickly, both in France and elsewhere, than its intrinsic merits could have done.

The bareness of the plot meant that Gounod could not rely on dramatic incident and exciting events to sustain the interest of his audience. He looked, instead, to characterization and atmosphere. Mireille is one of his most attractive heroines. After the opening chorus of Act I, where the peasant girls have sung about the handsome lovers they dream of meeting, she makes her appearance with a type of melody of which Gounod was master.

> '*Et moi, si par hasard, quelque jeune garçon*
> *Me disait doucement: "Mireille, je vous aime!"*'

has the naturalness of the tune that accompanies Marguerite's initial encounter with Faust. The wistful lilt beautifully expresses the young girl's romantic longings, eager yet apprehensive. She has a sense of humour, too, for when Vincent praises her with loving exaggeration her '*Oh! c'Vincent!*' is amused and amusing. But in '*Mon coeur ne peut changer*', and '*À vos pieds hélas, me voilà*', she shows a strength of character surprisingly resolute in one so fragile.

Another well-turned portrait is that of the benevolent witch

---

[1] In 1898, at Saint-Saëns' suggestion, Gounod's widow asked Busser to reconstitute the original score. This he did with the aid of the manuscript orchestral score owned by Mme Gounod and of documents from Gounod's publisher. Busser also completed the orchestration of 'En Marche!' in the Crau episode and orchestrated the final scene of Mireille's death, which was missing, presumed destroyed, in the fire at the Opéra-Comique in 1887.

Taven. Drifting among the jolly peasant girls who babble of their romantic dreams, she darkly foretells the sorrows that lie in wait for the unsuspecting little victims. They will be caught, she warns, like birds in a trap, and tears will replace laughter—this to music which Gounod himself described, appropriately, as 'bat-coloured'. She comes into her own with the *chanson* 'Voici la saison mignonne', an example of the composer's gift for taking an archaic form and breathing new life into it. The melody bounds along in a jaunty minor key varied with chromatic runs in the accompaniment to underline her forebodings as she warns Mireille of the sorrows which love and suitors will cause her. To the brightness of the Provençal landscape Taven brings a disturbing hint of troubled undercurrents, of veiled mystery.

Although Vincent is limited chiefly to partnering Mireille in the superbly written duets which are a feature of the opera, he has at least one big moment to himself. This occurs in Act V. 'Anges du paradis' is a nobly lyrical cavatina imploring Heaven to protect Mireille on her journey across the burning wastes of the Crau.

The other men characters also have excellent opportunities. Ourrias, proud and strong, portrays himself in an aria of impatient vigour, 'Si les filles d'Arles sont reines'. He will brook no defiance from the woman he honours with his choice. Yet, against a blaze of mellow brass in the orchestra, he, the tamer of bulls whom no human has yet succeeded in taming, is ready to submit to Mireille. Ramon, Mireille's father, is another example of feudal masculine dominance. Mistral had told Gounod about his own father and of how, faithful to Provençal tradition, the old man ruled his family with patriarchal authority: wife, sons and daughters bowed instantly to his venerable will. 'And so Mistral's mother, who adored her husband, always called him "Master",' Gounod recalled. 'When he dined she never sat at table with him; she served him and then sat apart with the children. You've no idea of customs like this: it's just like the Bible . . . Old Testament, of course.' Gounod put all this into the music he wrote for Ramon, especially the commanding aria he gave him, 'Un père parle en père, un homme agit en homme'.

The music is filled with the sunshine of Provence although Gounod has caught as well the tragedy that broods under the warm colouring of the countryside. If at midday the sun dazzles brilliantly, it causes shadows of unsparing blackness, and by evening the twilight is grey and melancholy. The bright exuberance of the opening chorus, 'Chantez, chantez, magnanarelles', is momentarily chilled by Taven's dark predictions. The whole of Act III shows this other, more sombre aspect of Provençal life. In *la Nonne sanglante* and in *Faust* Gounod was not successful in his attempt to portray the macabre. Here he achieves his aim. When Ourrias comes by night to the haunt of goblins and sorcerers known as the Val d'enfer, Gounod hits on a flittering Mendelssohnian theme that admirably conveys a suggestion of bat-infested caves and evil things. Ourrias' attack on Vincent in this unhallowed place is followed by a scene where the eeriness of the music intensifies. He is confronted with the spirits of dead lovers rising from the waters of the Rhône. A phantom chorus of

> '*Voici minuit,*
> *Un feu qui luit*
> *Traverse l'ombre*'

greets the would-be murderer with an unearthly motif depicting the midnight river shrouded in mists and peopled by frozen shapes half-glimpsed and formless.

In the 'Chanson de Magali' Gounod makes use of a traditional song which Mistral, after the fashion of Robert Burns, had drawn from regional lore. (Massenet was later to incorporate it in his opera *Sapho* as a theme representing Provence.) The composer ingeniously extends the tune, building it up into a duet and finally an ensemble through a series of swiftly changing time signatures implying the sudden transports, then hesitations, of love. The same flowing limpidity is to be found in the shepherd's dawn song in Act IV and Mireille's 'Heureux petit berger'.

The purely orchestral passages also help to re-create the spirit of Provence. The overture, beginning with a slow introduction used later in the opera to set the scene for the desolateness of the Crau, flowers into a broad sweeping melody that is the musical equivalent of those genre pictures of sun-burnt harvesters and hay wains. Dawn and the chirping of crickets are portrayed in a murmurous 'Musette'. And there is a magnificent farandole, bursting with energy and full of exciting rhythms.

Mireille has imperfections. It is possible that the heroine's death scene, complete with obligatory voice from on high, borders on religiosity and too closely resembles Marguerite's edifying dissolution in *Faust*. (Nor is the effect improved when the chorus of stricken worshippers appears to be singing the tune of 'I came from Alabama with a banjo on my knee'—whereas, of course, they are asking the saints of Paradise to hear their prayers.) The unfortunate waltz-song is out of character for Mireille, though happily it is not included in the restored version. It may also be thought that the drama is at times over-emphatic. But criticism cannot deny to *Mireille* the idyllic portrait Gounod has drawn of his womanly heroine, that captivating 'chato de Prouvenço', nor the skilfully blended chiaroscuro in the picture he gives us of her land. The opera, which showed the way for Bizet and *l'Arlésienne*, is one of his loveliest achievements.

A few months later *Mireille* crossed the Channel accompanied by Gounod for its London première in an Italian version as *Mirella*. This was on the 5 July and featured Tietjens in the leading rôle. Critical opinion was divided, although the opera ran for seven performances. As with *Faust*, Mapleson was the impresario in charge. On this occasion he seems to have been suffering from the disease that affected Carvalho, since his persistent demands for changes in the work led Gounod to talk of 'my humiliating profession of decomposer of music'. Mapleson was particularly keen on loudening the music at one of the curtain-falls so as to underline the dramatic effect. 'O human stupidity!' snapped Gounod. 'Why not bring a squad of artillery on stage for once and all each time the curtain comes down?'

A foot ailment he had contracted did nothing to improve his temper. At Mont-Dore in the Auvergne, where he went to take the waters, he worked between treatments on the incidental music for a drama by Ernest Legouvé entitled *les Deux reines*. Legouvé wrote many plays. None has survived. His father was the celebrated author of *le Mérite des femmes*, a poem so widely read that it went through more than forty editions. Polite society frequently quoted the immortal exhortation; '*Tombe aux pieds de ce sexe à qui tu dois ta mère.*'[1] His son's contribution to morality was to act as witness for the lady who became the second wife of Dumas *fils*. The author of *la Dame aux camélias* was pushed into wedding her by the daughters of his first marriage, who, bored by his constant prating of her virtue, insisted that he marry quickly and shut up.

Towards the end of August Gounod was back from Mont-Dore and consulting with Legouvé on the finishing touches to *les Deux*

[1] 'Fall at the feet of the sex to whom thou owest thy mother.'

reines. Then the government, always sensitive to political under-tones, stepped in and forbade its production. Although the plot related events that took place hundreds of years before, a nervous censor feared that unwelcome parallels might be drawn with the contemporary situation. Composer and author had to be content with private performances at which Legouvé declaimed the text and Gounod sang the male solos helped out by his usual team of the vicomtesse de Grandval, Bizet and Saint-Saëns. *Les Deux reines* did not appear in public until 1872, by which time Louis-Napoléon was out of the way and there was no Imperial government to offend.

Still troubled by the rheumatism that Mont-Dore was unable to cure, Gounod made preliminary sketches for an opera, *Fiesque*, to be based on Schiller's tragedy. Soon he dropped the idea in favour of a four-act work that Barbier and Carré had already adapted from Shakespeare's *Romeo and Juliet*. He had never forgotten the impression made on him by the Berlioz symphony he heard while still in his youth, and the subject attracted him as strongly as ever.

After a detour by way of Belgium to see a production of *Mireille* he arrived in the Spring of 1865 at Saint Raphaël. Here, where a rue Charles Gounod commemorates his stay, he wrote most of *Roméo et Juliette*. In the 'Oustalet dou Capelan', a neat little villa surrounded by a terrace with breath-taking views over the gulf of Fréjus, he worked in a state of happy feverishness. Nearby was a house Jules Barbier had built. Once more at home in that atmosphere of Provence which he always found an inspiration, he composed quickly and surely.

Sometimes he would rise with the sun. In the mild April weather he strolled at the sea's edge. A transparent sky hung above, and all around the peace of morning was disturbed only by the gentle lap of crystal water. He would settle down under an umbrella pine and cover the pages of his score with the finely detailed script in which he wrote. The second act, which includes the balcony duet, came to him swiftly and easily. Like the rest of the music, he wrote it straight off, almost without pause, so spontaneous was the thought that drove his pen.

On the 2 May, at half-past twelve, he finished the big duet in Act IV. 'I read over this duet, I read it again, I listen to it with all my attention; I try to find it bad; I'm afraid of finding it good and being mistaken! And yet it fired me! It still does! It was born of sincerity. In short, I BELIEVE IN IT. Voice, orchestra, everything plays its part; the violins turn passionate; it's all there: Juliet clasping her lover, Romeo's anxiety, his delirious embraces. . . . '

The countryside around Fréjus, dotted with the plentiful traces of ancient aqueducts, looked like the Roman campagna. 'There's nothing more beautiful than this in Italy,' he wrote. 'It's a purer version of Naples with quiet thrown in as well. It's brilliant like the East and lonely as Rome . . . I know of nowhere that has more charm than this spot: I like it even better than Mistral's Maillane. . . . '

Three days later he was deep in the scene where Juliet drinks the potion. The opera was developing as he had wished: 'The first act ends *brilliantly;* the second is *tender* and *dreamy,* the third *bold* and *animated* with the duels and Romeo sentenced to exile: the fourth is *dramatic,* the fifth *tragic.* It's a fine progression. . . . '

The warm weather crumbled into days of sultriness and storm. Depressed by the rain, worn out by the intense efforts he had put into completing the greater part of his opera within a month, Gounod surrendered to an attack of nervous debility. His wife arrived, and, escorted by his doctor, took him back to the country house at Saint-Cloud for rest. A fortnight later he was able to work again on *Roméo et Juliette* with fresh vigour.

The year passed quietly, as if it were to be the lull before the storm which production of a new opera would inevitably arouse. In August an exotic honour came his way: he was made a Commander in the Mexican order of Our Lady of Guadeloupe. Some time later the hero of Guadeloupe showed his mettle by adding to the *Messe solennelle Sainte-Cécile* a violin solo with a generous accompaniment of twelve harps. It soon rivalled in popularity the 'Méditation' on Bach's prelude.

In August 1866 the score of *Roméo et Juliette* was delivered to Carvalho. Disagreement was not slow to materialize. Carvalho wanted Victor Capoul to sing Roméo. This was reasonable enough since Capoul was young, handsome, and enjoyed a large following. Was not the hair style he made fashionable imitated by all young dandies who aimed to copy his dashing manner? Gounod was unconvinced. He defended his own candidate for the part, the tenor Michot. After discussion he won this first round. Another discord arose over the question as to whether the opera should contain spoken dialogue or recitatives. Rather surprisingly, Gounod would not decide one way or the other. Recitative, he said, tended to lengthen performance and slow up the action. He preferred to see

Roméo et Juliette on the stage with spoken dialogue before selecting the passages that needed recitative. His reasoning seems to have been dictated by practical rather than aesthetic motives since he also remarked that very many theatres in his experience opted for speech.

After making his ritual sacrifice at the altar of Madame Carvalho—this time in the shape of Juliet's waltz-song 'Je veux vivre dans le rêve'—and after many other alterations of the sort to which he had become resigned in his chequered relationship with the prima donna and her husband, Gounod looked forward to the production of his opera in April 1867. A few scenes were first given privately at Barbier's house near the Vallée-aux-loups. Composer and librettist were not dissatisfied with the result.

The dress rehearsal did not bear out this impression. It took place behind closed doors in an atmosphere of gloom. Nothing seemed to be ready. The singers were nervy. Some of the costumes didn't suit. It was the year of the Exposition Universelle, and the date chosen for the first performance, the 27th, clashed with an important State ball and reception. Gounod was anxious for his opera to be postponed, believing that all the important people would be at the ball and none at his première.

Carvalho listened and said nothing. He thought, on the contrary, that the situation promised well. If the performance ended in good time guests would go on to the ball and there spread the news of *Roméo et Juliette*. At midnight, when all the cast had gone home, he summoned the backstage crew.

'Can you guarantee to have everything ready by tomorrow night?' he asked them.

When they replied that they would, he went ahead and, overnight, sent out press tickets and arranged for the printing of posters. Gounod and his colleagues awoke next morning to be confronted with a *fait accompli*.

'It's thirty *louis* for you if the opera ends before midnight', Carvalho promised his stage-hands on the evening of the 27th. They earned their money, for the curtain fell at a quarter to twelve. The large audience rose and trooped off to the ball, where there was much talk about the merits of *Roméo et Juliette*.

It was, in fact, the only complete and immediate success Gounod ever enjoyed on the stage. None of his other operas, even the ones that eventually triumphed, were lucky enough to make such a speedy impact at their first performance. Carvalho described it as 'a firework of success'. In the year when the Exposition Universelle represented the Second Empire's most impressive flash of grandeur and when Paris was thronged with foreign guests tempted by the wonders on show, *Roméo et Juliette* drew full houses at ninety consecutive performances. It has since been played well over a thousand times in Paris. Although *Faust* has had more than double that number of presentations, *Roméo et Juliette* stands alone among Gounod's operas as having brought him an uncontested triumph in his lifetime.

Apart from a few isolated voices—Blaze de Bury, successor to Gounod's old enemy Scudo, kept up the tradition by finding the opera devoid of tenderness and passion, while another called it 'as cold as white marble'—the critics applauded. Ernest Reyer, who had followed Berlioz in his post as music critic on the influential *Journal des Débats*, shrewdly remarked on the unity of *Roméo et Juliette* which makes it a satisfying whole. He was even prepared to overlook Madame Carvalho's waltz-song in his praise for the inspiration which runs uniformly throughout the whole work and which extends even to the smaller details.

There have been more than eighty operas based on Shakespearean plays. *Romeo and Juliet* has, naturally, attracted many Italian composers. Bellini is the most famous of them with his *I Capuletti e i Montecchi*, where the part of Romeo is, refinement of refinements, sung by a lady. Others include Vaccaj, Zingarelli and Pauline Viardot's polyglot father. It is, of course, impossible to equal Shakespeare's beauty of language or to preserve the complicated sub-plots and large number of characters. The bold approach, as Verdi and his librettist found, is to reduce him to the barest, most important elements and hope for the best. This was the method followed with *Roméo et Juliette*. The narrative is a straightforward tale of tragic love between two young and attractive people, while the remaining characters—Friar Laurence, Gertrude, Capulet and so on—are kept firmly in their place as minor cogs in the machinery of the plot.

Within the inevitable limitations imposed by the venture Barbier and Carré produced a workmanlike sketch for the two hours' traffic of the stage. They even emerge respectably from the ordeal of turning into singable French the passage about Queen Mab, who:

comes in shape no bigger than Agat-stone, on the fore-finger of an Alderman, drawne with a teeme of little Atomies, over mens noses as they lie asleepe: her Waggon Spokes made of long Spinners legs: the Cover of the wings of Grasshoppers, her Traces of the smallest Spiders web, her coullers of the Moonshines watry Beames, her Whip of Crickets bone, the lash of Philome, her Waggoner, a small gray-coated Gnat, not halfe so bigge as a round little Worme, prickt from the Lazie-finger of a man. Her Chariot is an emptie Haselnut, made by the Joyner Squirrel or old Grub, time out a mind, the Faries Coach-makers: and in this state she gallops night by night, through Lovers braines: and then they dreame of Love.

For the purpose of opera *Roméo et Juliette* becomes a series of four great love duets. The Madrigal sung by the lovers at their first meeting, 'Ange adorable', is a stylized piece with an attractive archaic flavour. Gounod himself called it a 'duetto galant'. The mannered style is justified by Shakespeare's preciosity at this stage when he makes Romeo say:

> If I profane with my unworthiest hand
>   This holy shrine, the gentle sin is this,
> My lips, two blushing pilgrims, ready stand
>   To smooth that rough touch with a tender kiss.

and so on in polished elaborate vein. To which Juliet replies, continuing the image with alarming subtlety in a fourteen-year-old.

The balcony scene in Act II opens with Romeo's 'Ah! lève-toi, soleil!', a cavatina that reproduces, in finely graded steps of mounting passion, the spirit of the soliloquy 'Arise, fair sun, and kill the envious moon'. The second love duet of the opera, 'Ô nuit divine!', brings the act to an end. Here, in the mingling of recitative and aria, in the changes of mood and rhythm, Gounod evolved a suppleness of style that mirrored every fluctuating emotion. The music flows with the naturalness of speech and fits the words like a glove.

The third duet, this time comprising a good half of Act IV, portrays the fearful joy of the two lovers when Romeo defies the sentence of exile and dares to visit Juliet by night. '*Va! je t'ai pardonné*', Juliet greets him, offering forgiveness for his murder in a duel of her cousin Tybalt. Then they launch into a mellifluous '*Nuit d'hyménée! Ô douce nuit d'amour!*' which is suddenly shot through with anguish as Romeo hears 'the lark, the herald of the morn' and the signal for them to part. Juliet pleads:

> It was the nightingale, and not the lark,
> That pierced the fearful hollow of thine ear.

She sings, in a phrase of exquisite pathos, '*Non ! non, ce n'est pas le jour, ce n'est pas l'alouette*'. It is, she argues ingeniously, the nightingale: '*C'est le doux rossignol, confident de l'amour*'. The words are set to three simple bars which carry the poignant touch of genius.

The final duet is the climax of the opera at Juliet's tomb. The fatal misunderstanding that leads to double suicide is underlined by solemn music that changes, with the speed of April weather, into a triumphant affirmation of love. Once again the lovely phrase returns, '*Non ! non, ce n'est pas le jour*', this time with a still keener edge of emotion as Juliet strives to postpone not only dawn but death. Other themes which have already been identified with earlier incidents reappear and add to the tissue of longing, passion and regret that makes up the tale of the two lovers:

> For never was a Storie of more Wo,
> Than this of *Juliet*, and her *Romeo*.

The four duets are the glory of *Roméo et Juliette*. While composing them Gounod lived like a man possessed, sorrowing with his characters' unhappiness and rejoicing in their pleasure. Romeo and Juliet, Friar Laurence and Tybalt, were people of flesh and blood to him. He believed passionately in what he was creating. When writing his opera, said the forty-seven year-old composer, he felt like a young man of twenty again. This fresh quality, this sharpness of feeling unblunted by the cynicism of middle age or the disillusionments of the years, gives *Roméo et Juliette* a moving and innocent beauty.

But the love duets, although they provide the basis of the opera, are by no means the whole story. A happy stroke gives us a prologue—

> Two households, both alike in dignity,
> In fair Verona, where we lay our scene . . .

—sung by unaccompanied voices with occasional interjections from the harp. The harmonies, strangely novel for the time and austere only in their prophecy of later developments in French music, wander tragically through unusual modulations. More traditional is Friar Laurence's 'Dieu qui fit l'homme à ton image', an aria where the Mozartean resonance is strong. At one point the melodic line

145

closely parallels 'In diesen heilgen hallen', in *Die Zauberflöte*. Friar Laurence is usually dismissed as an unimportant lay figure, but in this tribute to Mozart, conscious or otherwise, there is fine music for the bass who sings him. Mercutio has a similar piece of luck with the Queen Mab song, all quicksilver and urgent rhythms. So does Stéphano, an additional character not found in Shakespeare, who, as a soprano *en travesti*, sings an Italianate '*chanson*'.

The orchestral writing is fluently responsive to the demands that are made on it. Moods and atmosphere are quickly established with economy. The overture warns of the tragedy to come by plunging immediately into the heart of the matter with an ominous downward theme on the brass. By contrast with the voluptuous ending of Act II, the introduction to the following scene in Friar Laurence's cell is briefly frugal and immediately sets the tone for more sober events. There are also three themes which come and go throughout the opera. The first of these, which appears as the concluding section of the overture-prologue, emerges again as the short andantino prelude to Act IV in Juliet's room. It is night still, and the '*petite ritournelle assez tendre et passionnée*', as Gounod himself described the theme, opens and closes the duet 'Nuit d'hyménée'. The same melody heightens tragic circumstance by returning as the accompaniment to Romeo's lament at Juliet's tomb, 'Ô ma femme! ô ma bien aimée!' Another theme, 'le jardin de Juliette', serves to frame the Act II meeting between the two lovers. Finally there is 'le sommeil de Juliette', a languorous figure heard when Friar Laurence administers the potion, and later, on its own, as the prelude to Act V and the scene by the tomb.

Apart from such minor blemishes as the waltz song and the pompous Second Empire mazurka that booms unrepentantly throughout the ball at the Capulets' in Act I, *Roméo et Juliette* is notable for its consistency of inspiration. It is all of a piece and remains faithful throughout to the joint authors' original conception. This, no doubt, was a factor in its quick success both at home and abroad. Soon after its production in Paris the opera was heard at Covent Garden as *Romeo e Giuletta* with Mario and Patti in the roles of the star-crossed lovers. It travelled across Europe and the rest of the world to become a regular attraction in opera houses everywhere.

Gounod's other works benefited from this reflected glory. People who enjoyed *Roméo et Juliette* in the theatre asked to hear his songs in the drawing-room. Choral societies turned with a new interest to the religious music. Extracts from earlier operas were given at concerts. One inspired musician conducted at a festival the soldiers' chorus from *Faust* sung by a monster choir to an accompaniment of three hundred and forty strings, sixty woodwind, fifty-six brass, twenty-five performers on harp and percussion, and a brass band of sixty.

The composer became a subject for newspaper gossip. His activities, chiefly mythical, were 'news'. It was exuberantly reported that he planned to write a *Francesca da Rimini* which began, modestly enough, in hell and purgatory, to end with a fifth act in heaven. There was even talk of a collaboration with Victor Hugo. *Roméo et Juliette* represented a peak of success that Gounod was never to reach again.

X

The Institut at Last – War and Exile in London – *Gallia* – Songs – Enter Mrs Weldon

In the year before *Roméo et Juliette* Gounod's career had been definitively honoured by election to the Académie des Beaux Arts. As a member of the Institut de France he was, officially, raised above the struggle to which lesser mortals were condemned in the fight for recognition of their talent. Formal consecration of 'le Maître' gave him automatic prestige. He sat on committees, presided at meetings and graced public occasions with his presence.

The vacancy at the Académie had arisen through the death of Clapisson, a teacher of harmony at the Conservatoire and a bumbling cause of mirth to the disrespectful Bizet. He wrote twenty or so operas ranging in style from the light tinkle of Adolphe Adam to the grandiose thunder of Meyerbeer. Since they had only a small success he relied for his living on other activities. He had formed a unique collection of musical instruments of every age, type and country, which he ended by selling to the government in return for a lump sum, a pension, and a post as curator which included rooms at the Conservatoire. The instruments can still be seen there. The prudent amateur of shawms and theorbs did not live long to enjoy this pleasant arrangement. Five years later he died from the effects of an ill-advised purge.

Gounod awaited the result of the ballot for Clapisson's seat at the home of his friend Ludovic Halévy, the librettist with Henri Meilhac of numerous operas, operettas and other stage works. Halévy noted a pleasant historical symmetry in the coincidence that Gounod sat in the same room as the one where years before the poet Alfred de Musset also spent the long hours expecting to hear whether his attempt on the Académie had succeeded. 'In our time', Halévy reflected, 'we've given house room to many an academic emotion and anxiety.' The news came through: Gounod was elected by a respectable majority. Three months later he was promoted *officier* in the Légion d'honneur. There were few official honours which he did not, to date, possess.

The atmosphere of the Académie and his emergence as a public figure seemed to release in Gounod that tendency to the oracular, that fondness for the pulpit manner, which had never been far from the surface. At lunch one day with a former schoolfellow at Saint-Sulpice, now the Archbishop of Rheims, he monopolized the conversation by declaiming sonorously and permitting no one to interrupt. The Archbishop's annoyance at seeing his role usurped and being forced to hear a sermon across his own table was distinctly un-Christian. Unperturbed and relentless, Gounod droned on.

By his late forties he had already adopted the patriarchal manner of Friar Laurence or of Ramon in *Mireille*. His bearing was not unlike that of Gladstone, who, Queen Victoria was said to complain, had the habit of addressing her as if she were a public meeting. He overpowered his listeners with a stifling aura of benevolence. His every word was delivered as if it had been a papal blessing. As he spoke his eye gleamed with a distant vision of celestial things. People who had a sense of humour were amused by the performance. Others, who wanted to get a word in edgeways, were not.

With the archiepiscopal style there went a taste for remarks which veered from stark absurdity to baffling grandiloquence. At a performance of Meyerbeer's *le Prophète*, the fourth act inspired Gounod to declare: 'What genius, what loftiness—*such music hits the ceiling*.' Mozart's *Don Giovanni* he described as *'garlanding music'*. Seated next to Bizet's wife at the opera, he expressed his admiration for one of the singers with the comment: 'Wouldn't you agree that she produces lilac-coloured notes in which you could wash your hands?' Madame Bizet, as sharp-witted as she was beautiful, instantly replied: 'You've taken the very words out of my mouth, cher Maître.'

The dreamland in which he existed sometimes collided embarrassingly with real life. One afternoon Sir Charles Hallé gave a piano recital in Paris. That evening at a party he met Gounod, who, wrapping both his hands in a warm clasp, thanked him effusively for the pleasure the recital had given. There was one passage in particular, cried Gounod, that affected him deeply. He hummed an extract from a Beethoven sonata. 'No one—no one, my dear friend, except you, could have interpreted that passage in so masterly a way. Even with my eyes shut, I should have known that Hallé was playing.' Then Madame Gounod bustled up and apologized to Hallé for her husband's absence from the recital. He had, she helpfully explained, a previous engagement.

Young composers who called to do homage were greeted by a venerable figure in sombre clerical raiment and skull-cap. Gounod would stand solemnly at the piano and strike the note of D three times. 'Don't you realize, young man,' he would say, 'that those three Ds stand for eternity ?'

One of those to be disillusioned by the blossoming of Gounod's personality was Bizet. Still anxious to help his protégé, Gounod had introduced him into Princess Mathilde's famous salon. The influence she could draw on through her cousinly relationship with the Emperor Louis-Napoléon enabled her, when she was in the mood, to further the careers of the artists, writers and musicians whom she gathered round her. She could be generous and sympathetic, as many of the Second Empire's most famous writers testified. She could also, as poor Sainte-Beuve was eventually to find, carry a vendetta to the unforgiving end with true Corsican fire. Gounod was one of her favourites. She found him 'the gentlest, the most modest and the kindest-hearted man in the world. . . . '

Since Bizet's acquaintance with Gounod was not limited to the courtier side of him, he took a different view. While far from ungrateful for the kindness the older man had shown both him and his wife, he was unable to stomach the Gounodian manner. It was the Institut, Bizet thought, that had led him astray and encouraged him to strike his insufferable attitudes. Careerism, in Bizet's view, had spoilt his friend. When *la Jolie fille de Perth* was produced in the same year and at the same theatre as *Roméo et Juliette*, Bizet even went so far as to suspect Gounod of jealous rivalry.

Soon after *Romeo et Juliette* another piece of luck came Gounod's way. Carvalho faded into one of his spectacular bankruptcies and the performing rights of *Faust*, which he owned, became once more available. Or at least, under pressure from Barbier and Carré, who argued that his business failure voided all contractual obligations, he reluctantly yielded them up. The director of the Opéra had let it be known that he was prepared to mount the work. Instead of leading a risky existence in the repertory of short-lived commercial theatres,

Faust was now to benefit from the glamour of a national opera house and from regular performances in settings that would do it justice.

It became necessary to include a ballet since subscribers to the Opéra insisted on this diversion. But feelings of religious scruple were stirring once more in Gounod. By some contrary quirk of nature, no sooner had he achieved his greatest success with *Roméo et Juliette* than he began to long to get away from the theatre for the peace of the cloister. Could he really bring himself to write more music for the profane and frivolous atmosphere of the stage?

In the summer of 1868, through the medium of an artist friend who knew them both, Gounod explained his delicate situation to Saint-Saëns. The young composer hastened to Saint-Cloud, anxious to help but acutely embarrassed by Gounod's suggestion that he write the ballet music. He found Gounod deep in a card game with an abbé. In between deals, Saint-Saëns tactfully pointed out that the work of another was bound to create an awkward effect if inserted into *Faust*. Gounod went on shuffling the cards and nodding gently as Saint-Saëns continued with his objections. In the end no more was heard of the proposal. Gounod himself wrote the ballet and it proved to be one of the most successful items in the new Opéra production.

A stomach complaint—perhaps a psychosomatic result of *Faust*'s revival and the awakening of his religious tendencies—sent Gounod out of Paris in November for convalescence. From Morainville, where he stayed long enough to recover, he set off on the journey most likely to restore his spirits for good: a trip to Rome. In the company of his painter friend Ernest Hébert, who had just been appointed director of the Villa Medici, he travelled to Rome and found it looking more beautiful than ever. The weather was as mild as if it had still been September. Under the watchful guard of Hébert he was protected from importunate visitors and allowed to wander and meditate in peace. He felt much better already.

An afternoon was spent in the company of Liszt who was then living quietly in Rome after the sensational years of virtuoso fame. He shared his life with that dragonish Princess who devoted her existence to his well-being and to the publication of her twenty-four volumed history of the Church. There was a great deal in common between Liszt and Gounod. Gounod had written an opera based on *Faust* and Liszt had composed a symphony inspired by the poem. Liszt's piano transcription of the waltz in *Faust* was the most spectacular of the pieces he adapted from Gounod. The others include the Berceuse he took from *la Reine de Saba* and the treatment of the 'les adieux' theme from *Roméo et Juliette*, which are on a much smaller scale than the thundering *Faust* waltz.

Both composers wavered eternally between the secular life and the religious. The excitements of the theatre for Gounod and the easy triumphs of the concert platform for Liszt often muffled the call of the monk's cell. And then, at the height of the applause and the glory, a sudden stab of conscience would send them hurrying away from the deceptive world to bury themselves in pious austerity. The disconcerting switches from devoutness to apparent hypocrisy were signs of the constant struggle that went on in both men. After spending hours at his breviary Liszt would abruptly concoct some meretricious fantasia. In the midst of studying Aquinas Gounod could produce a trumpery 'Méditation' on a Bach prelude. These artistic flaws testified to the basic contradictions that kept their personalities in turmoil.

Liszt had some slight advantage over Gounod in that he was actually a priest in minor orders, whereas the Frenchman had never attained even that modest level. Otherwise there was nothing to choose between the degrees of confusion and uncertainty that haunted them both. They were alike in their religiosity, in their yearnings for the holy life and in their ambition to write sacred music which they fondly, and vainly, believed to be greater than their other works. In the course of the Roman afternoons with Liszt Gounod heard him play from his oratorios *The Legend of Saint Elizabeth* and *Christus*. He admired their intensity and expressiveness but commented, enigmatically, that these qualities seemed to go 'perhaps beyond the limits and wisdom of great art'.

His companion on the visit to Liszt was his old friend the abbé Charles Gay. In the church dedicated to Saint Cecilia, Gay conducted mass and Gounod served at an altar which concealed the tomb of the Saint. During the early days of his sojourn in Rome he had, in fact, started writing an oratorio to be called *Sainte-Cécile*. By January 1869, he had given it up. An inexplicable discouragement came over him. Yet he was more than anxious to be composing again, 'It will soon be eighteen months since I wrote an important piece, a major composition! Let's see what 1869 will bring me.'

Gradually the magic of Rome began to work. On the 9 January he was already sketching out a new oratorio. It was entitled *Rédemption* and had words by the composer himself. Within a few days he had completed one of the main sections and was confident of orchestrating it before his return to Paris. He worked at his score long into the silence of the Roman nights. On the eve of his departure from Italy he gave a recital in the Villa Medici, promising to play and sing anything the audience might wish to hear. From ten o'clock on Sunday night until one in the morning he played for an enthusiastic crowd that filled the ornate salon and overflowed into the dining-room beyond. They acclaimed him as the leading French composer. They confirmed, with delighted applause, the promise he had shown as a student twenty-five years ago in that same spot. This double triumph held a peculiar sweetness for him.

He was back in Paris, reluctantly, for the première of *Faust* at the Opéra. Such was the public curiosity about the new version that every day a stream of requests for seats flowed in. Even the proud novelist Barbey d'Aurevilly humbled himself with a plea to the director that ended: 'Be very kind and reply to me, and be assured of the feelings of great sympathy which you inspire in me.' Expectation was further nourished by the months of rehearsal that had gone into the production. Among the sensations that made it the talk of Paris before the curtain rose were the headlines provided by Madame Carvalho. The swedish prima donna Christine Nilsson had been cast for the part of Marguerite. For some reason or other she thought it politic to make way for la Carvalho. Her offer was haughtily rejected by the original Marguerite, and the two ladies wrote letters to each other, duly published in the newspapers, which contained examples of that feline malice which is the speciality of rival prima donnas. Madame Carvalho was to have the last word, though. After twenty performances at the Opéra she stepped in and took over what she deemed to be her rightful place.

Including the scene-changes necessary for the elaborate presentation, *Faust* occupied more than five hours in performance on the evening of the 3 March. In the course of the ballet, while Helen was miming graciously to the music, a cloud of reddish smoke billowed from the stage across the auditorium. Everyone leaned eagerly forward to smell the exquisite perfume the goddess was inhaling. Unfortunately this novel effect had not been intended. The nostrils of the *tout-Paris* were assailed by a stink reminiscent of exploding fireworks. Something had gone wrong with the lighting apparatus. Instead of enjoying a new theatrical sensation of the type forecast by

Aldous Huxley in one of his futuristic stories, the lady spectators were reduced to fumbling and spluttering into delicate but inadequate lace handkerchiefs.

Apart from this unwelcome diversion *Faust* was immensely successful. The maximum receipts were taken during its first run of thirty performances, and ever since then it has been a mainstay of the Opéra. A number of parodies confirmed the impact it had made. On the boulevard there were skits entitled *Saf'aust et Marguerite* and *Faust du Faust, pas trop n'en Faust*. The prolific Hervé, who wrote and produced over a hundred musical stage works, mounted a *Petit Faust* which was soon to be translated and performed in London. Parody, Gounod learned, was the tribute that wit paid to success.

The Opéra management now began to think of producing *Roméo et Juliette* as a successor to *Faust*. But the composer was busy with other things. A selection of Bach chorales, with notes and commentary from his pen, occupied much of his time. He was also planning a new opera. Barbier and Carré had suggested a libretto taken from Corneille's *Polyeucte*. The tale of Christian martyrdom in ancient Rome appealed to Gounod, fresh from reviving his 'old Roman roots' and still not yet fully settled in Paris. He started the score in July and took it with him to the peace of Morainville. By the autumn, when he was staying with friends at Évreux in Normandy, he had made a certain amount of progress. In December he completed the important scene of Polyeucte's baptism. The second act was finished in January 1870. A painful whitlow prevented him from carrying on. He was exhausted both physically and emotionally, and the early months of 1870 found him in a state of weary despair.

He wrote gloomily: 'My work costs me the most painful efforts and racks my brain. I fight against the void, I think I've written something acceptable, and then, when I look at it again, I find it execrable. My mind wanders and grieves, *I don't know where I am*. It would be a help if only I knew how to deal with such a horrible condition. I can't see clearly any more; I don't know where I'm going . . . twenty times melancholy overwhelms me, I weep, I despair and I want to get away . . . I open my notebook and shut it again. Nothing! my mind is empty! Oh Lord, what better can be done than to accept this desolation and nothingness! . . . I thought I was worth something! I didn't want to be a nobody. I am very wretched.'

For several weeks he remained helpless in one of those periods of impotence that blight from time to time creative careers. Prayer and meditation helped a little to ease the dark passage of the days. Then, in July, the gloom lifted and he was able to report that even if he had not written down the whole of *Polyeucte*, the opera was now complete in his mind. In that same month, on the 8th, the Opéra contracted to produce *Roméo et Juliette*.

Roméo, however, was not to love and die at the Opéra for another three years, and *Polyeucte* had to wait nearly a decade before he was martyred on stage. Less than a week after the contract was signed Bismarck arranged the affair of the 'Ems telegram'. It read like an insolent rebuff to French diplomacy over the Hohenzollern withdrawal from the offer of the Spanish throne. As the Prussian chancellor hoped, opinion in France was outraged and angry patriots demanded revenge for the apparent humiliation. Louis-Napoléon, ill and enfeebled, saw with horror the approach of a conflict for which France was totally unprepared. On the 19th came the French declaration of war on Prussia.

In Paris the theatres were soon to be transformed into hospitals. The Opéra became the scene of patriotic concerts before it did duty as an arsenal and food store. Here, on the 8 August, was heard a new patriotic song called 'À la frontière!', with music by M. Charles Gounod *de l'Institut*. The words were written by a distinguished author whose other productions included pamphlets offering useful advice on such topics as how to be beautiful, the art of being unhappy when married, how to cure gout, and methods for prolonging life. 'À la frontière!' was cheered by rows of excited Germanophobes.

The composer evacuated his family to Varangeville near Dieppe, and wrote to them twice a day from Paris. His letters were full of the rumours that circulated daily. One morning, he announced, there was news of a great victory and the capture of 25,000 Prussian soldiers. The city was quickly hung with flags. At two o'clock in the afternoon Parisians learned that the news was false. 'Prayer is your *only* weapon,' he exhorted his wife, who by now had become used to his Old Testament style. 'You must load it! The *soul of the French* must be the gun-powder that fires French bullets!'

Prayer, indeed, was the only means of saving the country, for nothing else had been done to preserve it. A romantic unwillingness to acknowledge the invention of railways and a touching devotion to the tactical methods of half a century before produced a situation in

155

which the Prussian army, somewhat dazed by the speed of its own advance, had occupied Alsace and Lorraine before August was out. On the 1 September Louis-Napoléon capitulated at Sedan.

Gounod left Paris and rejoined his family in Varangeville. News of the Prussian invasion decided him to seek, at least temporarily, a safer retreat. On the 13 September he embarked with his wife, children and mother-in-law at Dieppe and sailed to Liverpool. They went to Blackheath, where a friend of Madame Gounod's mother, the hospitable Mrs Louisa Brown, gave them shelter for a time. At the beginning of October they moved into a house Gounod rented at No. 8 Morden Road. In this retired thoroughfare, which lies not far from Blackheath railway station and the promisingly named Tranquil Vale, the Gounods braced themselves for the prospect of an abruptly changed existence and life in a strange land.

Bad tidings from home added to their worries. Not only was Paris besieged and France the scene of desperate battles. The Gounod home at Saint-Cloud was also threatened with destruction by invading troops. Gounod wrote a letter to the Crown Prince of Prussia begging for his intervention. He had always, he claimed, regretted the war from the very first day. Had not his own artistic development stemmed from German art and the German spirit? The Crown Prince, who obviously bore no grudge on account of *Faust*, responded to the humble appeal. The Saint-Cloud property stood in an area mercilessly exposed to cannon shell. It still, happily, remained in one piece, but the interior had been damaged by French and German patrols in turn as first one side, then the other, gained the upper hand over bitterly contested territory. The Crown Prince ordered his troops to clean it and seal it off. When Gounod's self-abasement became known in France it did nothing to make him more popular with his compatriots.

In England, 'our worthy and excellent Browns' helped the Gounods adjust to their new way of life. Mrs Brown took them in her carriage to see the fountains at Crystal Palace. It was the last time they would be playing that year, she urged, so an early viewing was essential. 'There are certain English people who, for the French, are not really *England*,' wrote Gounod, who was beginning to revise his earlier unfavourable opinions of the country.

Pleasant though it was to enjoy the hospitality of that rare phenomenon, a civilized Anglo-Saxon, and to go on excursions to Crystal Palace, Gounod felt he needed to be in London if he were to earn a

proper living. There he could meet publishers and concert pro-
moters. If need be he could give music lessons. Until such time as
France was liberated and conditions restored to normal, he would
carry on with his work. Or, as he put it, unable to resist a Biblical
parallel, he would continue to compose 'so that when the waters sub-
side I can open my ark and release the dove (which perhaps will only
be a crow), but which at any rate will mark the return of the rainbow
for me and the peace of nations.' The London address where Gounod pitched his ark was at 9 Park Place, near Regent's Park, a district
he already knew from earlier visits to the capital. The first dove he
chose to launch from there, even though the waters had not yet
dropped, was his setting of 'There is a Green Hill Far Away'. Charles
Santley, the famous Victorian baritone, gave it at a Philharmonic
Society concert on the 8 March 1871, with Gounod conducting.
This venture into the style of Protestant hymnology was a foretaste
of the musical pleasures that were to make Gounod revered among
English church-goers and patrons of oratorio.[1]

Less successful was a premature attempt to enlist the favour of
Queen Victoria. Hearing that she was to be in St Paul's at a service
giving thanks for the recovery from illness of the Prince of Wales,
Gounod wrote a 'Te Deum' to mark the occasion and hopefully
offered it to the cathedral organist. In return that gentleman, writing
'dear Sir, believe me, with all veneration for your genius', tartly
observed that there existed Englishmen who were quite capable of
fulfilling the sacred duty.

The 'Te Deum' in question belonged among the religious music
Gounod turned to composing at this time. His reading of St Paul
consoled him for the snub. 'What a friend he is!' was how he
described the author of the Epistles. 'How well he knows Our Lord!
How well he teaches His message! How I thank God for having
created him and made him His apostle of the Gentiles! How deeply
he knows, investigates and turns over with the plough of his incisive
speech all the old heathen corners of poor Nature.'

Gounod's reputation in England was already substantial. *Faust*
and *Roméo et Juliette* established him at least as a composer of opera,
and by the time his London exile began frequent revivals of these
works had made his name familiar. Yet English publishers were
strangely reluctant to approach him. Only Henry Littleton, the most

---

[1] Gounod's setting may have been a little too elegant for many congrega-
tions. Horsley's muscular version is the one most often sung today.

enterprising of them, asked him for new compositions. Littleton's firm was Novello's, and the reason for their prosperity was hinted at by the legend in bright Gothic lettering which ornamented their premises in Berners Street: 'Sacred Music Warehouse'. The company had, rather accidentally, been founded in 1811 by Vincent Novello, an organist ,who, finding no publisher willing to bring out a collection of chapel music, produced it himself. In the years that followed his son built up a healthy business by providing inexpensive sheet music for the numerous oratorio societies that emerged as a result of the popular interest in amateur singing. When the son retired Henry Littleton took over. He started his career at Novello's as an odd-job boy whose duties included sweeping out the shop— 'the old sweep', as Gounod with ambiguous humour sometimes called him—and rose to be sole proprietor. The acquisition of Mendelssohn's copyrights further increased Novello's importance. Under Littleton's guidance the firm became the largest of its kind in England. Gounod was for a time to be one of the most remunerative names in the catalogue.

A feature of Littleton's reign at Novello's was the large-scale promotion of concerts. These functions stimulated publicity for Novello composers and encouraged the sale and hire of the sheet music that his printers were manufacturing in great quantity. He saw an excellent opportunity in Gounod. The International Exhibition was soon to open in London and a Gounod concert would benefit from the publicity such an occasion was bound to rouse. Would *le Maître* care to write a work for performance in the newly built Albert Hall ? At first the Master was coy. Was it right for him to tune his lyre on foreign ground while his native country bled and suffered from the misery of invasion and civil war ? The arguments turned persuasive: the new hall was immense, the choir would be huge . . . the auditorium seated ten thousand people. Gounod wavered. He thought of Jerusalem in ruins, of the prophet Jeremiah and of the Lamentations. His libretto was ready-made for a cantata which he would call *Gallia*. It would represent the invincible spirit of a France only temporarily crushed and humiliated by a brutal enemy. The music came to him at speed, like 'a sort of shell' exploding in his brain.

Gallia was heard at the Albert Hall on the 1 May 1871. The rest of the programme consisted of a Triumphal March by Ferdinand Hiller and Arthur Sullivan's cantata *On Shore and Sea*. Each composer directed the performance of his own work. The Hall's ten thousand seats were full. When Gounod walked on to the platform enthusiastic applause burst out from all round. Even the choir cheered. The topicality of the theme, Littleton's skilful exploitation and the publicity stimulated by the opening of the Exhibition made *Gallia* a triumphant occasion. The huge audience readily sympathized with the libretto's appeal for that 'Princess among the provinces'. 'And no one off'reth consolation, yea, all her friends have betray'd her', added the thousand voices of the massed choir. An operatic cantilena,

> Jerusalem, Jerusalem,
> O turn thee, o turn thee to the Lord thy God!

brought the piece to a stirring end. *Gallia* is not an important work. The emotional circumstances in which it was written and composed gave it an undeserved reputation. It was, however, a useful means of introducing Gounod to the general public and other benefits were to flow from it.

Accustomed to receiving only twenty pounds from his French publisher Choudens for all rights to his songs, Gounod was enchanted to be offered double that amount by Littleton. The popularity of home music-making supported a large market for ballads and duets. Gounod produced quite a number of these while in England. His setting of Kingsley's 'Oh, that we two were Maying' was performed in many drawing-rooms, together with 'Oh, happy home, Woe is me!' and 'There is dew for the flow'ret'. 'The sea hath its pearls', with violin and harmonium accompaniment, caused a parlour sensation, and the soothing tones of 'If thou art sleeping, maiden, awake', were often to be heard.

The quality of the English songs is not up to the standard of his earlier works. When he did not have to consider the needs of the market, as he was obliged to in England, he could write with delicacy and unforced charm. It was probably such pieces as 'l'Absent', with its forward-looking harmonies, that caused Ravel to hail him as 'the true founder of song in France'. Tact and a French sense of proportion characterize his best songs. They are small and well crafted. There is pleasure to be had in the unassuming workmanship and limpid grace. His setting of Lamartine's 'Au rossignol' does not, for example, fall into the easy trap of imitating the song of the nightingale. It moves with tranquil smoothness through a steady series of chords to portray the quiet of the lonely night, the swaying flowers and a sense of the mystery that lies behind the bird's voice. The music's reserve echoes the conventional poetic diction Lamartine chose to adopt. Exoticism, when needed, is discreetly brushed in, as with 'Medjé, Chanson arabe' or 'Boléro'. Sometimes Gounod was so pleased with a song that he expanded it as a full-length aria for one of his operas. 'Ce que je suis sans toi' was adapted as Léandre's serenade in *le Médecin malgré lui*. The aria 'Héro sur la tour solitaire' in *Sapho* was originally a setting of Lamartine's 'le Soir'. Gounod's version of Béranger's 'le Juif errant' became the nun's lugubrious air in *la Nonne sanglante*, and Valentine's cavatina in Act II of *Faust* began life as 'Invocation', which had been written in the early eighteen-fifties. The theme of 'Rêverie' turns up as 'Les Troyennes' in the *Faust* ballet.

Gounod's Italianate tendencies, which can be seen at more than one point in *Roméo et Juliette*, also found expression in a song cycle called *Biondina*. The ninth and tenth songs have a curious similarity to Liszt's *Tre sonetti di Petrarca*. Both layout and figuration suggest that, in their different ways, the two composers may have been inspired by a traditional Italian melody—although, of course, Gounod's version is modest compared with the elaborate superstructure imagined by Liszt. *Biondina* tells a little tale of love for an Italian girl adored from a distance, and of her death. Emotion is lightly sketched and there is a spice of humour, as in the amusing maestoso pomposo opening of 'Si j'avais l'univers sous mon empire', where the boastful admirer is accompanied by a tango rhythm. The twelve songs that make up *Biondina* successfully absorb the Italian idiom without degenerating into pastiche.

Gounod's performance of his own songs was, of course, a feature of his social life. Once he had been launched on the round of London society he became a lion worthy of the hunt. At *conversaziones* and receptions he was much in demand. On one such occasion the future Baroness Orczy was present. As a girl she had musical gifts and ambitions to be a virtuoso pianist, although recording the adventures of the Scarlet Pimpernel was later to take up her considerable energies. 'He was never a brilliant pianist,' she wrote a little de-flatingly of Gounod, a judgement suggesting that the charm of his impromptu recitals was due as much to personality as to musical technique. A female admirer, she went on, said to the composer as he sat benignly at the piano: 'Oh! Monsieur Gounod, do tell me how

9. An 1872 caricature of Gounod referring to his cantata *Gallia* and its first performance in London during his stay there. (Photo: Stella Mayes Reed.)

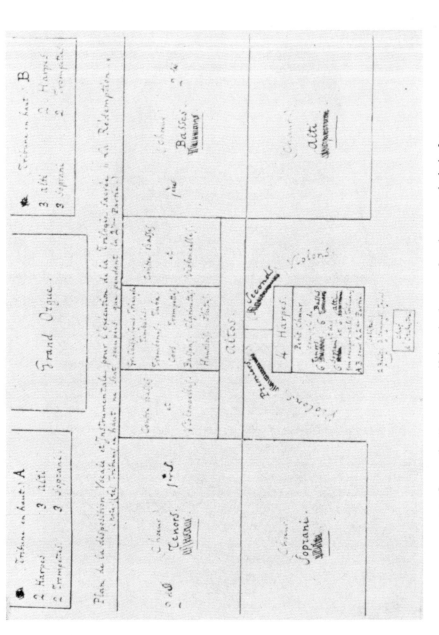

10. Gounod's diagram specifying the layout of orchestra and choir for *Rédemption*, which he conducted at Birmingham in 1882. (Photo: Stella Mayes Reed.)

your composing is going on? How do you think of those lovely melodies which Madame Nilsson sings so divinely?'

Gounod, not at all put out, meditated for a second or two and then turned his liquid eyes on the enquirer. 'God, Madame, sends me down some of His angels and they whisper sweet melodies in my ear.' All those present found it a lovely thought.

On the 26 February 1871, Gounod was at the home of Sir Julius Benedict, the conductor and composer recently knighted for his versatile services to English music. Among the guests were Mrs Georgina Weldon and her husband. As usual when a new and attractive face arrived, Gounod offered it his full attention and sang his song 'À une jeune fille' with many a significant glance at Mrs Weldon. 'He seemed to be specially addressing himself to me,' she wrote. 'I did not know which way to look. My tears, which had begun to flow at the first line, had become a rivulet, the rivulet had become a stream, the stream a torrent, the torrent sobs, the sobs almost a fit!'[1]

This effusion of sentiment, generous even by Victorian standards, petrified her husband and astonished the company. She calmed herself by retreating to a window and drinking a glass of water behind the curtain. When she emerged nearly everyone had left. Her meeting with Gounod was as historic in its way as the first encounter between Mr Rolls and Mr Royce . . . or that between Gilbert and Sullivan. The scene was now set for two past-masters in the art of comic improvisation to show their skill. All the elements were assembled of a long-running episode that for the next three years was to fascinate spectators with its sudden swoops from drama to farce and back again.

[1] The words of the song are by Emile Augier. The poet addresses an eighteen-year-old girl and wonders why she does not respond to the call of love. What sufferings has she undergone to make her so obdurate, he wonders: ' 'Tis better to break one's heart than close it up.' Mrs Weldon was then a tender maid of thirty-five.

❧ XI ❧

The Gounodyssey, Part I – 'You shall not burn *Polyeucte!*'

Mrs Weldon had been born Georgina Thomas in Clapham on the 24 May 1837. The dates are important. She shared with Queen Victoria not only her birthday but also the year of her Coronation. The coincidence gave Georgina 'a vague idea of superiority' which she nurtured all her life. Her father was a rich barrister who had no need to practise and preferred to dabble in farming and politics. If provoked to anger by his family of six children he would order them to bed 'for a fortnight'. When his daughters grew up he did not stand in the way of true love: all he asked, as a reasonable man, was that their husbands should be worth ten thousand a year.

Georgina spent her childhood in Italy where her mother had gone for the sake of her health. It was Mrs Thomas, a sensitive musician, who helped her develop a talent for singing. Fluency in both French and Italian followed. Soon Georgina had grown into a very pretty young woman. She made her début in London society as Georgina Treherne, since her father, who had a taste for the mysterious gesture, had suddenly decided to take the surname of an ancestor who fought at the battle of Crécy. Miss Treherne was presented to the Queen, met the artist G. F. Watts who painted a handsome portrait of her, and flustered many young men about town with her blue eyes and plump good looks.

One of her admirers was an army officer called Harry Weldon. He called on Mr Treherne for interview as a prospective suitor. Far from possessing the necessary ten thousand a year, it seemed that he had not even two thousand. So Harry, 'the only object of my wild fancy and fervent dreams', was dismissed. Despite a year's separation they kept in touch. Georgina sent him letters twenty-eight pages long and full of eloquent passion. Her beloved Hussar, though as an officer and a gentleman he made valiant attempts to match her fluency, proved taciturn by comparison. At one stage he even wrote to Mrs Treherne withdrawing his claim on Georgina. But his sweet-heart was determined. There were secret meetings and urgent messages. Few men are modest enough to disbelieve a woman who declares undying love for their heroic qualities, their handsome features and their brilliant minds. The object of an undeserved passion cannot help feeling sympathy towards the woman perceptive enough to detect in him sterling traits which people have till then unaccountably ignored. Harry wavered. Two years after meeting Georgina he married her at Aldershot. Harry was in the bag. The first example had been given of Georgina's iron will in action.

She did not care that her outraged father cut her off. All that mattered was to get what she wanted. For the time being this took the form of Harry. She did not seem to realize that they were an ill-assorted couple. Her feeling for him was sentimental and affec-tionate. She gave him the same loving care as she did the pug-dog she christened Dan Tucker. There was nothing sensuous in her nature. Harry, on the other hand, was a blundering tactless man full of desire. Temperamentally they were opposites. The dull and un-ambitious husband had married a mercurial and high-spirited wife. Motherhood might have eased the strains between them. But early on in their life together she had a miscarriage, and even that frail hope dissolved.

Their first married home was at Beaumaris in Wales. Harry hunted and was popular with the local gentry. His wife's vivacity endeared her to the reigning queens of the area. A lot of her time Georgina spent in London, where her social triumphs were just as complete and more important. One of her most reliable friends was Fred Clay, the composer of 'I'll Sing thee songs of Araby' and 'The Sands of Dee', which he dedicated to her. Her vocal talent opened the doors of great houses and introduced her to the circles of the famous. She sang for the Prince of Wales and dined at Cliveden. Wherever she went she made a point of mentioning Harry, of suggesting to her influential hosts that her husband was a man of remarkable talent and versatility that fitted him for the highest posts.

So Georgina bustled through season after season in London, advising Mr Gladstone on how to raise new taxes, earning a 'Long live Mrs Weldon' from Arthur Sullivan, and receiving tribute of many silver girdles from Mahmoud Ali Khan. Her friendship with Julius Benedict was more purposeful. The urge to mother deserving cases was already strong in her, and she sympathized with the problems of a German-born musician struggling to make his career in a strange land. In return, he recognized her musical ability and later encouraged her to become a professional singer. Throughout the early years of the eighteen-sixties she sang for her supper in the houses of the nobility and appeared publicly in oratorio and operetta. They were happy times, divided between the little nest at Beaumaris, holidays abroad and the whirl of London.

By 1870 the prospect was flawed. She still had no child. She longed for one, and the cruel years of hope deferred made her sick at heart. Constant disappointments at last made her realize that she must seek elsewhere an outlet for her maternal yearnings. She felt, besides, a sense of growing distance between herself and Harry. With a touch of bitterness, an emotion that was rare in this expansive woman, she wrote: 'Being beautiful only helps men who are no good to fall in love with you.'

Then the practical side of her nature came into play. Beaumaris was deserted for London where she set up as a teacher of singing. Harry was found a useful occupation at the College of Heralds. It was beside the point that he neither wished to become a Herald nor wanted to live in London. Within a short time he was taking instruction in heraldry, had become Rougedragon Poursuivant, and had leased a spacious London house.

The home Georgina chose was Tavistock House. Charles Dickens had been a recent tenant. The large garden, said his guest Hans Andersen, had 'a countryfied look in the midst of this coal- and gas-steaming London. . . .' Dickens wrote *Bleak House* there—a title as sombre as that of the pamphlet Georgina was to write ten years later when she described the adventures that befell her as *The Ghastly Consequences of Living in Charles Dickens's House*. (The voluminous literary productions of her middle and old age were noted for hair-raising titles.) There were eighteen rooms, one of them capable of holding more than three hundred people, which included a private theatre. The railings fronted on the select surroundings of Tavistock Square. At the back were the tall trees and lawns that Hans Andersen appreciated. With the aid of an inheritance from his grandmother, Harry Weldon obediently acquired the lease for £2,500.

At Tavistock House Georgina planned the singing school which was to spread the 'Weldon System'. Her theory was plain and sensible. Clarity, simplicity and naturalness formed the basis of her teaching. She had no sympathy with the style of a Madame Carvalho. Showiness and vocal embroidery were the enemies of truth as Georgina saw it. A good singer, she claimed, should be able to speak, recite or sing with an equally natural grace. 'I maintain', she declared, 'that every word that is sung should be *said* as if in the course of common conversation or as if read.' Her emphasis on clear diction and a sober style was later to be vindicated by her most distinguished pupil, Jean de Reszke.

Ignoring Harry's feeble protests, she took in a number of promising young girls. The next step was to give a public concert at which she hoped to raise £3,000 for her venture. The takings amounted to a miserable £199. A tour of North Wales succeeded a little better, and despite the smelly schoolrooms and draughty halls where her charges were forced to perform, Georgina felt moderately satisfied with the experiment. Yet there was discord between teacher and pupil. The girls were reluctant to submit to Georgina's autocratic rule. Parents had a tiresome habit of interfering. Not long afterwards she was deserted by her pupils. The lesson was obvious: she must in future concentrate on orphans who had no family to hinder the great work she proposed.

To the horror of her own family, Georgina appeared professionally at a Beethoven concert and was paid for it. This was her first public engagement. Julius Benedict, who arranged it, was delighted. He thought she had 'the most remarkable talent in the United Kingdom and I might say in the whole of Europe. . . .' Benedict was a true friend who responded to the kindness she had shown him by helping with her career and giving her the benefit of his advice. Their friendship even survived his attempt to introduce her to Wagner's music. Georgina confessed: 'One had to pay for, by hours of spiritual and labyrinthian passages of almost unbearable weariness, a quarter-of-an-hour of dazzling music—majestic in its splendour and brilliancy. I have conscientiously studied it, but soon left it to take care of itself!'

The music of Gounod was a mellifluous contrast. It spoke to her, she wrote in her exuberant prose, of a mossy dell, 'a dell, where lay encrusted precious stones,—a dell, sparkling here and there with pebbles overlaid with soft moss, green as the lizard, yellow brown, pale blue green, hardy lichens. . . .' In Gounod's music she saw 'violets, periwinkles, foxgloves, tangled ferns waving in picturesque disorder by the side of the purling brook. . . .' Exploring her own very personal vision of *Faust*, she announced that she could also discern there cathedrals, incense, anthems, plainchant and processions. With these, she added, were mingled hints of farmyards, castles, hell and heaven. She always defended Gounod when he was criticized. Once her singing school was firmly established, she vowed, her pupils would become 'the Apostles of this Messiah of the Gospel of New Music'.

One of Gounod's warmest supporters in England was Benedict, whom he had known since the time of his early visits to London. It was inevitable that one day Benedict should bring together the two people of whom he was so fond: the eminent composer and the talented lady who admired his music. A few days after their meeting in Benedict's drawing-room, when, it will be remembered, Georgina's emotion overpowered her, Gounod happened to look in at St James's Hall where she was rehearsing. She sang Mendelssohn's 'Hear My Prayer'. 'I was struck by the purity of her voice,' he wrote later, 'by the sureness of her technique and the noble simplicity of her voice, and I was able to prove to myself that Benedict had not been exaggerating when he spoke to me about her remarkable talent as a singer.' He was also to describe her voice as a *voix des deux sexes*.

Next day she called on him to ask a favour. Would he arrange for her to sing at a charity concert that was being organized by an acquaintance of his for the benefit of French war-wounded? He invited her there and then to perform it. At their meeting in Benedict's drawing-room it was Georgina who had burst into tears. Now, in Gounod's home, it was everybody else's turn—at least according to Georgina. Her singing made Gounod's mother-in-law weep. Madame Gounod wept. Gounod's eyes were full of tears. 'It was a perfect shower of tears and compliments,' Georgina recorded. The composer sat down at the piano and together they sang through *Faust* from beginning to end. Wife and mother-in-law both told her she was 'born for Gounod'. He, believing he had found the singer of the heroine in his opera *Polyeucte*, raved: 'This is the Pauline I want! this is the Pauline of my dreams!'

The Pauline of his dreams was no less exhilerated. Gounod was 'the angel from heaven'. She looked on him 'as a saint, as a father'. They met frequently, Georgina explaining, as evidence of the propriety of their relationship, that a sprained foot and the presence of her husband kept her decently immobilized. She was thrilled to have won the friendship and respect of the man whose music she adored. Not only that: his helplessness in everyday affairs, his artist's inability to cope with the mundane aspects of life, made him an ideal target for her maternal care.

Unfortunately there were already people in his life who believed that looking after him was no one's business but their own. Madame Gounod knew only too well her husband's lack of financial acumen. She blamed him for his spendthrift ways. Her feelings cannot have been improved when he pointed at Georgina and said: 'Here is a dear little woman who will help us wonderfully!' In spite of his wife's disapproving shadow he went on seeing Georgina. They found that religion, as well as music, was another joy they shared. One day he brought to her a prayer he had written:

> Oh! Lord Jesus,
> May I know myself, may I know Thee,
> May I not desire aught but Thee,
> May I hate me, and love Thee,
> What I do, may I do it because of Thee...

Like a pet dog expecting its reward for some particularly clever trick, he submitted to her his sixteen lines of pious invocation. He was not disappointed. She pronounced them 'splendid'. In the months that followed they would keep up a correspondence whenever separated for a few days. His letters to her when she had for some reason to go to Brighton sometimes flowered into delightful Anglo-French made piquant by his literal translation of idiom: 'Have you written to Saint-Saëns? I feel sad like a night-cap, so is the season.

> The sea hath its pearls,
> The heaven hath its stars,
> But London, London, London hath its fog.'

As their acquaintance grew so did her happiness. She seemed to be finding the fulfilment she sought. He showed her the music he was writing, asked her opinions, and almost every day came to see her. They sang and performed together at concerts. There was no doubt that he admired her, though this was not the only feeling he entertained. Gounod at the age of fifty-three had not changed in outlook from the handsome young man who, on his return from

Rome, enraptured the ladies with his charm and appreciation of their beauty. One of the sad facts of growing old is that while a man's physical attractions may wither, his desire remains as strong as it ever was. In appearance Gounod was no longer a youthful Adonis. His bushy beard was rapidly turning white and his hair had retreated from the forehead to leave only a few waif-like strands behind. The complexion was muddy and the hands looked not quite clean. His clothes always seemed a little too short and clung tightly to his round stomach. Yet his appetite for women had lessened not at all.

His private life was said to be full of incident by turns amusing and outrageous. It is difficult, after a lapse of more than a century, to establish in accurate detail the history of his liaisons. That there were many was, among his contemporaries, a known fact. Bizet mentions it with amusement, and Gounod's colleagues—writers, librettists, musicians—were inclined to wink, metaphorically, when the topic arose. The 'unfrocked priest', as he was sometimes described, could not resist a pretty woman. He was, George Moore protested, himself an expert at the practice, 'a base soul who went about pouring a kind of bath water melody down the back of every woman he met.' Neither, as he grew older, was he proof against the unripe charm of girls still at school. It is not known whether his name figured in police records on account of this imprudent taste, as did that of at least one celebrated French philosopher at the time.

His intentions towards Georgina were at first the usual ones. It was a long time before he realized that they would never be fulfilled. He had not yet understood the Victorian habit of self-deception nor the unusual nature of Georgina's character. She belonged to that type of women who speak with flamboyant emotion, who strike attitudes of fiery passion, but who act with a chasteness and propriety as definite as the clang of an iron door barring the way. He was only a simple male and early made the mistake of thinking that her extravagant declarations were the sign of a passionate nature. He could not have been more mistaken. Unlike the Paulines, the Céciles, the Catherines and the Rosalies who had up to now brought a pleasing if dangerous variety into his life, Georgina would never have allowed the slightest liberty.

She sometimes cursed the beauty that was hers. It seemed a tiresome irony that she, who had not an ounce of sexual passion in her, should be continually pestered by men. What she wanted to give her hero was motherly affection. She wanted to build his career, to nurse him in times of difficulty and to bask in the glory of his fame. Gounod could not understand this.

Neither could his wife. She thought she saw with alarm a situation developing that was familiar from past experience. Her husband's usual excuse that 'pure affection' was the reason for his behaviour failed to convince her, just as it had failed on so many earlier occasions. And as always, she made life hell for him. She was, wrote Georgina indignantly, 'the most ill-natured, cross-grained woman I had ever met'.

On the 16 May, by which time they had known each other for nearly three months, Gounod came in a state of distress to see Georgina. He was accompanied by his friend the abbé Boudier. He could not stand his wife any longer! After twenty years of hell on earth he was determined to separate from her! She had made a martyr of him! He walked back and forth, storming incoherently, foaming at the mouth. The abbé shrugged his shoulders and said, 'It's the same story every three months—they will make it up again!' The scene continued with Gounod boiling up into paroxysms of rage. Even the abbé was impressed by now. 'Madame Gounod', he remarked to Georgina, 'is terrible! TERRIBLE!' She agreed. Gounod was an *angel*. His wife was a *demon*.

Five days later Madame Gounod went back to France and took her son Jean with her. 'She was odious, I confess; but I pitied her,' said Georgina. 'Why had God made me so amiable and her so disagreeable?' She could afford to be magnanimous in victory. She felt sorry for the woman she had described as ugly (like 'a Japanese crockery dog'), vulgar and impudent. However had Gounod ever brought himself to marry this 'little old brown woman'?

Next month Gounod's mother-in-law also departed. On the 19 June Gounod moved bag and baggage into Tavistock House. What came to be known as the 'Gounodyssey' had started in earnest. He arrived trailing clouds of sanctity. The rope which held his trunk together, he gravely explained, was a scourge with which he flagellated himself. Georgina shivered deliciously. He gave her a copy of *The Imitation of Jesus Christ* and a rosary. 'We were up to our necks in religion', quipped she. When he confessed that his wife had ruined his digestion and turned his blood to vinegar, she put him on a regimen of india-rubber baths and cold ablutions. He was allowed to continue smoking and taking snuff, though she did manage to suppress his habit of spitting everywhere. He became, for Georgina, 'the Divine Being', 'my chicken' and 'my dear old papa-mamma'. She was known to him as 'Mousie'. Husband Harry entered into the spirit of the thing by calling Gounod 'the old man'. This partiality for wholesale baptism extended to the absent Madame Gounod, who, licking her wounds in France, was gratified with the nickname of 'the crockery dog'. In such time as he could spare from making advances which Georgina always evaded with a mixture of deft footwork and tact, Gounod took up work again on the score of *Polyeucte*.

An example of his complete dependence on her was his rejection of an offer to become head of the Conservatoire. A feeler was put out from Paris indicating that if he wished to give himself the trouble of applying the job was his. As an extra treat he was invited to dinner with President Thiers, the astute little lawyer who had made peace with Bismarck and stimulated the creation of a new Republic, the third of its kind. Under normal circumstances Gounod would have found the proposal irresistible. But now he only considered it in the light of his relationship with Georgina. If he accepted, he told her, he would be able to give her a class at the Conservatoire and obtain engagements for her everywhere. She dissuaded him. His duty would be to avoid favouritism, she argued, and any way, as he often complained, the Institut took up so much of his time already. With the Conservatoire as well he would have no leisure at all for composing. He did as he was told and refused the offer.

In July he had to return to Paris where urgent business awaited him. Leaving Georgina and her husband in full control of all his English affairs, he landed in France after an absence of nearly a year. The long letters he wrote to Georgina told of complicated negotiations that were still dragging on over *Roméo et Juliette* and its production at the Opéra. There were arrangements under way for a revival of *le Médecin malgré lui*. The new director of the Opéra seemed enthusiastic about what he had heard of *Polyeucte*. As for Choudens, Gounod had a stormy interview with him over publishing rights. The villain 'was *inflexible* and so WAS I', wrote Gounod to his 'chère et dévouée' Georgina.

Towards the end of August he was back in London for a short stay and consultations with Georgina. Then he went to Paris again with an exciting project in mind: Georgina was to sing in the French première of *Gallia*! It would be performed at the reopening of the Conservatoire on the 29 October. The occasion was a special one, since the Conservatoire had been shut for eighteen months during the Franco-Prussian War and the Commune. *Gallia* was to signal the official resumption of musical life in Paris.

Georgina arrived for rehearsals and settled alone in the flat which had been specially rented for her to allay gossip. She was nervous and irritable. The importance of the event and her inexperience as a singer combined to rob her of her usual assurance. *Gallia* was, moreover, a particularly French work that, despite its slender musical qualities, involved patriotism and deep feelings. Where was the place of an English singer, even had she been one of international fame, in all this?

The Conservatoire depressed her. She found it 'a real hole altogether', uncomfortable and chilly. The audience, however, was unexpectedly kind. Her dignified appearance made a good impression and her singing won applause which, if modest, was polite and well intentioned. Although she was quivering with nerves, although the choir sometimes drowned her voice, she came through the ordeal with credit. Real proof of her success was given when the Opéra-Comique decided to stage *Gallia*.

A week later Georgina sang in the two Opéra-Comique performances. There was specially designed scenery and she wore a costume with an elaborate train—it gave her privately a lot of trouble when she had to move backwards—which, a sympathetic journalist wrote, made her look as if she had come out of Vernet's picture 'Rebecca at the fountain'. Again her singing and acting were praised and there was even mention of other parts to follow. A final performance in the church of Saint-Eustache crowned the success of her Parisian début. The whole episode was the greatest triumph she ever knew as a singer. What pleased her equally was the obvious satisfaction of Gounod, 'my angelic old man', who had conducted each performance.

He was not so happy, needless to say, in his family life. Reunion with Madame Gounod and his children had only brought more scenes, more argument. For some time now, though living in the same house, he had slept away from his wife. They occupied separate apartments, she on the ground floor and he on the third. One day, at the height of a quarrel, he slapped her face and tore her dressing-gown. He had never forgiven her for saying that Georgina was 'a woman of the town' who slept around at a fiver a time. Was it not that 'execrable woman', his wife, who had driven him mad in the

171

past and forced him to be locked up in a strait-jacket at Dr Blanche's clinic? Was it not that harpy who had several times caused him to attempt suicide by ripping himself open with a knife that left 'enormous scars' on his body?

Of course, we know only Gounod's side of the affair as Georgina reported it. Madame Gounod was not so articulate as the other two partners in the grotesque situation which had arisen and she lacked the eloquence of either. It is clear that she did not seem a very pleasant woman to many of Gounod's friends and that the impression she left was one of small-mindedness. Bizet heartily disliked her. Nowhere can one find a word of genuine praise for her, and even the conventional tributes Gounod paid her in his autobiographical writing have a merely dutiful ring. Their marriage had been one of convenience. Yet she had genuine grievances, of which the *Gallia* episode was not the least. It was bad enough for Gounod to live in England beneath Georgina's roof. Even more humiliating for his wife was his action in bringing Georgina to France and starring her in a series of much talked about concerts. By flaunting Georgina in public on his home-ground he had painfully embarrassed Madame Gounod.

The confrontation with his wife and the strain of launching his protégée in France were too much for Gounod's ragged nerves. He collapsed utterly. The one fixed point in his existence, the one source to which he looked for help and comfort, was Georgina. He could not bear to be separated from her. She took him back to London with her, and at the beginning of December he was installed at Tavistock House. 'He fluttered into our nest like a wounded bird; he crouched down in his bed like a poor hunted animal, and there he lay for several days without moving,' Georgina wrote.

The Weldons' doctor was called. Since everything to do with Georgina tended to be larger than life, one is not surprised to learn that her medical adviser belonged to the Plymouth Brethren and was a keen believer in hydropathy. He diagnosed eczema and congestion of the lungs. The state of Gounod's pulse led him to fear a cerebral attack. Each morning from then onwards husband Harry packed up Gounod in a swaddling of wet sheets and blankets. The treatment was designed to make him sweat, but sometimes, despite being smothered for six hours at a time in extra bundles of furs and waterproofs, the invalid's pores remained obstinately dry. Hot baths and a constant room temperature of sixty degrees Fahrenheit were devotedly sustained. Before setting off to the College of Heralds, Harry would enquire: 'I hope the old man will perspire today.' His first question on returning was: 'Has the old man perspired?' Sometimes, if the news was good, Georgina would await him at the top of the stairs and, when he opened the hall door, would joyfully shout: 'The old man perspires!'

The fact is that Harry was not at all jealous of Gounod. Long ago, when his infatuation with Georgina had cooled and he realized she could not give him what he wanted, he had found consolation elsewhere. Since he now had no sexual feeling for Georgina he regarded her with kindly indifference. He welcomed Gounod's presence. It gave husband and wife a common interest which till then had been lacking and helped to preserve a marriage that might by now have crumbled. Though the rest of the world may not have known it, the so-called philandering Frenchman was instrumental in keeping the Weldons together. Moreover, Harry rather enjoyed nursing.

Gounod was certainly in need of it. His skin had dried to the consistency of parchment. The itching caused by eczema drove him mad with irritation and made him scratch until the blood came. The doctor forbade him tobacco and snuff, two things that would have helped him bear the painful monotony. He sweated gloomily in his hot little room and the hours passed slowly, very slowly. Georgina, his 'chère Mimi', was his salvation. She cooked all his meals, became his goddess, his nurse, his slave. She gave him baths, soaping him vigorously and rubbing him with a fierce energy as the doctor advised. He spluttered contentedly through the suds. Then she dowsed him with pails of cold water and brushed the mane of hair, long at the back, short in front.

In the last days of 1871 he was attacked by colic and dysentery. The New Year brought him a chill. Within a few days he was unable to move for the agony of piles. Rheumatism increased his pains. A glandular swelling in the neck created more suffering. The doctor offered little comfort. The patient, said he, foreshadowing later advertisements for that famous bedtime drink, had nothing *organically* wrong with him. It was just that he had reached a mental state comparable to that of a woman at the change of life. Who knows, softening of the brain might follow.

Harry in his new-found role was a miracle of devotion. At the end of the day he would intone a litany of anxious questions. Had the old man been out for his walk? Had the old man had his eleven o'clock egg? Had the old man taken his powders before lunch? Had he eaten his four o'clock broth? Had the old man drunk his five o'clock brandy whipped up in egg?

From time to time there were callers. Emissaries, for the most part, of Gounod's family, they came to gather news and report back to his wife. First the abbé Boudier put in an appearance. Then Dr Blanche, owner of the clinic where Gounod had stayed in the past, arrived at Tavistock House. 'Another spy from the *crockery dog*!' snapped the composer. But Dr Blanche reassured him: 'We *all* know what Madame Gounod is!' he slyly remarked. The least sympathetic visitor was Jules Barbier, the librettist and a belligerent henchman of Madame Gounod. His comments about 'chère Mimi' left Gounod muttering furiously about duels and choice of weapons. His anger lifted when Georgina, referring to Barbier's faithful championing of the deserted wife, nicknamed him 'Madame Gounod's parrot'—another candidate for the bestiary which already included the crockery dog and those real-life canine pets of Georgina which she baptized 'Dan', 'Mittie', 'Jarby' and 'Whiddles'.

By the February of 1872 Gounod was well enough to go down to Brighton for a performance of *Gallia*. Throughout Spring he convalesced. With the return of his strength came an urge to clarify, in some sort, his position. In March he wrote to his wife. He could not, he explained, face the prospect of returning to Paris and its atmosphere of 'odious wickedness'. Her lack of faith, her extreme readiness to believe the worst, had for years poisoned his existence. He was divided in his loyalties to a wife whom he honoured and loved, and to friends whom he also honoured and loved. It was an intolerable situation. Should his wife wish to live with him, she must come to England.

Having discharged this bombshell he felt that he was, for the time being at least, fully restored to health. He could now meet Georgina on her own ground. The clash of temperament between these two brilliant actors resolved itself into a number of dramatic scenes which they both played for all they were worth. The smallest incident was enough to inspire an episode which they would build up and nurse with an untiring ability to squeeze drama from the slightest detail.

One of their joint masterpieces in this line concerned the score of *Polyeucte*. An argument over a letter was magnified by Gounod into accusations of tyranny on Georgina's part. He decided to go to see the writer of the letter, despite her objections and despite the bad weather outside. Slowly and deliberately he put on boots, winter coat and Georgina's sealskin cap, taking his time in the hope she would say something so that the argument could be resumed. She did not rise to the bait. Without a word he stalked downstairs, shut the door and ventured out into the storm.

In the afternoon he returned. He refused the broth Georgina offered. Before she knew what was happening he had rushed out-doors again. This time Harry ran after him, and when 'the old man' had walked as far as the railings he seized him under his arm, like a vice. Once back in the house Gounod erupted into fury. He darted to the cupboard where he kept the score of *Polyeucte*.

'*Polyeucte* first,' he shouted, '*Polyeucte* shall burn!' (He would always threaten to burn a manuscript whenever he was crossed. 'It was his best way of getting anything he wanted out of me,' Georgina explained.)

The climax was dramatic: 'With strength lent me by the horror of despair, I threw myself on Gounod with all my weight. I knocked him down; I rolled on him; we tussled violently for possession of the treasure. I tore it from him; I flung it on the sofa; I suddenly picked myself off the floor; I sat up on it and screamed: "You shall kill me first, but you shall not burn Polyeucte!" My strength then gave way, I burst into sobs, I stretched out my arms to him—"My old man! My old treasure! Why are you so wicked to me?"'

Gounod enjoyed the fight. It had done him good and he calmed down. *Polyeucte* was saved.

⚜ XII ⚜

The Gounodyssey, Part II – Libel – Joan of Arc – Gounod to be Horsewhipped?

The founding and administration of an Academy for orphans with vocal talent absorbed only a portion of Georgina's bounding energy. The rest of her attention was given to 'the old man' and his business affairs. An important event in the Spring of 1872 was the series of concerts he gave at the Albert Hall with a body that became known as 'Gounod's Choir'. Georgina was closely involved in all the arrangements. Naturally there was drama, and next year her experiences were to form the subject of another of her fiery pamphlets: 'The Quarrel of the Royal Albert Hall Company with Ch. Gounod'.

Even at the first concert on the 8 May there were murmurs of discontent. It is expecting too much of a composer to give him the task of organizing programmes and to imagine that he will ignore his own music. The result was that most of the items to be sung were from the pen of the Master himself. Those that were not had benefited from his 'arrangement'. The National Anthem and the 'Old Hundredth' emerged in brand-new Gounodian settings. Except for the Hallelujah Chorus, which was left for some reason untouched, everything at the concert bore the mark of Gounod. *The Times* deplored the absence of compositions by any English composer living or dead. The *Musical Times*, ever a champion of home-grown genius, entered a waspish protest that there was a number of 'native professors' qualified to direct an English choir 'in a building under royal patronage'. The remaining three concerts brought the Royal Choral Society, which had sponsored them, redoubled criticism and a large financial loss. In July Gounod resigned. He had planned to give a concert of his own which would feature more popular items. But the Albert Hall authorities had had enough. He was succeeded

11. Gounod's study in his Paris home, complete with organ, his own bust in the corner, and, at the far left, the combined desk/piano at which he worked. (Photo: Stella Mayes Reed.)

12. The drawing-room of Gounod's country house at Saint-Cloud. He is playing cards with his wife. Other members of the family are grouped around. (Photo: Stella Mayes Reed.)

by Joseph Barnby, a once-famous Victorian musician who earned Gounod's intense dislike.

Gounod's quarrels with the Albert Hall were insignificant when compared with the heroic battles he waged against publishers. A favourite topic of his at Tavistock House was the similarity he had detected between them and vampires. A guest has preserved one of his characteristic orations on the subject.

'At the present day', Gounod would comment, 'vampires are said to inhabit only certain villages of Illyria. Nevertheless, it is by no means necessary to undertake so long a journey in order to engage in conflict with monsters of this kind. They come across us in all parts of civilized Europe under the form of Music Publishers and Theatrical Managers.' This was the preliminary to a searching dissection of the evil incarnate represented by publishers.

At first he had been pleased with the royalty system he found in England. It appeared to be a most civilized and equitable arrangement which, in an imperfect world, enabled the composer to draw a steady reward from his toil. He was soon to discover that the purity of theory was contaminated in practice. The well-known singers who performed songs demanded also a share of the royalties. They argued that since their own reputation and skill contributed to the popularity of the numbers they sang they were entitled to their percentage. This early form of 'payola' infuriated Gounod. If it were justified, he pointed out, he in turn would be able to insist that a prima donna who sang in his *Faust* share her fee with him. This was clearly absurd. Why, then, should the stars of the concert platform be allowed to rob the composer of his modest share? He summed up the age-old dispute by remarking that the composer was the soul of the work and the singer only the body. The former was the idea, the latter nothing but a voice. A voice without an idea was mere noise, and the body without soul a corpse. Singers were lost without composers to write the works that enabled them to show their talent.

Gounod's discontent and Georgina's instinct for battle created a fiery mixture that was bound one day to explode in some publisher's face. In the Autumn of 1872 the big bang occurred. The victim was Littleton of Novello's. Gounod's initial satisfaction at gaining better terms than Choudens ever offered him had turned into a sense of injustice. The details of the situation are obscure, and even today, more than a century later, the firm politely refuses access to its archives. The wounds must have gone deep. What is clear is that

Gounod and Georgina voiced their dissatisfaction in unmistakable terms. The articles and letters they wrote—for even though the composer put his signature to them they were the result of collaboration—went beyond the limits of fair comment. Novello's issued a writ for libel.

When Harry Weldon learned that the famous and formidable Sergeant Ballentine was to represent Novello's he retreated out of London and went to ground. Alone, undaunted, Gounod and his Egeria set off to the courts. The composer did not shine in the witness box. The strange legal language and the odd procedure were confusing to a foreigner. Georgina, though, had found her element. She confused the terrible Ballentine, tripped him up in his questioning, and soon, instead of being a defending witness, she seemed to have taken charge of the attack. The judge smiled. The jury tittered. There was laughter in court.

This was her first appearance in the surroundings where, during the years to come, she made herself the most famous lay lawyer of her time. She put up a brilliant performance. So effective was her pleading that the verdict awarded Novello's a mere £2 damages against the defendant. There remained the unfortunate problem of costs amounting to £100. These Gounod refused to pay. The two conspirators chuckled together at Novello's embarrassment when it became known that they would be responsible for sending a famous composer to prison. Bailiffs arrived at Tavistock House to distrain. There was nothing for them to sell. Gounod had signed a document admitting a debt of £350 owing to Georgina.

He actually looked forward to the prospect of a stay in an English prison. 'On the 28th of the month I shall go into my *convent*,' he joked to a friend. 'In prison I shall orchestrate the imprisonment of Polyeucte and my Mass of guardian angels.' He was denied this novelty. Littleton, 'the old sweep', withdrew from the suit and the costs were paid by a third party. This anonymous guardian angel was, it seems, Gounod's mother-in-law Madame Zimmermann. When Gounod heard of this he was beside himself with rage. His language turned so blue that Georgina had to leave the room.

Throughout all the distractions of legal proceedings and the turbulent existence at Tavistock House he went on writing music with remarkable facility. Amid the squawking of Georgina's orphan pupils from the room below, the barking of a tribe of dogs and the noisy interruptions caused by a stream of visitors of every type and

nation, he composed industriously. Undisturbed by noise and clat-
ter, he would quietly work out themes in his head. Having first
written out a work in short score, he could then play and sing it in
full as it existed, complete already in his brain. One of the scores he
wrote under these conditions was the incidental music for Barbier's
drama *Jeanne d'Arc.*

As usual he went through the text in meticulous detail before
writing a note of music. The lines of choruses to be set were studied
singly and broken down first into phrases and then into syllables.
Over each syllable he pencilled, in words, the note it was to be given.
This care for words is one of the reasons behind his mastery of vocal
writing. Henri Busser, who knew him well in the last years, remembers a striking example of Gounod's respect for the word. As
candidates for the Prix de Rome, Busser and his colleagues were
visited by Gounod in his official capacity as a member of the
Institut. He read aloud to them the text they were to set. First he
dictated it to them slowly, repeating each sentence. Then he read it
over again with free expression. Busser, closely following Gounod's
voice, noted the accents, the pauses, the long stresses and the short,
and all the changes of rhythm. The indications he had made immediately suggested to him melodic themes appropriate to the
situation and to every word in the text.

Although the manuscript of *Jeanne d'Arc* gives an interesting
glimpse of the composer at work it is not, of course, a major piece.
The bells heard by Saint Joan are developed into an imposing chorus
of saints, and there are curious touches of Franckian chromaticism.
Hints of plainchant and a clever pastiche of medieval ballade help
create the atmosphere of the age. The chorus in Act IV, 'Sans verser
le sang elle prend les villes', is so very Gounodian that for a moment
it sounds almost like a caricature. The finale takes the theme which
earlier embodied Joan's 'voices' and, following Gounod's customary
habit with a climax, repeats it in different keys.

Jeanne d'Arc, featuring Rachel's sister in the title role, was given
in Paris on the 8 November 1873. The critics were lukewarm and
described Gounod's music as a bundle of reminiscences. One sees
their point of view, particularly as the ballet consisted of that trifle
l'Enterrement d'une marionnette. Immensely popular with English
drawing-room pianists as *The Funeral March of a Marionette*, within
two years it had earned Gounod at least £350. The significance of
this little skit is that it was intended as a musical portrait of Henry

F. Chorley, critic of the *Athenaeum,* whom Gounod had for some reason begun to detest. Chorley, said Georgina, had a 'thin, sour, high-pitched, sopranish voice' and moved like 'a stuffed red-haired monkey'. Gounod played the music over to her and made her 'nearly die of laughter'. He planned to dedicate it to Chorley, but the critic's death robbed the joke of its point. So Georgina wrote a little programme and gave it a marionette title. She always believed she deserved credit for her contribution and, by an ironic reversal of circumstances, in later years reproached Gounod for not sharing the royalties with her.

The score of *Jeanne d'Arc* carried the dedication: 'I offer this manuscript to my two dear and courageous friends Henry and Georgina Weldon in memory of the Stake at which public ill-will has condemned them to burn with me, ever since I had the good fortune to have them for friends. 6 October 1873.' This was a reference to the comments about Gounod's long absence in England which the French press was making. A visit to Spa, where he went to take the waters accompanied by Georgina, provoked sarcasm about his relationship with her. He was nicknamed 'The Englishman Gounod' and attacked for having turned his back on the native land that had given him success and honours.

There were many references to his passionate love affair. Had the journalists who wrote so maliciously about it gone with him to Spa they would have realized that romance was the one element lacking. No sooner had the party arrived at Spa than Georgina saw that her beloved dogs had been mislaid at the frontier. Little 'Tity' was expecting. Old 'Dan' would be in despair. What had become of the poor dear creatures? She rushed out to send a telegram to the frontier while Gounod fumed: 'Those brutal dogs. Why have [you] brought them? Why submit ourselves to such a *nuisance*? All the better if they are lost! You, you can't live without your pugs! Is there a thing in this world more insupportable than a woman who cannot move without dragging after her animals of all kinds, birds, beasts, parrots, frogs, tortoises, hedgehogs? If they are found I insist on your opening their basket and letting them run wherever they please! As for me, if those pugs darken our doors again, I take the first train, I return to Tavistock, and you'll do the season of Spa without me!'

Was it jealousy? Perhaps it had not struck him that, for Georgina, he was himself another sort of pet, though human this time, on whom she lavished her frustrated affection. Soon he was down with indigestion again, and eczema and heartburn. 'Chère Mimi' was there to cut his meat for him and tidy up the breadcrumbs. He played the part of fractious little boy, not that of romantic lover.

The long-delayed production in Paris of *les Deux reines* with his incidental music aroused pointed remarks about his exile. *Roméo et Juliette* had at last entered the portals of the Opéra-Comique, and Bizet, who was in charge of the performance as well as that of *Jeanne d'Arc*, wrote a friendly letter to Gounod. His earlier disillusionment had faded to be replaced by sympathetic appreciation of the older man's genius. He had not, he wrote, been able fully to understand *Roméo et Juliette* at its first hearing, though today he knew it better, with the 'delightful' opening chords of its *Sommeil de Juliette* and its 'excellent' *Epithalame*. Most important of all, he told Gounod: 'The ties that bind us are such that neither absence nor silence can loosen. You were the beginning of my life as an artist. I spring from you. You are the cause and I am the consequence. Now I can tell you that I feared being absorbed by you, and you must have noticed the result of that uneasiness. Today I believe I am more a master of my craft, and I feel only the benefits of your helpful and decisive influence. . . . I don't know the causes that have brought about your separation from us, my dear Gounod. We often think of you. We miss you and love you still.'

At about this time Gounod acquired another protégé. Édouard Lalo, though not so young as Bizet, remained a struggling and obscure composer. Germany was more receptive to his work than France, where public indifference and lack of recognition wounded a man of pride who suffered in silence. He published the opera *Fiesque* at his own expense and was never to see a complete performance of it. Gounod took up his cause and tried to interest theatre managers in *Fiesque*. He pleaded, did all he could to awaken enthusiasm for a work he believed in, but finally he had to write to Lalo's mother-in-law: 'A theatre manager is in some ways forced to *play safe*: instead of giving *faith* to the public, he expects and receives it from *them*; in other words, it's no longer the pilot who steers the ship, but the ship that steers the pilot. The world revolves in a host of vicious circles like this.' Nearly a decade later, in 1881, he was able to give more positive help. A serious illness prevented Lalo from finishing the orchestration of his ballet *Namouna*. It could not be performed unless completed within a short time. Gounod, then the most famous French composer of the period, generously offered to do the ungrateful task. Humbly, he insisted on working under Lalo's direction.

These reminders of musical life at home in Paris made Gounod restless. The idyll with Georgina had worn perilously thin. Existence at Tavistock House became still more farcical. An argument over one of her pupils sent him storming out. The police had to be alerted before he came back again. An altercation at the whist table led to Gounod emitting 'a sort of roar like that of a wild bull' and packing his bags with his clothes and a loaded pistol. Late one evening he wandered in his nightshirt through the passages giving 'unearthly cries' until Harry appeared and led him back to bed. A dispute about a pair of trousers reached monumental proportions. Although he was able to wear Harry's cast-off coats and waistcoats, the trousers were too long and wide for him. Accordingly he wore his own until they reached an alarming state of decay. He refused to buy a new pair. 'I haven't a farthing!' he replied to Georgina's rebukes: his mother, he told her pathetically, had been so poor that she lived in *tatters*, but she was honest, as he hoped to be. He couldn't afford £2 for new trousers and was terrified of getting into debt. Georgina won this round by entering into a majestic rage. Gounod fell on his knees, wept, and asked forgiveness. The trousers were bought.

Not surprisingly, in the March of 1874 he was very ill again. Fainting fits were succeeded by hallucinations. He imagined that his son Jean was tuberculous. A fear possessed him that Harry Weldon would kill him if he were unkind to Georgina. As for that lady herself, she appeared to his vision surrounded with rays of white light. 'Old man off his head all day,' Georgina wrote in her diary, not very perturbed by Gounod's oddities. After all, he was a composer, and, like all artists, composers were queer fish.

He convalesced at St Leonards and soon felt well enough to cheer up Harry, who was going through one of his black moods. 'Poomps', as Gounod nicknamed him, was more embarrassed than helped by the attempt, though the composer wrote optimistically to Georgina: 'I told your Poomps I could not bear to see him sorrowful, because it made me so unhappy; and I took him in my arms and kissed him so hard, so hard, it really seemed to do him good.' Poor Poomps! He confessed to Georgina: 'When the old man takes me in his arms to comfort me, I don't know what I would not do to him; I'd as soon be kissed by a viper as by one of my own sex.'

At St Leonards Gounod turned to Molière again. This time it was the prose comedy *George Dandin* that occupied his thoughts. Dandin, a rich peasant, hopes to improve his social status by marrying a girl of higher birth. The ill-considered marriage plunges him into a sea of troubles, and his rueful comment, '*Vous l'avez voulu, George Dandin, vous l'avez voulu*', has become a proverb for use whenever anyone complicates life with problems of his own seeking. Gounod's idea was to make an opera out of the play—but an opera with a difference. Instead of setting verse, he would set the original prose.

If verse had its advantages, thought Gounod, it also had serious drawbacks. Its symmetry was a dangerous temptation because the regular rhythm it suggested to the composer tended to make him the slave of dialogue rather than the master. He might well be carried away by the purely rhythmic consequences of his first impression. Rhyme wasn't necessary to music. The oratorios of Bach, Handel and Mendelssohn showed that music could be written quite as successfully to prose. Why not follow their example in the theatre? The variety of stress and rhythm in prose opened up new horizons that could save the composer from monotony and uniformity.

What better prose could he choose than Molière's? Like *Tartuffe* and *le Misanthrope*, *George Dandin* is described as a comedy, although in fact it is a drama as rich in pathos as in laughter. The characters attracted Gounod because they belonged to that universal human comedy which Molière had called into existence. He started by writing a duet for Dandin and the servant Lubin in the second act. This was followed by a trio between Dandin and his parents-in-law the Sottenvilles (a perfect name for those dull-witted socialites) which he found gave him little difficulty. There were, he admitted, obstacles to setting concerted numbers in prose, but he felt he had succeeded so far. Unfortunately he did not continue the experiment and George Dandin was to lie unfinished among his papers.

The party went on to Hastings where he made a setting of Lord Houghton's *Ilala*. He sat on the beach, mellow in the warm sun and bright with the reflection from the sea, and dedicated *Ilala* to 'Mrs Weldon, whose daily inexhaustible charity I grow to revere more and more. . . .' The previous month he had written to her: 'It was today, the 26 February, this evening, at eleven o'clock, three years ago, that I saw you for the first time.—Three years!—Already! and in another way it seems to me that I have known you for a lifetime.'

Never, it appeared, had Gounod been more content with his

183

'chère Mimi'. A great scheme was in hand to enlist the patronage of Queen Victoria. A letter went to Balmoral offering the dedication of his new oratorio, *la Rédemption*, and soliciting the Royal command for a performance at the Albert Hall. Shamefully and iniquitously treated in the past, (a reference to his brush with the Royal Choral Society), Gounod aspired, so the letter said, to found an institution devoted to sacred music and dedicated to the memory of 'a venerated and revered Prince'. This elaborate piece of flattery evoked a not unfavourable response. Then, apparently, one of Georgina's numerous enemies mentioned at court her vitriolic pamphlet about the Albert Hall management. Despite further correspondence, to which Gounod contributed choice quotations from the Psalms and Saint Paul, the project aborted.

Perhaps this failure was one of the circumstances that made Gounod ill at ease with the atmosphere in Tavistock House. His association with Georgina passed through several stages. First, impressed by her beauty, he saw her as merely another conquest. Then, when he realized that her chastity was inviolable, he accepted the tribute of her admiration and came to rely on her vigorous guidance through the puzzling ways of a foreign land. Finally, as nurse and businesswoman who fought on his behalf with publishers and lawyers, she became an essential prop. Besides, how much prettier she was than his wife! In personal relations he always gave way to the stronger force and let himself be carried along at will. And Georgina had shown that she was even more formidable than Madame Gounod or his mother-in-law.

But Madame Gounod held a card that Georgina could never trump: despite her lack of attractiveness she was his wife, the mother of his children and the mistress of his household in France. In the battle for possession of Gounod she was bound, eventually, to win. She knew that simply by waiting she would triumph in the end. She was a very patient woman.

As for Gounod himself, his moods changed as swiftly as the tints of a chameleon. At one moment he would make a statement with passionate conviction. At the next he would contradict it in tones of equal sincerity. He was, said a friend, 'a man of sand'. When the holidaymakers returned from Hastings to Tavistock House he appeared docile enough. On the 27 May Mrs Louisa Brown, his friend during the early times in England, invited him to Blackheath for the day. Georgina drove him there in a carriage together with two of her dogs. On the way little 'Whiddles' had a fit. Outside Mrs Brown's house a crowd gathered and there were cries of 'Mad dog!' Gounod loathed her dogs and the scene added to his annoyance. His nerves were upset by the shrill barking, he was embarrassed by the incident and irritated by Georgina's obvious distress over her pet. It was agreed that he should stay the night at Mrs Brown's. Georgina left him there for the time being, 'more dead than alive'.

He stayed there a week. Each day he sent her a postcard, one of them playfully signed 'Whiddles'. Then a telegram announced that he was ill. She flew there and saw him in bed. A silver crucifix lay on his chest. His mind wandered and his speech was incoherent. Harry came too, and when she returned to Tavistick House he stayed to keep watch over the 'cher vieux old man'. Next morning Gounod still slept. Harry reported ominous news: an envoy had come to Blackheath from Gounod's family. During the next few days Georgina haunted Mrs Brown's home. She was allowed a brief interview with the invalid and found him pale and grey. He was thin. His trousers flapped on shrivelled legs.

On the 8 June she saw him again. He accompanied her as she sang 'Watchman, what of the night?' and a setting of Mrs Felicia Hemans' 'Better Land'. Dr Blanche had arrived and Georgina knew that the prize was to be taken from her grasp. She silently acknowledged defeat. Her eyes remained dry while Gounod wept copiously. It was a comfort to her that he was wearing one of Harry's Panama hats. At least he was taking something of theirs with him. On the platform at Charing Cross Georgina brought Dr Blanche up to date with the history of Gounod's cerebral attacks. The railway clock stood at twenty minutes past one. The train moved off and Gounod, the tears flowing down his withered cheek, insisted that they meet again soon.

He was gone. No longer would he be there to call her 'H-mee— H-mee' with his little habit of putting a grunt before each syllable of the name 'Mimi'. No longer would she soap his back and brush his hair until it gleamed. On the 22 June a carefully written letter from him confirmed that 'your dear old man who kisses you', while paying tribute to her good intentions, would not come back.

This was the opening shot in a correspondence that lasted for years. Human nature is inexplicable. We each of us believe that we act as a result of logical and sensible reasoning. It is only other people who behave foolishly and irrationally. The truth, we are assured by Chesterfield, that icy scrutator of the human heart, is that man is not a rational creature. He is guided by his ruling passion of the moment. The situation between Gounod and Georgina illustrates how confusedly the mind and the emotions work. It was a tangle of genuine feeling, hypocrisy, play-acting, warm affection and commercial instinct. Sometimes he looked on her as a mother, sometimes as a business manager. For her, he was a dearly loved if wayward son and, at the same time, a figurehead who would help to further her dream of a singing school for orphans.[1]

Had he not agreed that after a sum was put aside for his daughter's dowry he would give all the proceeds from English sales of his music to Georgina's school ? Was it not a fact that, apart from small and inadequate payments, he had enjoyed free board and lodge at Tavistock House ? Their letters grew acrimonious. Legal opinions were taken. A forthright acquaintance advised Harry to 'horsewhip Gounod on the staircase of the Grand Opera'. The ruffled composer told his friends that Georgina, whom he had once described to them as 'an angel', was now 'a demon'. Instead of affectionate little notes from 'your poor old man', there clumped into the hall at Tavistock House letters nineteen pages long demanding the return of his manuscripts, his drawings, his gold snuff-box, his evening dress. Stung by Georgina's complaints about the expense he had given her, he incautiously asked her to present her bill.

Georgina pounced. 'So I was to send in my *bill*,' she exclaimed bitterly. She had been his sick nurse, secretary, publishing representative, advertising agent, poet, business manager and singer. The bill she drew up covers sixteen closely printed pages in her memoirs. It gives evidence of a photographic memory and an eye for detail that the Duke of Wellington would have envied. The entries include pawnbrokers' fees, an 'advertising cart', visiting cards, a spring-mattress, and 'a square wooden affair on wheels'. Provision was made not only for these exotica but also for the notional damage caused her by 'infamous calumnies, lies and libels'. The total came to £9,787 5s 9d. As a matter of interest she reckoned Gounod had earned nearly £6,000 while in England.

For a time she refused to give him back the manuscripts of *Polyeucte*, *George Dandin* and other works. In Paris he resignedly set about scoring *Polyeucte* from memory and completed it within ten

---

[1] A brilliant and compassionate analysis of Georgina's character will be found in Edward Grierson's outstanding biography. (See list of books at end.)

months. Then, with what seems feminine perversity, she sent it to him along with the others. Even so his ill-luck persisted. As he came away from his attorney's office bearing the precious load in his hands, his delight caused him to miss a step and fall down the stairs. In bed with a dislocated shoulder he joked: 'What do you expect? Polyeucte suffered for his faith and I can suffer, in turn, for Polyeucte!'

The Gounodyssey was over. The composer's departure meant also that the last bond between Harry and Georgina was dissolved. She separated from her husband and was left with Tavistock House and an allowance. Her subsequent career proved that destiny had not intended her to be either a teacher of singing or the manager of a famous composer: it had sent her into this world for the express purpose of changing the laws of England. For in the thirty or so years that remained to her she generalled no less than seventeen lawsuits, most of them running concurrently. Disdainful of bungling solicitors and ill-briefed counsel, she appeared in person and pleaded her own cases with brio. She was admired for her gallantry by a somewhat bemused public, respected for her mastery of the law by judges, and detested for her implacable zeal by opponents.

Georgina's first sensational appearance in her new role was as leader of the movement for reform of the lunacy laws. This startling development arose from a court battle with Harry Weldon. Relations between them had degenerated to a point where he tried to get her put away in a lunatic asylum. Her behaviour in court showed that, far from being mad, she was a woman of clear and dominating intelligence. Harry was to regret his action. On one day alone she issued five writs against him and his colleagues. Charges alleging trespass, libel, slander, assault and false imprisonment showered upon the bewildered heads of those who had associated with Harry to do her down. Georgina emerged as a formidable cross-examiner. Though her knowledge of the law was not immaculate her technique for eliciting the truth from witnesses, however eminent, was awesome. She won her case.

Her experiences during this period were set forth in a lively pamphlet entitled 'How I escaped the Mad Doctors'. For it was the doctors, she claimed, who were mad, and not herself. Certainly she had demonstrated the cruelty of the Victorian lunacy laws and shown how easily they could be perverted to cause innocent suffering. Lunacy reform was the topic that made her a public figure. She erupted on lecture-platforms, gave concerts to finance the campaign, and, from time to time, spent tranquil months in Newgate and Holloway as a result of uttering incautious libels. She did not mind imprisonment. In a hectically busy life it gave her a rare chance for the peace and quiet she needed to plan her future lawsuits.

Having won the cause of lunacy reform she went on to tackle other issues. She won the first case in legal history for the restitution of conjugal rights. The Salvation Army engaged her sympathetic attention. The Land Reform Union found her an active member. At meetings of the Bow Cemetery Grievance Committee she was a forceful debater. She spoke in support of Charles Bradlaugh, the free-thinking M.P., and of his call for repeal of the blasphemy laws. Spiritualism was another keen interest and the subject of a defiant pamphlet: 'Death-Blow to Spiritualism—is it?' She even spared time for historical research and propounded her novel findings in 'Louis XVII; or the Arab Jew'. With every post came letters asking for help from people who had been unjustly treated by authority or cheated of their rights. Despite the endless flood of litigation in which she was engaged, she dealt with them all.

She still sang at concerts and even music-halls. Her beauty remained. At the age of fifty she testified, in an advertisement seen by the whole of London, that she owed her youthful complexion to Pears' Soap. In old age she divided her life between England and France. Known as 'Grannie Weldon' to the children of her friends, she was adored by them. Her Sunday visits were looked forward to with pleasure. She would arrive surrounded by quantities of luggage and mysterious packages. Once she was installed—and the ceremony took some time, involving the nice positioning of cushions—the children gathered round to admire her still beautiful features and to enjoy the stories she told with a pronunciation which, even in Edwardian times, was delightfully old-fashioned. She treated the children as equals and never forgot a birthday. News of their exploits, however naughty, was eagerly welcomed. She wrote them long letters and treated them, as one of the circle now remembers, 'as though we had been her own children'.[1] When the moment for departure came she would give the cab-driver her address in ringing tones. And then, to make quite sure, her bonnetted head would peek out from the window and she would boom a final detail: 'O-o-o-ver the milkshop.'

[1] Miss Marjory Pegram, who has vivid memories of 'Grannie Weldon's' kindness and whose recollections are utilized here.

Gounod was only a brief though significant episode in Georgina's long life. As will be seen later, he was to have yet another terrible clash with her before she had done. Though he went to his grave loathing her it is possible for us to take a different view. When you examine her career you have to admire her energy and determination, however wrong-headed it may sometimes have been. She was a gallant creature. In an age when women were regarded, officially at least, as inferior chattels, she fought bravely and contrived single-handed to alter the laws of the land. At first you are amused by her. Then you respect her. In the end you cannot help feeling affection for her.

⚜XIII⚜

France Again – *Cinq-Mars* – *Polyeucte* – *le Tribut de Zamora*

In England Gounod's private life had been exposed for all the world to see and was eventually to be documented in painful detail by the six volumes of Georgina's memoirs. Once he had returned to France it lapsed into decent obscurity. Even so, it was some time before he again lived normally with his wife. On his arrival in Paris he was 'shattered with sorrows, sufferings, trials and distress of every kind'. He went to recuperate with friends at Morainville and did not see Madame Gounod for another two or three months. He assured her in a letter that while he was uncertain about where his state of health allowed him to settle, it would certainly not be in England, to which he hoped he had bid '*un éternel adieu*'. 'Pray for the woman who persecutes me,' he exhorted Madame Gounod. 'Ah, how I overflow with joy in Jesus amid my tribulations.'

Round about October 1874 he was at last reconciled with his wife. Their meeting must have been a piquant occasion. No doubt there were many tears, many quotations from Holy Writ—something, perhaps, about the return of the lamb to the fold and metaphors concerning shepherds—and many declarations enriched with florid metaphor. Madame Gounod was a sensible woman. Her cause was gained when Gounod returned to their home in the rue La Rochefoucauld. The world now saw that the master of the house was restored to his family. Madame Gounod could afford to ignore the malicious gossip that continued to appear in the newspapers.

Slowly he picked up again the threads of a life shattered by three years of war and Georgina. A revival of *Jeanne d'Arc* put him in touch with audiences once more. Offenbach produced it at the Théâtre de la Gaîté during one of his more serious moods as a theatre manager. At the dress-rehearsal a telegram from Offenbach recalled that he had earlier conducted *Ulysse* and spoke of his pleasure in staging another work by Gounod. In February 1875, Gounod attended a performance of *Gallia*. The conductor, seeing him in the audience, called him up to the platform where he bowed and waved to the applause. The music-loving public welcomed him back unreservedly.

Next month he went to the first performance of *Carmen*. His reaction to the work of his young protégé was unfavourable. During the interval he hugged Bizet, spoke to him affectionately and praised the opera. As the evening went on, in the privacy of his box, he muttered to his companion that Bizet had stolen themes from his own music. The best tunes, he grumbled, were not Bizet's at all: when they weren't Spanish they owed their origins to Wagner or to himself, Gounod. Was Gounod jealous? Did he now realize that the disciple had long since outgrown the master to create a work of original genius? It is difficult to believe that Gounod, sensitive and skilled musician that he was, failed to glimpse at least a spark of the great qualities in *Carmen*. He did not even have the excuse that Carmen had scored a success, for it was received with incomprehension. His attitude towards his former pupil became spiteful. The conventional endearments he lavished on Bizet masked a stubborn refusal to give him credit for a talent Gounod must have been forced to acknowledge in the secrecy of his own heart.

As Bizet's short life drew to a close his relations with Gounod reached their lowest ebb. Gounod at that moment was engaged in one of his interminable quarrels with the publisher Choudens and Bizet found himself involved as go-between. The unfortunate result was that Gounod, ever ready to suspect the worst of anything or anyone to do with publishers, thought Bizet was tarred with the same brush as the detested Choudens. His last letter to him was full of protests about illegality and defamation. It referred darkly to solicitors and attorneys. Soon afterwards, at the age of thirty-six, Bizet died. Gounod spoke at the burial. His graveside speech was tender and generous—elaborately so, for it contained a number of those fanciful inventions with which his imagination could never resist embroidering the cold truth. His voice broke with emotion and he was unable to finish his graveside tribute. The grief that struck him dumb was genuine . . . for the moment.

That summer he spent at Dieppe. On the 8 June it was exactly a year since his return from England, a date to which he referred as 'the anniversary of my crossing the Red Sea'. Soon he was busy on a new opera. The unsinkable Carvalho had risen again, this time in charge of the Opéra-Comique, and asked Gounod for a contribution. The proposed libretto came from the novel *Cinq-Mars* by Alfred de Vigny. It was a joint work, the plot being minced by Paul Poirson and the scenario run up by Louis Gallet, an old hand at the game who supplied many libretti for Bizet, Massenet, Saint-Saëns and others.

Cinq-Mars, which is sub-titled '*Une conjuration sous Louis XIII*', features a historical personage, the marquis de Cinq-Mars, and his friend de Thou. They mounted a conspiracy against Cardinal Richelieu, were discovered and executed for treason. *Cinq-Mars* raises the old problem that dogs the writer of historical novels: should the leading characters be imaginary or should they be taken from life? It is difficult to present a convincing Napoleon or Wellington in fiction. What is the point, when fact is at once more compelling, and restricting also, than the fantasies of an author? Walter Scott, whose novels so impressed Vigny and his friends in the Romantic movement, found a solution by keeping true historical characters in the background and giving the stage to his fictional heroes and heroines. In this way he avoided the pitfalls of trying to convince readers that the kings and queens in his tales were creatures of the imagination.

Vigny, on the other hand, as if to challenge Scott on his own ground, deliberately gave prominence to real people. His hero Cinq-Mars is well documented in history, as are his mistress the famous courtesan Marion Delorme and his friend de Thou. Richelieu is also a major character, and at various times one is disconcerted by the appearance of such interlopers as Milton and Descartes. *Cinq-Mars* is long and beautifully written. Great care has been taken to fill in historical detail and contemporary politics are described with anxious attention. Yet the novel has something immobile about it. The scaffolding of fact has been constructed with too much earnestness. By contrast the novels of Alexandre Dumas, a much inferior stylist, brim with vitality. One turns the page eager to know what adventure lies in wait for Dumas' pasteboard characters. One reads *Cinq-Mars* with a dutiful respect for the poet's exquisite prose. One lays the book down conscious of a duty done.

Meyerbeer had once been tempted by the novel. He soon gave up

13. Gounod in his sixties.

14. Gounod at the age of 72, two years before his death. Portrait by Carolus Duran.

work on it, perhaps foreseeing the difficult problems of characterization which the historical factors involved. Gounod had no such reservations. He threw himself into the subject and completed the score within a very short space of time. Although Madame Carvalho, the usual source of trouble, was not appearing in the opera, rehearsals were still soured by clashes of temperament. The conductor Charles Lamoureux was as autocratic a man as Carvalho. He had disagreed violently with the impresario and the composer on other occasions. One evening early in the run of *Cinq-Mars* he abruptly stalked out after the first act and left his deputy in charge. Gounod took over at later performances, and the box-office receipts, already healthy, acquired a still warmer bloom.

For *Cinq-Mars* was a success. Its début at the Opéra-Comique on the 5 April 1877, was the first Gounod première in ten years. Public interest was keen and large audiences filled the theatre to see what Gounod after his long absence had to offer them. They do not seem to have been disappointed. There were fifty-six performances throughout the year and Carvalho had a fair return on the big sums of money he laid out. A publisher—not Choudens this time but a new man called Léon Grus—paid Gounod 100,000 francs for the score and sold over three thousand copies of it, a figure that shows the popularity of *Cinq-Mars*.

This popularity was short-lived. Next year the opera received only four performances, after which it dropped from the repertory and was not heard again. One important reason for the disappearance of *Cinq-Mars* is the libretto. This consists of episodes hacked out of the novel and pieced together with little regard for uniformity or dramatic conviction. The quality of the narrative is uneven and the characterization at best tentative. Richelieu becomes, at the hands of Poirson and Gallet, a lay-figure with nothing about him to suggest the powerful statesman or the formidable intriguer. The flaws of the novel are taken over and magnified by the libretto.

The music reflects this weakness. Gounod found himself unable to escape the shadow of Meyerbeer, and the scene in Act II, where the conspiracy is hatched and oaths are taken, cannot but recall similar passages in *les Huguenots*. The cantilena, 'Nuit resplendissante', is a throwback to the Italian operas of Gounod's youth. Sometimes, when he is not following other models, he even plagiarizes his own earlier work. When Marie is betrothed to Cinq-Mars and, with de Thou, sings the trio in Act III, the echo of *Roméo et*

Juliette is too persistent to be ignored. One hears again Romeo (Cinq-Mars), Juliette (Marie) and Friar Laurence (de Thou) celebrating the approach of marriage. De Thou underlines the similarity with his '*Puisse Dieu vous bénir comme je vous bénis!*' which exactly parallels the Friar's interjection.

Among the better things in *Cinq-Mars* is a short prelude in the form of a slow march hinting at mysteries and conspiracy. The theme recurs from time to time throughout the opera as a unifying factor and serves, at the end, as the funeral measure accompanying Cinq-Mars' walk to the scaffold. Best of all, perhaps, is the tableau where Marion Delorme entertains her *précieux* friends. Here Gounod had an excuse to relax from attempts to outdo Meyerbeer and to write the sort of music that lay well within his grasp.

The *précieux* movement in seventeenth-century literature set ideals of elegance and purity not confined to language alone. The salons of the marquise de Rambouillet and of other leading hostesses became a meeting-place where ladies and gentlemen gathered to enjoy not only polite conversation but also elaborate debates on the psychology of love. Was beauty, they asked themselves in polished phrases, essential to the birth of love? Could love survive marriage? The subtle problem of what effect absence had on love was the topic of endless discussion. So too was argument about the exact proportion of joy caused by the presence of the loved one or of pain caused by his or her indifference. In one evening alone twenty-five madrigals were written on a similar theme. Naturally these excessive refinements caught the eye of Molière, who satirized the more obvious absurdities in *les Précieuses Ridicules*,

One of the monuments of *précieux* literature—a monument that runs to ten substantial volumes—is a novel by Madeleine de Scudéry entitled *Clélie*. In it she outlines the famous '*Carte de Tendre*' which illustrates the theories on '*galanterie*' which she and her friends had elaborated over many evenings of sophistical argument. Her map of the emotions showed the routes to be taken in order to reach the three towns of 'Tendre'. The road to 'Tendre-sur-inclination' was straight and easy. The direction for 'Tendre-sur-estime' was, by contrast, fraught with difficulties. If it was a simple matter to achieve tenderness by inclination, admiration called for a devious route by way of villages named Flattering Attentions, Probity, Generosity, Respect and Kindness. Most impregnable of all was 'Tendre-sur-reconnaissance': to reach it involved passing through Assiduity,

Eagerness, Obedience and Constant Friendship, with the ever-present danger of straying on to the path of Negligence which might land the gallant in Coolness, Fickleness, Oblivion, and eventual drowning in the Lake of Indifference.

This intricate strategy for conquering the citadel of the human heart is the theme of the second tableau in Act II of *Cinq-Mars*. A gathering of *précieux* hear Marion Delorme outline the analysis offered by the '*Carte de Tendre*'. She charts for them the stages by which Inclination becomes Happiness, always provided that Negligence does not engulf the heedless traveller. For her aria 'Bergers qui le voulez connaître', Gounod rediscovers the freshness of *Mireille* and expresses in music the delicate simplicity of the *précieux* before it staled into exaggeration. The chorus evokes the spirit of older French music, the tradition of Rameau and Lully, and continues with a ballet delightfully representing the various obstacles that face the hopeful gallant on his journey. A sonnet, 'De vos traits mon âme est navrée', sung by a lovelorn shepherd, completes this charming interlude.

For a long time after *Cinq-Mars* Gounod was preoccupied with the subject of another opera. Having considered, and then rejected, Charlotte Corday as a possible heroine, he became fascinated by the story of Héloïse and Abélard. Their tragic love affair would, he felt, provide the necessary drama, though what really attracted him was the religious and philosophical aspect. His opera would tell the story of Abélard, the brilliant medieval theologian and scholar. It would recount Abélard's love for Héloïse, their secret marriage and the birth of their child. How, though, was Gounod to present Abélard's fate? (He was castrated by Héloïse's uncle to avenge the family honour.) How was he to incorporate the theological issues discussed at such length in the letters exchanged between the two lovers as Abélard wandered from monastery to monastery and Héloïse lived out the rest of her existence in a convent?

Up to a point the subject was Gounodian. It looked at first sight like another *Roméo et Juliette* with a series of extended love duets. Abélard's fate would be somewhat less painful than in real life: in order to avoid upsetting family audiences he would be killed neatly and cleanly in the good old-fashioned way by a dagger in the back. And Gounod, the former seminarist, planned to make the reconciliation of faith and reason the main theme of his opera. He went so far as to send his collaborator Louis Gallet the opening lines of an aria:

O Raison, puissance sublime,
Soeur immortelle de la foi !

As soon as the news of Gounod's latest project became known
there was amused comment by journalists. The delicate question of
precisely how the family of Héloïse were to be shown exacting their
revenge was good for a frivolous paragraph or two. In the autumn of
1878 the German critic Eduard Hanslick arrived in Paris to find out
the latest musical developments. He interviewed Gounod and heard
respectfully a long sermon the composer delivered about his opera.
Hanslick then asked, with a straight face and with something more
than academic interest, the question that the more flippant newspapers were also propounding. Gounod solemnly explained that
Abélard was murdered at the end of the fourth act. His ghost returns
in time for Act V and visits Héloïse. In a vision the audience was to
see his tomb surrounded by pilgrims at the cemetry of Père-Lachaise.
When the remains of Héloïse were laid there his corpse was to rise up
and welcome them. The opera, added Gounod, would end on a chord
full of harmony and forgiveness.

Maître Pierre, as he tentatively called his opera, lingered in his
thoughts on and off for the rest of his life. He succeeded in completing the last act which was found among his papers after his death.
Madame Gounod passed the manuscript to Saint-Saëns in 1904
asking him if he would like to complete it. He wisely did no more
than add a few recitations necessary to link isolated arias. Reynaldo
Hahn, that faithful admirer of Gounod, made a piano arrangement
of the score. In 1939 he conducted a concert performance of the last
tableau. It showed Abélard appearing in a vision to Héloïse and
continued with mystical exchanges between the two lovers. The
music was, thought one who heard it, '*du grand Gounod*'.

Work on *Maître Pierre* in 1878 was in any case held up by the
excitements involved in staging an opera which, after many vicissi-
tudes, had at last reached production. Something like ten years had
elapsed since Gounod first conceived the idea of *Polyeucte*. Those
years of his exile in England had witnessed many hazards for the
opera. It survived, as we have seen, and the episode was to end
happily, for the moment at least, on the stage of the Opéra.

Gounod found himself yet another publisher, Achille Lemoine,
who was prepared to pay him 100,000 francs for the score. In view of
Polyeucte's later career it was as well that Lemoine possessed a solid

back-list of educational works, the only musical publications guaranteed to yield steady income in a business where risks often outweigh notional profits. As if foreseeing the losses the future held in store, Lemoine prudently demanded 5,000 francs for use of the orchestral parts. The favour was denied him.

Polyeucte opened on the 7 October 1878 before a distinguished audience. They had come expecting another masterpiece from the composer of *Faust*, of *Mireille*, of *Roméo et Juliette*, of *Cinq-Mars* even. They were disappointed. The lofty 'fresco' (Gounod's own description) wearied them. When audiences found an opera tedious there was always the hope that the ballet, with its promise of charming spectacle and pretty dancers, would reward them for sitting through hours of vocal boredom. When the ballet finally came on it was difficult even for the keenest admirer to reconcile with the early Christian era the sight of Venus dancing a contemporary mazurka and nymphs pirouetting in a salon waltz.

The choice of subject did not help either. Though Corneille is traditionally spoken of with reverence, he is not, even in France, a temple to be frequented with much more than the respectful manner assumed by nominal believers on rare attendance at church. He deals, on an exalted level, in the conflict between duty and passion, between honour and the promptings of a wayward heart. His characters, often drawn from remote classical antiquity, wrestle in superhuman terms with their tragic fates. The remoter their origins, in fact, the better for Corneille's purpose since he is free to concentrate on the ethical problems that torment his Nicomède, his Andromache and his Théodore. Appreciation for the grandeur of his language and his mastery of dialectic demands an intellectual effort which the general public, except for school examination candidates, are not always prepared to make.

Polyeucte is a very Cornelian affair. The hero, son-in-law of the Roman governor of Armenia, is converted to Christianity. His conversion will, he realizes, lead to martyrdom, but he knows that above his duty to king and state lies a higher devotion to God:

> *Je dois ma vie au peuple, au prince, à sa couronne.*
> *Mais je la dois bien plus au Dieu qui me la donne.*

The dilemma of his wife Pauline is that although she is the most faithful of companions she still loves her former admirer Severus whom she believes to be dead. When Severus unexpectedly arrives in Armenia honour forbids her to renounce the marriage which family dictates have arranged for her. She will continue to bear respect and loyalty to Polyeucte, knowing all the time that she can never subdue her love for Severus. Corneille gives her a speech where she analyses the situation with serene clarity:

> *Ma raison, il est vrai, dompte mes sentiments,*
> *Mais quelque autorite que sur eux elle ait prise,*
> *Elle n'y règne pas, elle les tyrannise.*

In the last act she is inspired by Polyeucte's martyrdom to become herself a convert to Christianity.

Such was the rugged drama Gounod proposed to set before opera-goers reared on the pre-digested pap of Scribe and his fellow specialists in anodine entertainment. Even at the Comédie-Française Corneille's icy masterpiece only attracted the crowd when an actress of Rachel's stature took the role of Pauline. Nearly forty years ago Donizetti's version of the play had failed to hold the stage despite the aid of a slick libretto from Scribe. A spectacle that worked out lofty issues with the austerity of a Bach fugue and limited dramatic action to argument about love, honour and duty, was not very rewarding in operatic terms. Gounod's intellectual interests and his affection for Corneille, the translator of Thomas à Kempis' *The Imitation of Christ*, had overcome his sense of theatre.

The music in which he draped Polyeutce was singularly lifeless. It seemed that his gift of invention had been overawed by association with the marmoreal dignity of Corneille's verse. Sometimes he recalls his idol Gluck, and not unworthily, as in Pauline's invocation to Vesta. Occasionally a lusher spirit breaks through and the sensuous Barcarolle of Act II brings a more full-bodied tone to the opera. When Saint-Saëns heard Gounod play the Barcarolle to him for the first time he remarked: 'You make paganism sound so attractive that one wonders how Christianity will look beside it.' 'Well,' replied Gounod, 'I can't take away its weapons.'

In a way Saint-Saëns' reaction is a valid criticism of the opera. It is much more difficult to arouse enthusiasm for goodness than it is to hold an audience with the convincing presentation of evil. A saint is no longer interesting because his struggles are over, whereas a villain can always be relied on as a source of interesting complications. *Polyeucte* often falters. It wanders into anaemic expanses where the music, striving for simplicity, becomes monotonous. The opera congeals into oratorio. The momentous confrontation between Rome and the challenge of Christianity is reduced to a matter of sustained notes and recurring unisons. Audiences quickly tired of Gounod in his role of pontiff. After Polyeucte had been martyred on twenty-nine occasions the box-office ruled that enough was enough. He was never resuscitated.

Three years later, in 1881, Gounod made a final determined effort to retrieve his prestige as a composer of opera. *Le Tribut de Zamora* contained all the ingredients which *Polyeucte* had lacked: exotic settings, virtue in danger, reunion between a long-lost daughter and her mother, a slave auction, assassination, and love triumphant. The libretto had already been offered to Verdi. He was interested but insisted on buying it outright for 4,000 francs from one of the collaborators, Adolphe d'Ennery.

'I'm offering you this large sum because it's you,' the wily Italian said to d'Ennery. 'Usually I pay less, but the piece will belong to me and you'll be free of all risk.'

D'Ennery refused. He was a veteran of the theatre who, in the course of a life extending over three quarters of the nineteenth century, wrote hundreds of plays. The facile pathos of his *les Deux orphelines*, often filmed since, caused many tears to flow. He made numerous adaptations for the stage including *Uncle Tom's Cabin* and the fantasies of Jules Verne. He could turn his hand to anything: operas (with two other collaborators he wrote Massenet's *le Cid*), comedy, tragedy, ballet scenarios, pantomimes and farce. In private life a man of wit and culture, he was careful to allow none of this to appear in his plays. He knew the mass public well and did not wish to scare them off. His collaborator on *le Tribut de Zamora*, Jules Brésil, was a former actor who specialized in villainous roles. Brésil's long experience of the garish melodramas in which he had played fitted him well for the task of writing sensational libretti.

The plot concerns an orphaned heroine Xaïma (d'Ennery was an expert on the dramatic potentiality of orphans), her lover Manoel, Ben Saïd the commander of the Moorish army, his sympathetic brother Hadjar, and the madwoman Hermosa. As a penalty for Spanish defeat at the battle of Zamora, Oviedo and its neighbouring towns are condemned to pay annual tribute of a hundred virgins. When Ben Saïd marches in to levy the year's crop Xaïma is among the girls selected. Virginity being then a state more plentiful than today, the required number of maidens is soon rounded up and marched off to Ben Saïd's camp. Xaïma awakens his love. She also attracts the notice of Hermosa. This vindictive female, taken captive at Zamora, is protected by Ben Saïd, a pious Mohammedan who observes the lesson of the Koran by respecting her madness as a sign of divinity. Hermosa puts in a bid for Xaïma at the slave auction because, like Miss Havisham, she wants to make another woman suffer the unhappiness she has herself experienced from life. Ben Saïd outbids her and carries off the beautiful virgin, who, remembering her fiancé Manoel, threatens to throw herself into a rocky chasm. Then Hermosa recognizes Xaïma for the daughter she mislaid as a baby in the ruins of Zamora. Her sanity is restored. She murders Ben Saïd and spirits Xaïma and Manoel, disguised as a Moor in the attempt to rescue his betrothed, out of the camp. The mixture is well thickened with a sub-plot in which Manoel is revealed as the soldier who once saved Ben Saïd when he lay gravely wounded on the battlefield—a twist that helps to spin out the action with several layers of conflicting emotion.

Everyone associated with *le Tribut de Zamora* believed it would be a cast-iron success. Had not Verdi's interest proved that the clever showman recognized its dramatic value? Ever since the production of *Aïda* a few years ago at a rival theatre, the director of the Opéra had been anxious to find a similar goldmine. In Gounod's new work he was sure he had discovered it. D'Ennery and Brésil were confident, from their years of giving the public what it wanted, that they had hit on the right formula. The Austrian soprano Gabrielle Krauss, lately settled in France where she was to follow a very successful career, had been cast in the plum role of Hermosa which gave her many dramatic opportunities and helped to make up for her previous disappointment as Pauline in the ill-fated *Polyeucte*. As for Gounod, he had said after the failure of his Corneille opera: 'I'm unhorsed; now I shall have to get back into the saddle.' It was *le Tribut de Zamora* that would, he hoped, put him there.

Le Tribut de Zamora was heard at the Opéra on the 1 April 1881. In spite of the inauspicious date the evening was a success. Among the audience could be seen the bearded features of President Grévy, all unaware of the scandal which his enterprising son-in-law was eventually to unleash upon him as a result of shady financial dealings. In another box sat the fiery politician Léon Gambetta. The audience that night was a characteristically 'brilliant' assemblage of Third Republic celebrities. Gounod appeared in person to conduct his own work—the presence of the composer as conductor always sold extra seats—and was suitably emotional at the ovation he received. A certain restlessness and much craning of heads in the direction of the amphitheatre focussed attention on a handsome woman in a black dress wearing a purse on a silver chain and at her bosom a medal of remarkable size. It was none other than Georgina Weldon, a target for curious glances and hasty murmurs. She did not like the opera. The auction of virgins, she thought, was 'disgusting', and she deplored the absence of a moral. But she was thrilled to see 'the old man' again, even at a distance. He looked tired and bad-tempered, she felt. His appearance was untidy and she wished she could spruce him up and make his hair shine again.

Gounod's admirers would have found in his new opera reassuring evidence of his youthful style. Xaïma and Manoel exchange their vows in an aubade full of pretty sentiment, and there is a 'bell' chorus that has an innocent lilt in the happy spirit of *Mireille*. The virgins march into durance accompanied by a stately tune of elegant melancholy. Another typically langorous melody sung by women's voices greets the Moorish splendour of Ben Saïd's palace.

The leading character is not Xaïma, in different circumstances a made-to-measure Gounod heroine, but the domineering Hermosa. She has the biggest scenes in the opera and the most spectacular arias. As a madwoman she thrills the audience with her bloodthirsty ravings. As a mother she stirs their pity. Finally, as murderess of the villain Ben Saïd, she wins their sympathy. Or that, at least, is how the librettists planned it. All the big moments are reserved for Hermosa, ranging from the pathetic '*Pitié! pitié!*' lamenting her lost child, to the bombastic '*Debout! enfants de l'Ibérie!*' This latter, immediately hailed by Gounodians as a Spanish *la Marseillaise*, was, in the words of a hostile critic, 'bawled' with great energy by Gabrielle Krauss. It has all the crude bounce of the prize-giving marches the composer used to write in his Orphéon days. Encores were demanded before the opera could continue. And Madame Krauss, supposed to be in a faint from her exertions, came forward to shake hands with Gounod on the rostrum before returning upstage and going on with her interrupted swoon. An irreverent laugh swept through the audience.

Gounod enjoyed his evening. He belonged to the type of conductor who favours elaborate gesture and a wealth of intricate fingerwork. The smallest bassoon entry was charmed into existence with the care of God creating the world. Arms at full stretch conjured the harps to sing and fierce jabs with the baton set the percussion in a roar. He was on his feet all the time in lordly contempt of the chair provided by a kindly management to lighten the strain on his sixty-three-year-old frame. The sweat bubbled on his forehead as he bowed to the applause and clasped Madame Krauss in a hug of iron.

Le Tribut de Zamora at first gratified expectations by achieving forty-seven performances in two years. In 1885 three more brought it up to a total of fifty. These were not the result of any popular demand but of a resolute tactic by Gounod and his librettists. Their contract included a fee to be paid by the publisher—in this case Choudens—when the opera had been played fifty times. Well aware of the ploy that was being used against him, Choudens wriggled hotly and invented a host of legalistic reasons for not paying up. In the end he capitulated and was forced to admit that the composer had beaten him at his own game. The story goes that early in their acquaintance Choudens asked why Gounod wore such a shabby old hat. 'It's my *Faust* hat', Gounod replied in a tart reminder of how Choudens outwitted him over royalties from that opera. When, not long after *le Tribut de Zamora*, Gounod saw the publisher wearing an equally shabby overcoat, he was wryly informed: 'This is my *Zamora* coat.'

Although *le Tribut de Zamora* at least enabled Gounod to settle an old score with Choudens it brought little else to comfort him. The opera added nothing to his reputation. It is too reminiscent of his earlier work. The lovers' duets could have been taken from *Philémon et Baucis*. Frequent and often grotesque reminders of *Faust* occur in the most unlikely places. The conception of the work was already old-fashioned when it appeared in 1881, and at the height of the Wagnerian revolution Gounod was still trifling with cavatinas, romances and arias that breathed the musty air which had settled on the operas of his compatriots who flourished in the eighteen-fifties. *Le Tribut de Zamora* was his last work for the stage. Henceforward he was to be a public monument.

XIV

The Patriarch – Oratorios – A Little Symphony

Until the eighteen-sixties the plaine Monceau was a stretch of open countryside to the north-west of Paris. It was sparsely dotted with the outbuildings of market-gardens and dairy farms where ladies of frail health sometimes called to buy fresh milk. The only other Parisians to venture here were sufferers from consumption whose doctors had advised them to sleep in cow-sheds.

Then Paris began to break its bounds. The avenue de Villiers cut through the fields and levelled trees that once had sheltered grazing cows. Expensive mansions lined the sides of its broad expanse. Millionaires indulged their secret fantasies with a riot of Greek pediments and Flemish turrets. Mansarded roofs lay next to massy Egyptian pillars. Pseudo-Renaissance façades glowered across the road at buoyant reproductions of the Alhambra. Soon after its starting-point in the boulevard de Courcelles the new avenue passed through the place Malesherbes. Here, at number twenty, Gounod set up house in 1879.

The whole of one side was taken up by a reduced copy of the château de Blois, the whim of a rich sugar tycoon. It now houses the Banque de France. Among the lawns and flowers stands Gustave Doré's monument to Alexandre Dumas with d'Artagnan keeping watch below. His son lived nearby. Each day as he passed he threw a cheery 'Bonjour, Papa!' to Daddy's graven image. Now Dumas *fils* has his own statue. A granite 'Dame aux Camélias' lies on the pedestal. At one time, wherever you looked in the square, the place seemed full of the Dumas family, for there was also a statue of grandfather Dumas, the general, and people talked of re-naming the place Malesherbes the 'place des Trois-Dumas'. A fourth statue represents Sarah Bernhardt as Phèdre.

Gounod's neighbours were successful theatrical folk, bankers, celebrated authors and fashionable artists. The home at number Twenty was designed and built by his architect brother-in-law. Behind the Renaissance façade were three storeys, each occupied by various branches of the clan. Gounod took over the second floor. His sister-in-law moved in below, and his son Jean lived on the third floor. When his daughter Jeanne married she and her husband established themselves on the ground floor.

A massive wood staircase carved in Henri II style led up to Gounod's apartments. It had been decorated by his nephew Guillaume Dubufe with sketches of characters from the operas: Marguerite was silhouetted at her spinning-wheel, a white and gold Juliette peered out from a blue background, and Sapho stroked her lyre. A winter garden on the first floor enclosed the brightness of flowers and palms as a contrast with heavy oak and sombre carpets. Gounod's workroom, high-ceilinged and lit through stained-glass windows, had oak panels and churchlike vaulting. A platform at the end of the room supported an organ. (The bellows were pumped in the basement by a hydraulic machine.) A medallion of Christ's head was prominently fixed to the instrument. The writing table, which contained a movable keyboard to be pulled out when needed, stood directly beneath the window. Scenes from the Passion were carved on a wooden Renaissance mantelpiece embellished with a bronze medallion of Joan of Arc. A Pleyel grand piano filled the centre of the room. One of the walls had book-cases crammed with religious and philosophical works and scores. The rest of the furniture included a pair of divans draped in Persian rugs, small tables and chairs.

Here Gounod received the visitors who called in large numbers. His manner was easy and welcoming. He usually wore a black velvet smoking-jacket and a white flannel shirt. Around his neck was a loosely knotted silk handkerchief. A small black cap perched on the silvery hair at the back of his head. The beard, white and luxuriant, spread down to his chest. On his feet he wore patent leather shoes. (He had always been proud of those small, neatly-shaped feet.)

Just over half the year was spent in the place Malesherbes. When summer arrived he would escape to Saint-Cloud where a chalet in the garden of his country home became his study. The fogs of November drove him back to Paris. He liked walking, and often, when going home on foot, he would call in on his friend Lalo whose home was nearby. His visits there were looked forward to with pleasure. His voice, never very strong, was thin with age, but he could still delight listeners when he sat at the piano and sang in the delicate tone that hinted at rather than expressed feeling.

Official recognition during an artist's lifetime often comes long after his original powers are spent. A reputation takes years to reach the ears of government. This was the case with Gounod. In 1880 he was promoted to Grand-officier in the Légion d'honneur, only one step below the highest grade in that order. It was a rank usually kept for generals, admirals and other members of society more esteemed than mere composers. The honour was in fact being paid not to the Gounod of sixty-two but to the composer of twenty years before, the man who had written *Faust*, *Roméo et Juliette* and *Mireille*.

At home and abroad Gounod in the eighteen-eighties was the incarnation of modern French music. No one else could equal his reputation. Many years would have to elapse before Berlioz, who died in 1869, emerged as the giant whom posterity has belatedly acknowledged. True, Saint-Saëns had founded the Société Nationale de Musique as long ago as 1871. This was a rallying-point for composers such as Franck, Lalo, Fauré and Castillon. At its concerts was given the new music that took on where Gounod had left off and gradually supplanted his influence in advanced circles. Other rising men were Chabrier and Duparc. Yet it was a long time before the general public recognized their gifts. In the eyes of the average opera-lover Gounod was supreme.

The mantle of patriarch descended on willing shoulders. Gounod and his snowy beard, his clerical garb, and his episcopal manner, was a celebrity to be classed among famous politicians, actresses and society figures. He granted interviews readily. His conversation was full of quotable remarks and no journalist came away disappointed from the place Malesherbes. Explaining his preference for extemporizing in C major, he would say that it was the key in which God existed. He liked, he said, to think of Bach and Beethoven as marble columns of the temple of music with Mozart as its high priest. On subjects other than music he was just as fluent. 'Children', he would announce, 'are roses in the garden of life.' Social problems did not find him at a loss for words. He foresaw revolution. The family, the basis of society, was under attack from divorce. Property would be next to suffer. As for strikes he feared that, encouraged by the fomentors of disorder, they would end by tainting the whole of the French working class. Democracy was dying and ruin lay not far off.

It was all good sound doctrine that middle-class readers of *Figaro* were comforted to hear from the mouth of a distinguished man. And Gounod was no less pleased at the opportunity of expressing it. To some extent he was able to make up for the absence of the pulpit which he would have attained had not his musical career taken him in another direction. Indeed, he might congratulate himself on enjoying the best of both worlds. His reputation, achieved in the profane surroundings of the theatre, gave an air of authority to his public statements that an archbishop would have envied.

From the date of *le Tribut de Zamora* until the end of his life he showed a keen interest in extra-musical subjects. In 1882 the sexagenarian remembered his infancy with an autobiographical contribution to a symposium on the breast-feeding of new-born infants. He wrote about the place of the artist in society and the relationship between nature and art. One of his plans was to publish a series of 'philosophical poems' examining the links that bound art and philosophy. The former disciple of Lamennais rediscovered the fascination of social and political questions. He took up his theological studies once again and made copious notes, jotting down ideas for articles, books and addresses. Manuscript essays signed 'l'abbé Gounod' treated of faith and reason, the nature of prayer and the history of religions. The diligent abbé translated the Pope's Christmas sermons and examined Renan's *Vie de Jésus* with a critical eye. He addressed himself to such topics as State persecution of Catholics, the place of science in art, and the problems of representative assemblies.

His musical writings were prolific. At the annual October assembly of the Institut de France in 1882 he read a paper on Mozart's *Don Giovanni* that summed up his lifelong admiration for what he had always regarded as a miracle of art. (It was one of the few occasions when he gained the wholehearted approval of Bernard Shaw, himself a fervid Mozartian.) He gave up a trip to Italy in order to see the first performance of *Henry VIII*, a new opera by his friend Saint-Saëns, and wrote a long appreciative article about it. No publisher who asked him for a preface was refused, whether the matter concerned Berlioz' correspondence or an anthology of theatrical reviews.

His literary activities did not prevent him from writing music. The marriage of Queen Victoria's eighth child, the Duke of Albany, brought from him a Wedding March for three trombones and organ. *The Musical Times* ingeniously sought to explain this unusual combination by remarking that Gounod, writing 'not for a small company, however illustrious, but for an empire', had presumably felt that such an occasion positively demanded a unique choice of instruments. The march was said to have been commanded by the Queen Empress. It won great success, especially for the snatches from the National Anthem which clanged out towards the end. Stimulated by this favourable reception Gounod wrote a 'Wedding March No. 2' that was praised for its 'exceptional merits'. Many copies were sold. Two years later the music-loving Duke, ever frail in constitution, suddenly died, not from a surfeit of Wedding Marches but from the effects of a fall in the Nautical Club at Cannes. The title was extinguished and Victorians lamented the memory of an amateur singer who had taken his encore at a village concert 'with the perfect simplicity and unaffectedness that stamps the English gentleman'.

The manuscript of Gounod's nuptial tribute to the Duke of Albany occupied five pages. That of his oratorio *Rédemption*, which followed soon after, takes up no less than five hundred and sixty-six. The idea had first come to him in 1867 when he wrote two of the items. Twelve years later he completed it. The oratorio begins with a prologue describing the creation of the world and goes on to represent Calvary and the Crucifixion, the Resurrection, and finally the Pentecost.

There was much good will towards the composer in England. His misadventures with Georgina had not affected admiration for his music. The Committee of the Birmingham Festival offered him £4,000 to come and conduct the first performance of *Rédemption*. This perhaps explains why the manuscript dedication to his mother and his children was diplomatically changed, in the printed score, for one to Queen Victoria. Gounod's 'sacred trilogy' was so well received that two performances were necessary. On the 30 August and the 1 September 1882, he conducted four hundred singers and an orchestra of a hundred and forty. He had planned the layout of these large forces in careful detail. The effect thrilled the thousands who heard it. Cardinal Newman attended the rehearsal, by which time it was clear that the Festival was set for one of the biggest triumphs in its history. *Rédemption* travelled the length of Britain and proved just as successful in Europe and the rest of the world. The Festival committee recouped nearly all their expenses by ceding the international performing rights to Novello's. How Gounod must have regretted accepting a lump sum instead of a royalty! How, in private, he must have cursed that 'the old sweep' had 'done' him again.

A generation that regarded the oratorios of Handel and Mendelssohn as the twin peaks of musical achievement found *Rédemption* a model worthy to set beside them. Musicians both amateur and professional believed that Gounod had renewed an old tradition with the vigour of his modern genius. English composers of what the Victorians called 'sacred music' were in general much influenced by *Rédemption*. For many years afterwards a heavy flavour of Gounod permeated the works they wrote.

Today it is difficult to understand the immense enthusiasm *Rédemption* stimulated—as difficult as it is to enter into the spirit of a best-selling novel a hundred years back. Gounod's oratorio seems as foreign to us as the once-popular stories of Mrs de la Pasture. It does not even have that quality of nostalgia which sometimes acts as a slender barrier to hold back an inferior work from tumbling over the edge into oblivion. One can only assume that *Rédemption* answered a contemporary need and spoke to the minds and hearts of its hearers with a directness that overwhelmed them. It is astonishing to find Saint-Saëns, usually an acute and penetrating critic, singling out the oratorios and religious music as destined for survival when the rest of Gounod's work is forgotten. Even more surprising is the fact that Saint-Saëns, an atheist, readily admitted to experiencing emotion when he listened to Gounod's 'sacred' compositions. If so shrewd an artist was affected like this, no wonder the average music-lover went into ecstasies over *Rédemption*.

A theme presumably representing Jesus comes and goes throughout the oratorio. It is reminiscent of the leading motif from Liszt's symphonic poem *Tasso*: a tune effective enough once heard, but tedious when repeated over and over again on a yearning violin without variation or development. Worse still is the March to Calvary. This would have been adequate, even charming, in a comic opera as a portrayal of some *buffo* character. As an attempt at depicting one of the most tragic episodes in the story of humanity it is trivial. The scenes are linked by a Narrator who, frequently intoning on a repeated note, deserves to qualify as one of the most grinding bores in music. Throughout the Crucifixion a pair of sighing flutes burble the Jesus theme again. Odd contrasts strike the ear: a chorus, 'Lord Jesus, Thou to all bringest light and salvation', written in the hearty tradition of the Anglican hymnal, is followed soon after by a piece for women's voices, 'How shall we by ourselves have strength to roll away the stone from the tomb ?', which is strongly scented with the *odor di femina* so typical of Gounod in his swooning mood.

The blend of operatic and religious elements is clumsily mixed. The reason, as Bernard Shaw pointed out, is that 'those angelic progressions which lift the voice from semitone to semitone on ineffable resolutions of diminished sevenths on to six-four chords, though beyond question most heavenly, are so welded in our minds to Gretchen's awakening from her miserable prison dreams to the consciousness of Faust's presence in her cell, that it is not easy to keep in the oratorio frame of mind when they begin. In fact a knowledge of Gounod's operas is a disadvantage at the Albert Hall on Redemption nights, even to the ordinary occasional opera-goer.' What is even more of a disadvantage is the Apostles' Hymn in *Rédemption*. Though disguised as 'The Word is Flesh become', it is nothing more than an awkward reproduction of the march in Act I of *la Nonne sanglante*, where the assembled barons, also intent on divine matters, chant '*C'est Dieu qui nous appelle*'. A charitable explanation would be that absent-mindedness had caused Gounod to fall back on an opera written thirty years before.

Turning down an invitation to conduct *Rédemption* in America, he went home again and prepared for a revival of *Sapho*. Duly refurbished and expanded into four acts, his first opera stood up well to the footlights in the spring of 1884. Gabrielle Krauss enjoyed a personal success in the role originally sung by Pauline Viardot, and Gounod as conductor directed the proceedings with vigour. Next day, on the 3 April, the tireless composer faced a mass audience in the cavernous depths of the Trocadéro and led chorus and orchestra at the first Paris performance of *Rédemption*. Such was his prestige that this work, so alien to the French tradition, made the vast Trocadéro ring with applause.

Only a few weeks later his pleasant memory of excitements at the Trocadéro was soured by news from England. Over the past ten years Georgina Weldon had been pursuing him steadily through the English courts. Among his letters one day he found a writ summoning him to appear in the Queen's Bench Division. Prudently he stayed at home. In his absence judgement was given against him for £11,640, a sum covering Georgina's secretarial work on his behalf, board and lodge at Tavistock House, and damages for libels he had uttered about her on his return to Paris and since. The glorious news came to Georgina as she was setting off to spend six months in Holloway prison. She had been sent there for herself libelling another French musician, the conductor Jules Rivière. Her life was crammed with fearful symmetries like this.

'Oh the excitement in Paris and the rage of the old man!' she telegraphed to a friend. 'I shall be able to get judgement against him in Paris and bother him for the remainder of his life.'

Then she returned from the court to Holloway where she spent 'six happy months' and where the Matron treated her kindly. Her relationship with the Governor was excellent. When she left they exchanged photographs of each other signed with affectionate inscriptions. A crowd awaited her outside. In an open barouche drawn by four horses and attended by coachman and groom, she led a procession estimated to number seventeen thousand people. The barouche was unhorsed and cheering supporters dragged it, Georgina bowing gracefully to the acclamations, through Green Park.

She was literally to get no change out of Gounod. It soon became apparent that the judgement could not be executed in the French courts. She tried another tactic: when, in August 1885, the Birmingham Festival Committee invited him to conduct his new oratorio *Mors et Vita*, she sought a judgement giving her all the royalties he would earn on the work. This she was refused. But Georgina was a dogged fighter. She warned—and she was here within her rights—that if he came to England she would immediately have him arrested for debt. So he was unable to repeat his earlier appearance in Birmingham. Next year Queen Victoria gave her royal command for a performance of *Mors et Vita* in the Albert Hall. She was Gounod's most distinguished admirer in England. Would he be allowed to attend and conduct his oratorio this time? A solicitor (his name was Harding) was sent to Georgina. He pleaded with her to lift her embargo. She remained obdurate.

'I am more than astonished at your impudence!' she retorted. The moment Gounod set foot on English soil, she insisted, he would be clapped into prison. Her Majesty was obliged to forego the presence of her favourite composer.

Despite Gounod's absence from Birmingham on the 26 August the first performance of *Mors et Vita* under Hans Richter was as successful as that of *Rédemption* had been. Receipts amounted to £25,000 and Novello's struck another good bargain with the composer. ('Pray do not pay Mr Gounod who truly does not need it, so immense sums', Dvorak wrote plaintively to them, 'for what would be left for me?') Queen Victoria sent a personal message of congratulations. The English press endorsed her opinion.

Mors et Vita was intended as a continuation of *Rédemption*. 'It will perhaps be asked why, in the title, I have placed death before life,' Gounod observed in his preface. 'It is because in the order of eternal things death precedes life, although in the order of temporal things life precedes death. Death is only the end of that existence which dies each day; it is only the end of a continual "dying". But it is the first moment, and, as it were, the birth, of that which dies no more.'

The standard is a little higher than that of *Rédemption*. The home-made text of the former is replaced with passages taken from the liturgy. The Latin words give a dignity to music that otherwise is not often memorable. The first part, 'Death', is in effect a requiem that lasts for two-and-a-half hours. Part two, 'Judgement', mingles nineteenth-century harmonies with Palestrina. The final section of the trilogy, 'The Vision of Saint John', takes up in the chorus 'Ego sum Alpha et Omega' an attractive theme heard earlier in the Kyrie and elsewhere. The Judex begins with a broad operatic melody so rich and self-confident that one is tempted to feel a guilty pleasure in it. It is some compensation for the mournful repetitions on an endlessly sustained note that have given the listener a far more convincing impression of Eternity than anything Gounod deliber-ately intended.

The extent of his popularity in England may be judged by the manner in which Protestant audiences welcomed an intensely Catholic work. Saint-Saëns was struck by the paradox: 'On one of those days of awful black rainy weather that London specializes in, I saw the vast auditorium of the Albert Hall filled to its upper galleries with a host of eight thousand people, silent and attentive as they listened devotedly, while following the text with their eyes, to a giant performance of *Mors et Vita* given by a thousand performers, the huge organ and the best soloists in England.'

There is no doubt that Gounod wrote with sincerity and belief in the religious content of his music. But sincerity is not enough to ensure a great work of art. However expert the choral writing may sometimes be, however skilful the orchestration, *Mors et Vita* and *Rédemption* were fated to moulder unheard once the fashion that called them into existence had passed.

Much more attractive than either of these dropsical oratorios are two smaller works he composed at about this time. One of them, the *Petite symphonie* of 1885, is still played and recorded today. He would doubtless have been shocked had he known that this unambitious piece was to survive long after his sacred 'frescoes' were dead. He wrote it for a friend, the international flute virtuoso Paul Taffanel, who had set up in 1879 the Société de musique de chambre pour instruments à vent. Taffanel was the founder of the modern French flute school and trained a number of brilliant players. Besides teaching the instrument at the Conservatoire he also conducted the orchestra at the Opéra and the Société des Concerts du Conservatoire. His *17 Grands Exercices journaliers de mécanisme* were known to the weary fingers of generations of aspiring flautists and went through several editions.

The *Petite symphonie* was written for a chamber combination of flute and a pair each of oboes, clarinets, horns and bassoons. Gounod naturally saw to it that Taffanel had opportunities for display. The flute solo of the 'adagio cantabile' spins out a long cool melody of irresistible charm with ornamental flourishes that are an integral part of the line. As elsewhere the effect is vocal, operatic even, though here Gounod was able to control the embellishments and did not have to suffer the interference of prima donnas. Each instrument is allowed its moments and there is no favouritism in the way good things are distributed. The horns lead the celebrations in the Scherzo and get it off to a dashing start as well as highlighting vital points in the score and generally underpinning the other instruments with their friendly rumble. In the Allegretto it is the oboes and clarinets that take turns to hustle on the busy little theme of the movement. The bassoons are ever present to offer a witty footnote. The *Petite symphonie* is a perfect example of intimate chamber-music in which the scale of the work is absolutely right.

The other miniature that bobbed in the wake of *Mors et Vita* was the *Suite concertante*, a sort of concerto for '*piano pédalier*' or 'pedalier pianoforte' as the English version had it. This instrument grew out of a pedalling device which, attached to a piano, enabled the pianist to practise organ-playing at home and to improve pedal technique. It was very popular in France where a soloist called Lucie Palicot gave recitals of music adapted for it. Gounod's *Suite concertante* was one of the pieces specially written for the instrument. He also dedicated it to Lucie Palicot. She gave the first performance at the Salle Érard in 1885 with Gounod deputizing for the orchestra at a second piano. Two years later it was heard at a London Philharmonic Society concert. The 'Entrée de fête' starts with an endearing fanfare, a theme that surfaces again from time to time among passages of broken chords. This is followed by a 'Chasse' marked 'allegro con fuoco', though the stern admonition is belied by the rollicking nature of the horn calls and their intimations not of the hunt's fierce pleasures but of Marie-Antoinette's make-believe rustic diversions. A 'Romance' in aria form and a humorous 'Tarantelle' close a piece which, though not as sophisticated as the *Petite symphonie*, provides innocent enjoyment.

Gounod's talent for well-written music, small of dimension but finished in artistry, was forgotten when he composed his *Messe de Jeanne d'Arc*. A few months after the *Suite concertante* delighted listeners at the St James's Hall he came to Rheims to conduct his new mass in honour of France's patron saint. In a spirit of worship, he declared without the glimmer of a smile, he had wished to write his Mass in the cathedral while kneeling upon the stones where Joan herself had stood. On the 24 July, the anniversary of Joan's entry into the town and the coronation of Charles VII, he directed the chorus, the organ, the eight trumpets, the three trombones and harps for which he had scored the work. The mixture of plagiarisms from his incidental music for the play *Jeanne d'Arc* and of neo-Palestrinian techniques was greeted by the faithful and soon forgotten.

Undeterred, he went on composing the religious music that was all that really interested him now. Masses, prayers, motets and canticles dripped from him as the rain from heaven. He extemporized for hours at the organ in his study. The sunlight came in through the stained-glass window and lit up his snowy beard, dappled the sparse white hairs at the back of his head and gleamed around him like a halo. A visitor found him looking like 'one of those apostles, shining with eternal life and glory, that you can see in the pictures of a Rubens or a Titian.'

&XV&

'Old Man Gone and I Fast Going'

Though he appeared to want no more than the cathedral atmosphere of his organ room in the place Malesherbes and the reverence of admirers who came to hear the Master discourse Bach and Palestrina, reminders of profane success were always intruding on the old man. In 1885 Madame Carvalho gave a reluctant farewell performance. She was fifty-eight and her voice had decayed. One evening at the Opéra she sang for the last time extracts from *Mireille*—the work she and her husband so cruelly mutilated—and the garden scene from *Faust*. The woman who had helped to spread Gounod's fame and, at the same time, injured its merit, was suddenly no longer there to irritate him.

The five-hundredth performance of *Faust* at the Opéra in 1887 was timed for the day of Saint Charles on the 4 November, a thoughtful act that must have pleased him. It was celebrated with pomp. A revival of *Roméo et Juliette* in 1889, with Patti and Jean de Reszke, so excited him that illness interfered with his direction of rehearsals, though he recovered in time to conduct the first performance. The closing months as well brought a production of *Mireille* in the Carvalho version. It was, Gounod protested resignedly, 'inept'.

Yet another revival, that of Barbier's play *Jeanne d'Arc* with Gounod's incidental music, put the evangelizing musician in touch with the worldly circles of the 'straight' theatre. Disturbed by the wicked ways of the star Sarah Bernhardt, he tried to rescue her immortal soul. For weeks Paris was entertained with reports of the latest developments in the struggle to save her from the Devil. He exhorted Sarah to carry over into her private life those virtues which, as Joan of Arc on the stage, she portrayed so convincingly. He thought to see the flames already licking at her feet. His most eloquent arguments were deployed so that he might yet snatch this

214

brand from the burning. As history knows, he did not succeed. There was, however, a supporting player in the cast, a Mademoiselle Nevada, who, impressed by Gounod's pleading, renounced her sinful life and agreed to be converted. He presided, with genial satisfaction, over the service at which she was received into the Church.

He had long since given up writing for the theatre. Church music alone absorbed him, and in the last decade of the century he was gladdened by the reawakening of interest in Bach and Palestrina. Forty years ago he had pioneered their cause. Now a young man, Charles Bordes, musical director at the church of Saint Gervais and a former pupil of César Franck, was touring the country with his 'Chanteurs de Saint-Gervais' and revealing the beauties of old music to audiences which had rarely known such things existed. Inspired by a fervour that overcame material obstacles, Bordes was an adept at making something out of nothing, at recruiting choirs from amateurs and chance acquaintances. 'God will provide,' he would say. Somehow finance always seemed to turn up at the last minute and he was able to continue with his concerts. At the same time the renewal of church music was helped forward by work done in the abbey of Solesmes, where monks restored the texts of Gregorian chant and cleared away the errors and misconceptions which over centuries of performance had gradually obscured the music's true spirit.

All this made Gounod rejoice. During the Holy Week services at Saint Gervais, when the music was played as it should be in its correct form and style, he must often have thought of his own attempts on these lines at the Église des Missions étrangères. At last his hopes were fulfilled. What he had striven for as a young man he was, as an elderly composer, to see achieved by like-minded enthusiasts. Bach and Palestrina, he told Bordes, were for musicians the Fathers of the Church: 'It is up to us to remain their sons, and I thank you for your help.' Another echo of his youthful ardour was sounded by the fiftieth anniversary of Lacordaire's restoration of the Dominican order in France. He wrote a 'Consécration' and a 'Quam dilecta' with thankful heart.

The patriarch's family was growing. When his daughter Jeanne married the Baron Pierre de Lassus Saint Geniès, Gounod's music accompanied the ceremony and the couple left the church to the strains of 'Ave Maria'. The wedding party returned to the place

Malesherbes and was joined by Liszt, then in Paris to hear his *Graner Mass* at Saint-Eustache. He said to Gounod: 'I haven't had time to buy flowers for Jeanne, but here's another sort of bouquet.' He sat at the piano and played with dazzling verve his fantasy on the waltz from *Faust*. Next year Gounod announced the arrival of his grandson Jean, who with admirable timing had chosen not to disturb the peace of the Sabbath: 'On Saturday evening at seven o'clock, my Jeanne gave birth to a son who is doing very well, and so is his mother. . . . '

Nearly every Sunday he played the organ at mass in the church near his Saint-Cloud home. He had not lost his appetite for theological debate and he enjoyed brisk arguments with the curé about Saint Augustine and Thomas of Aquinas. When, in Gounod's opinion, mass was being said too quickly, he would call the abbé to order by playing on the organ a sustained 'Et cum spiritu tuo' and a lingering Amen. The offer of a million francs to go on an American tour did not tempt him. He preferred to divide his time between Saint Cloud and Paris. When in Paris he usually walked, very slowly, and paused frequently to address his companion in tones so loud that passers-by turned round in surprise. On his promenades through Paris he once heard a street-organ grinding out at a dizzy pace Siebel's aria 'Faites-lui mes aveux'. He stopped, horrified.

'Ah, friend', he cried, 'not so fast! Look, let me turn the handle.' The notes came out at the proper speed. 'This is the tempo', Gounod added, 'and let me tell you, my good fellow, I wrote it.'

Madame Gounod protected him from unwelcome visitors and defended the venerable sage with untiring care. Partly this was because absent-mindedness and meditation unsuited him for practical matters. Partly, too, she still feared the designs of other women. She knew that, however old a man may be, however busy his existence, he can always find time for dalliance. The adventure with Georgina took place a long time ago, but there were others. She had realized that no woman can fully trust a man until he is dead.

He never carried a wallet. On excursions into the outside world Madame Gounod would count out a small amount of change for his pocket money. Saturday was his day for attendance at the Institut, and he went by train from Saint Cloud to the gare Saint Lazare. Many people knew his face and greeted him as he passed by. At the station he took a cab. A cabman once said to him: 'Monsieur Gounod, I'm proud of having driven the composer of *Faust*.' The composer replied, handing him a good tip: 'My friend, you've a fine turn of speed—you'd have made a good conductor.'

He was above the battle, too far off in time to feel jealous of the young composers who were making their way. Debussy aroused his curiosity. As a member of the judge's committee at the Institut Gounod had voted in favour of the twenty-two-year-old composer's entry *l'Enfant prodigue*. 'You have genius, young fellow', Gounod is reported to have told him. He gave Debussy a recommendation that enabled him to find work as an accompanist. They wrote to each other, and it is probable that Gounod's letters were written in the paternal, encouraging tone he had used towards Bizet, the protégé of earlier years.

Another young musician caught his eye. Henri Busser, a promising musician of Swiss descent, had come to Paris from his native Toulouse and done well in his studies at the Conservatoire. He had much talent but little money. One useful source of income was a music lover who, refusing to study harmony for fear of spoiling his 'originality', paid Busser to write down and correct the little pieces to which he put his name. The amateur composer was a Boulangist in politics and, with Busser's help, created a 'Marche de l'oeillet rouge' as a tribute to the General and the red carnation that symbolized his movement. At the famous military review of 14 July 1886, Busser saw General Boulanger win the hearts of the crowds at the start of a lightning campaign that made him, temporarily, the darling of France. That evening the musician accompanied the entertainer Paulus when he sang *En r'venant de la r'vue*, the song that became identified with Boulangism. The General, with a politician's courtesy, told Busset that he liked music, especially that of Gounod and Massenet. Was he not like Werther, thought Busser, to die for love by committing suicide in Brussels on the grave of his mistress?

Busser graduated from the Conservatoire with a Grand Prix and memories of Erik Satie, who, playing the piano in cabarets at night, followed lessons during the day and showed himself, as everyone thought, to be a student of little talent. Busser's teacher was anxious to find a job more suitable for his pupil than revising the Boulangist composer's efforts and mentioned his name to Gounod. Some time later, when Busser thought Gounod must have forgotten all about him, a letter arrived addressed to 'Monsieur Bussère'. In it Gounod told him that the curé of Saint-Cloud was ready to offer him the post of organist. Scarcely able to believe his luck, Busser hastened out to

Saint-Cloud. At the little station he met his benefactor who had come there to post his letters.

'There you are, Mr Organist,' chuckled Gounod. 'You'll have to pray to God the way it suits me. I shall be listening to you each Sunday. You can play me Bach, Mendelssohn. . . . '

Gounod took him home and went over his compositions with him. After that they were to meet regularly. Sometimes it was difficult because Madame Gounod barred the way with her 'Come another day, my child, you'll weary your Master.' When the door shut in his face Busser would slip through the back kitchen and up the servant's stair to reach Gounod's room. They had long conversations together. It was pleasant for Gounod to hold forth in the certainty that his disciple hung on every word.

Wagner frightened him a little. He likened his effect on music to that of a storm suddenly rising in a forest. 'You only have time to clamber up a tree and hold on like grim death. Your hair is blown about, your face streaked with blood, but when the storm dies off and recedes a little, you get down from your shelter, you shake yourself and you enjoy the pleasure of having escaped a great danger. The hurricane, my dear child, is Wagner or Wagnerism. It is fearsome but it passes on. The important thing is not to let yourself be carried away. . . . '

What, Busser asked, was the unfailing secret of Gounod's art? The answer came quick and firm. 'Melody alone counts in music. Recently I heard a modern work at a big concert: it had lots of notes and the orchestra spread itself in great waves of sound. Well, I'd have given anything to hear a melody, however short. Whether in the concert hall or in the theatre, everything is based on melody. Music-loving audiences, even experienced ones, prefer works to have clarity and ideas that go right to the heart and not only to the brain. . . . Melody, always melody, my dear child, that is the sole, the unique secret of our art.' Melody, he added, would ever be the purest expression of human thought.

He practised what he preached, at least as a musician. Clear, flowing, spontaneous melody is the characteristic of Gounod at his best. The individual accent of Faust's encounter with Marguerite opened a new chapter in French music. Juliette's '*Non! non, ce n'est pas le jour*' continued this novelty of expression. Yet *Faust*, that flawed masterpiece, encouraged him to over-extend a talent that was for the lyrical and the intimate. The mirage of grand opera betrayed him into territory where his real gifts were stultified. The essence of Gounod and the purest examples of his genius will be found in parts of *Roméo et Juliette*, in *le Médecin malgré lui*, in *Philémon et Baucis*, in the adorable *Mireille*, and in a dozen or so exquisite songs.

Gounod's example helped to raise French music out of the slough into which it was beginning to decline. His plea for a return to the standards of older masters put in train the reform of church music that Bordes was later to complete. When he chose Mozart and Gluck as his models he directed attention towards influences that were healthy and needful. He was a cultured man whose acquaintance with literature and art gave added persuasiveness to his advocacy. He restored to his native music a quality of Frenchness it had been in danger of losing through sterile imitation of foreign trends. It was this Frenchness that, a few decades later, Jean Cocteau as spokesman of 'les Six' was to proclaim as an ideal.

The renewal Gounod inspired also brought in its train undesirable things. The facile side of his talent, the more obvious tricks of a style dedicated to charm, were imitated by ambitious composers. The shadow of his great success fell like a blight on musicians lacking his originality and stifled their aptitude. Others who were strong enough—like Massenet, despite the nickname that mocked him as '*la fille de Gounod*'—absorbed his example and applied it in their own personal manner. Fauré is another spiritual descendant of Gounod, as the early songs and choral writing show. This was a debt Fauré gladly acknowledged and he did not stint his admiration of *Faust*. Gounod's fluent treatment of speech rhythms, his loosening of poetic metre, and his wish, never realized except for the little 'Ave Maria de l'Enfant' of his closing years, to capture in music the freer cadences of prose, was to influence Debussy with *Pelléas et Mélisande*. It was not only gratitude for small practical favours that moved Debussy to respect Gounod. He applauded the way in which he had preserved his individuality against the contagion of Wagner and opened the door to Bizet. Gounod, for Debussy, represented an important phase in the evolution of French sensibility.[1]

He had so much wanted to be a churchman. The rituals of the Catholic church and their symbolism of mysteries beyond human understanding never failed to enthral him. Their appeal was as much

[1] According to Henri Busser, Debussy's favourite Gounod opera was *le Médecin malgré lui*: the wit, lightness and orchestral writing were a revelation to him.

aesthetic as spiritual. How he would have liked to be a keeper of the shrine, a hierophant with a jewelled mitre and a pectoral cross, revealing the word of God and murmuring beautiful words amid chain-swung censers teeming! The theatre, like the church, deals in showmanship (was not the theatre born of the church, as Sacha Guitry used to say, a fact that the church, through professional jealousy, could never forgive?), and both these spheres evoked a strong response from a man with Gounod's keen dramatic instinct. When asked the obvious question of why he had not become a priest he would reply that he did not feel he had the moral strength to hear confession from women. The chief reason, one that he may only have admitted to himself in private, was the strain of materialism that kept him earthbound when he most ardently wanted to rise. He failed to resolve the clash between his longing for material success and his spiritual yearnings. It was as well for music that he did not. A bishop would never have given us *le Médecin malgré lui* or *Mireille*.

The music sometimes reflects the troubled contours of a personality rarely at ease with itself. The flatulent periods of the oratorios and the bars of vapid note-spinning suggest the oracular statements and pontifical remarks he would make in life. The sudden plunges from refinement to the depths of vulgarity are paralleled by the indecision of a character not always able to distinguish between opposing values. Yet when Gounod achieves balance he is unique. His depiction of the stirrings of love springs from the sympathy of a fresh and uncomplicated nature. When he portrays the feelings of an amorous girl he draws on the resources of a delicately feminine sensibility. Though he did not often trouble to revise the music he wrote so quickly, the spontaneity that resulted is one of his most charming features. This was the basic Gounod, a being of artlessness and innocence.

The personal conflicts within him arose when the sensitive child that he was came up against a scheming world. Tensions were created that he failed to dispel. He took refuge in evasiveness and found that the easy way out was to go along with whatever force seemed strongest at the time. It was a relief for him to submit first to his mother, then to Madame Zimmermann, to his wife, and finally to Georgina Weldon.

He had a sense of humour. The friend of a talentless young man who believed himself to be a genius remarked: 'He has such a love of music.' 'Yes,' replied Gounod, 'but alas, it's unrequited.' At one time he was pestered by an amateur woman singer who kept asking him to hear her songs. The importunate female had an unusually large mouth that expanded to vast dimensions when she sang. He christened her 'the Aeolian carp'. His love of teasing found a ready butt in Massenet, who was notoriously sensitive in the matter of box-office takings. 'Look, mon petit,' Gounod would say to him, 'I've bested you. *Faust* has made 20,000 francs this week and your *le Cid* only 16,000 . . . suicide's the only thing left for you now. . . .'

He was also a kindly man. The help he gave to Lalo has already been noted. For years he kept on as his copyist an old and poverty-stricken musician, one of nature's failures doomed for ever to be down on his luck. Gounod was careful always to surround him with polite attentions and to pay him generously for his menial labours. He treated him as an equal, and the ageing copyist, warmed and flattered, came as an honoured guest to his dinner table.

In 1891, at the age of seventy-three Gounod recovered from a long attack of bronchitis only to suffer from heart trouble and temporary paralysis of one side of his body. He went on writing music. His eyesight began to fade and his right arm was affected by sciatica. Still he went on writing music. He wanted to compose a 'diptyque musical' about St Francis of Assisi in the manner of primitive pictures. The first section, inspired by Murillo, represented St Francis at the foot of the Cross. The second, after Giotto, portrayed the saint's death. Another work he succeeded in completing was the suite *les Drames sacrés*, a sequence of eleven tableaux for a play produced in 1893. It put on the stage Fra Angelico, Salome, Jesus and Mary Magdalen. The characters were dressed and grouped in the style of medieval frescoes.

These days he lived in seclusion at Saint-Cloud or rested in the peace of Normandy. Pre-printed cards were sent in reply to the heavy post that flowed in. His lifelong study of the Bible continued to yield new ideas and themes for reflection. Reluctant to give up his art completely, he investigated the problem of tonality and embodied his solution in an essay he entitled 'The constitution of the scale explained by the division of the circumference into forty-eight equal parts.'

His mind was alert though his body faltered. 'I feel as young as I was at the age of twenty,' he complained. 'What ages in us is the dwelling. The tenant doesn't.' Sometimes he was too tired for clear thinking and his remarks took on the surrealist quality of those apocalyptic announcements credited to Victor Hugo in his rambling old age. While he sat to the painter Carolus Duran for his portrait he meditated aloud. Art, he mused, was life and love—to be in love was all that mattered. Art was also the heart intellectualized. Besides Goodness and Truth, he went on, there was Beauty, which proceeded from the other two as the Holy Spirit from the Father and the Son. A crowd of reporters diligently noted his statements.

Forbidden by doctors to work, he strolled in the garden wearing his black suit and a Panama hat—was it Harry Weldon's?—and smoking his favourite clay pipe. An interviewer succeeded in approaching him. Gounod quoted from St Paul: 'For I am now ready to be offered, and the time of my departure is at hand. I have fought a good fight, I have finished my course, I have kept the faith.' His mind wandered. Sometimes he would break out with the exclamation: 'Holiness!' His mouth hung open as he struggled for words. 'Holiness . . . is a pre-celestial translucence . . . a foretaste of the immateriality of the future life.' He looked up, eyes staring at the sky. 'God loves those whom He admits into suffering.'

They talked about his career in the theatre. At the memory of what he had gone through, of the tortures and humiliations he had experienced, he burst out: 'Imagine handing over the work of one's brain and heart, confiding it to creatures who earn their living by tearing it to shreds for you, by degrading and dishonouring it! It is my child you are torturing, wretches! Take me, strike me, tear my beard . . . I am as nothing. But the work, the work! I give you one thing and it is another that you show to the public. You libel me . . . it's slander. That's not what I did. You are wicked forgers!'

He thought of the critics, the producers, the singers who had attacked or mangled his work, and he added: 'Performance is a crucifixion.'

Polyeucte was mentioned. Tears welled up in his eyes. 'The failure of *Polyeucte* is the greatest sorrow of my life.'

A reference to *Faust* calmed him. Even so, moved to feelings of repentance by the thought of death's approach, he feared that his opera might have led people into temptation.

'Yes . . . I've been the cause of many sins,' he muttered. 'Sometimes I feel remorse. . . .'

Then, very softly: 'I feel remorse . . . Only occasionally, because . . . there are also many people who owe their happiness to it.'

His last piece of music was a *Requiem* for his grandson Maurice who had died prematurely. Though his eyes were failing and he saw the manuscript as if through a fog, he drove himself to complete this last tribute to Jean's son, the little boy whom he had loved. On Sunday, the 15 October 1893, after nine o'clock mass, he sent a message to Henri Busser in the organ loft at the church of Saint-Cloud. He wanted him to collect the score and arrange it for organ.

Busser arrived in Gounod's drawing-room at one o'clock. There he found Gounod and his daughter Jeanne, baronne de Lassus. Madame Gounod and her sister were also in the room. With the orchestral score of the *Requiem* in front of him at the piano, Gounod sang it through in his tenuous voice while he sketched an accompaniment on the keyboard. When he came to the Benedictus his daughter joined in. The effort had tired him, but he walked with '*mon petit Busser*' to the front door and waved him an affectionate '*au revoir*'.

Waiting for his train at the station Busser happened to see a priest hurrying along the street. With him was an acolyte ringing a little bell. They were taking the last sacrament to someone who was dying. Busser instantly thought of Gounod and ran back to the house.

He learned that after his departure Gounod had sat down to read through his score again. The women started a game of dominoes while the composer, his clay pipe fuming peaceably, bent over his manuscript. Madame Gounod's back was turned to him. After a while, anxious at hearing no noise of activity from him, she called out: 'Gounod!' He murmured in reply.

A little later she called again. There was no response. She turned round and saw him slumped forward, the bowl of the pipe lying on the table. He never regained consciousness. For the next two days he lay in a coma. All that time his clenched fingers were tightly folded round a crucifix. On Tuesday, the 17 October, he died at twenty-five past six in the morning.

There was a State funeral. Plainchant was sung as he wished, at a ceremony in the Madeleine on the 27th. Then the coffin was taken to Auteuil cemetery and lowered into the Gounod family vault. The autumn evening was unusually mild. The last roses had not yet withered and the golden cockerel on the church tower reflected the subdued gleam of twilight.

Georgina Weldon heard the news in a hospice at Gisors where she lived as a paying guest with her dogs, her pet monkey and various birds. 'Poor old man—how I did love him and how hard all hope died,' she wrote in her diary. It was a satisfaction to her that, although he had not said goodbye to her at the end, neither had he been able to do so to his family. She was annoyed to learn that his wife, 'vile woman', had had him buried at Auteuil. In letters to the newspapers she thundered that Gounod deserved no less a resting-place than the Panthéon. To the relief of those involved, she did not attend the funeral.

She was at this time a convinced spiritualist. The shade of Gounod did not take long to materialize, thanks to the mediumistic talent of her maidservant Charlotte. It bore a strange resemblance to the Gounod she had known in this life: it reproached her for their quarrels, criticized her clothes, and told her she should go to bed earlier. Saucers moved, tables were rapped, ghostly writing appeared. Georgina's chair took wing and floated in the mysterious dark of the séance. She was addressed by her old nicknames of 'Raton' and 'Mimi'.

Soon Charlotte was receiving messages written in poetry. A sequence of regular alexandrines expressed a theme dear to Georgina's heart: the serpent-like evil of judges toward honest litigants. The range of subjects widened and she was pleased to hear that Gounod, like her, staunchly supported the cause of the unfortunate Captain Dreyfus. For nearly ten years the spirit kept in touch through exchanges that often followed the same tempestuous course as had their conversations in life. Then Georgina fell out with Charlotte. The communications ceased abruptly.

In the last years of her life, puffing at the cigarettes that eroded her wheezy lungs and disdaining the aches and pains inflicted by old age, Georgina did not forget her composer. 'Old Man gone and I fast going', she scrawled laboriously in her journal. 'His music is thought nothing of now.' Death was to solve all their problems and settle all their differences.

BIBLIOGRAPHY

Unpublished sources
Autograph letters, documents, proofs and manuscript scores preserved in
the Bibliothèque de l'Opéra; autograph material and other items in the
possession of Miss Marjory Pegram; the archives of the Royal Albert Hall;
the author's own collection of Gounodiana, including autograph letters and
manuscript music.

Published sources
Barnhill, J. B., *Gounod's Opera 'Faust': a plea for the lyric drama* (M'Caw
    & Co., 1894).
Bellaigue, Camille, *Gounod* (Félix Alcan, Paris 1919).
Boschot, Adolphe, *Portraits de musiciens, II* (Plon, Paris, 1947).
Bovet, Marie Anne de, *Charles Gounod* (Sampson Low, 1891).
Burgess, Francis, *Gounod's Faust* (Alexander Moring, 1905).
Busser, Henri, *De Pelléas aux Indes Galantes* (Fayard, 1955).
— *Charles Gounod* (E.I.S.E., 1961).
Clark, Ronald W., *The Royal Albert Hall* (Hamish Hamilton, 1958).
Curtiss, M., *Bizet and His World* (Secker & Warburg, 1958).
Dancla, Charles, *Les compositeurs chefs d'orchestre. Réponse à M. Charles
    Gounod* (Chatot, 1886).
Dandelot, A., *La Société des concerts du Conservatoire, 1828–1923* (Dela-
    grave, 1923).
Davies, L., *César Franck and His Circle* (Barrie & Jenkins, 1970).
Debillemont, J. J., *Charles Gounod* (Nouvelle Revue de Paris, 1864).
Debussy, Claude, *M. Croche antidilettante* (Gallimard, 1921).
Delaborde, Henri, *Notice sur la vie et les oeuvres de Charles Gounod* (Institut
    de France, 1894).
Demuth, N., *Introduction to the Music of Gounod* (Dennis Dobson, 1950).
Dubois, F. C. T., *Notice sur Charles Gounod* (Institut de France, 1894).
Dukas, Paul, *Écrits sur la musique* (S.E.F.I., 1948).
Ehrlich, Alfred H., *Charles Gounod* (Nord und Süd, 1885).
Fitzlyon, April, *The Price of Genius* (John Calder, 1964).
Gillington, M. C., *A Day with C. F. Gounod*, 'Days With The Great Com-
    posers' (1911).
Goddard, Joseph, *A Study of Charles Gounod's Sacred Trilogy* The Re-
    demption (Novello, Ewer, 1883).
[Gounod] *Catalogue de tableaux, dessins, estampes, recueils . . . par F. L. Reg-
    nault-Delalande.* (Auction sale of Gounod's father's art collec-
    tion, 23 Feb., 1824).
[Gounod] *Manuscrits musicaux de Charles Gounod.* Hotel Drouot; E. Ader
    and P. Cornuau; 27 Nov., 1963. (Auction sale including the
    complete manuscripts of *Philémon et Baucis, la Colombe, Roméo
    et Juliette, Polyeucte, Ivan le Terrible,* and *la Rédemption,*

[Gounod]—*contd.*
together with substantial autograph passages from *Faust* and many other important items.

Grierson, E., *Storm Bird: The strange life of Georgina Weldon* (Chatto & Windus, 1959).

Hahn, Reynalso, *Thèmes variés* (Janin, 1946).

— *L'oreille au guet* (Gallimard, 1937).

— *Du chant* (Gallimard, 1957).

Halévy, Ludovic, *Carnets 1, 1862–1869* (Calmann-Lévy, 1935).

Harding, James, 'Gounod' in: *Dictionnaire de la musique, 1* (Bordas, 1970).

— *Massenet* (Dent, 1970).

— *Saint-Saëns and His Circle* (Chapman & Hall, 1965).

Hervey, Arthur, *Masters of French Music* (Osgood, McIlvaine, 1894).

Hillemacher, P. L., *Charles Gounod* (Laurens, 1906).

Imbert, Hugues, *Nouveaux profils de musiciens* (Fischbacher, 1892).

Jullien, A., *Musiciens d'aujourd'hui* (Librairie de l'Art, 1892).

— *Musique* (Librairie de l'Art, 1896).

Lalo, Pierre, *De Rameau à Ravel* (Albin Michel, 1947).

Landormy, P., *Gounod* (Gallimard, 1942).

— *Faust de Gounod* (Mellottée, 1944).

Mapleson, J. H., *The Mapleson Papers*, ed. H. Rosenthal (Putnam, 1966).

Newman, E., *Opera Nights* (Putnam, 1943).

Northcott, Richard, *Gounod's Operas in London* (Press Printers, 1918).

Noske, Frits, *La mélodie française de Berlioz à Duparc* (Presses universitaires françaises, 1954).

Orczy, Baroness, *Links in the Chain of Life* (Hutchinson, n.d.).

Pagnerre, Louis, *Charles Gounod* (L. Sauvaitre, 1890).

Pincherle, Marc, *Musiciens peints par eux-mêmes* (Cornuau, 1939).

Prod'homme, J. G., & Dandelot, A., *Gounod*, 2 vols (Delagrave, 1911).

Reyer, E., *Quarante ans de musique* (Calmann-Lévy, 1909).

Saint-Saëns, C., *C. Gounod et le* Don Juan *de Mozart* (Ollendorff, 1893).

— *Portraits et souvenirs* (Société d'édition artistique, 1899).

Samazeuilh, G., *Musiciens de mon temps* (Renaissance du livre, 1947).

Scudo, P., *L'art ancien et l'art moderne* (Garnier frères, 1854).

Soubies, A. and de Curzon, H., *Documents inédits sur le Faust de Gounod* (Fischbacher, 1912).

Tolhurst, H., *Gounod* (Bell, 1905).

Treherne, Philip, *A Plaintiff in Person*, (Life of Mrs Weldon) (Heinemann, 1923).

Vallas, Leon, *La véritable histoire de César Franck* (Flammarion, 1955).

Weldon, Georgina, *The Quarrel of The Royal Albert Hall Company with Ch. Gounod* (R. Oxley & Son, Windsor, 1873).

— *Lettres de M Gounod et autres lettres et documents originaux*, 3 vols (Mrs Weldon, 1875).

— *The History of My Orphanage* (Mrs Weldon, 1878).

— *Death-Blow to Spiritualism—is it ?* (Music & Art Association, 1882).

— *Hints for Pronunciation in Singing* (Mrs Weldon, 1882).

— *How I Escaped The Mad Doctors* (Mrs Weldon, 1882).

Bibliography

— *My Orphanage & Gounod in England,* 2 vols (Music & Art Association, 1882).

— *The Ghastly Consequences of Living in Charles Dickens' House* (Mrs Weldon, 1882).

— Preface to: *Prison Horrors by H. Harcourt* (G. Weldon, 1883).

— *Charles Gounod (Esprit): Après vingt ans et autres poésies* (Leymaris, Paris/Nichols, London, 1902).

— *Mémoires de Georgina Weldon: Justice*(?) *anglaise,* 6 vols (G. Weldon, Gisors/34, Hart St, Bloomsbury, 1902).

— *Louis XVII: or, The Arab Jew* (Nichols & Co, 1908).

Wolff, S., *L'Opéra au Palais Garnier* (L'Entr'acte, 1962).

— *Un demi-siècle d'Opéra-comique* (André Bonne, 1953).

APPENDIX: LIST OF WORKS

OPERAS

SAPHO: Opera in three acts. Libretto by Emile Augier.

Opéra (rue le Peletier) Original version, 16 April 1851	Role	Opéra (Garnier) Revised in 4 acts, 2 April 1884
Gueymard	Phaon	Dereims
Marié	Alcée	Melchissédec
Brémond	Pitheas	Gailhard
★★★★★★★	Cratès	★★★★★★★
★★★★★★★	Cygénir	★★★★★★★
Aimès	Un pâtre	Piroia
Prévost	Grand prêtre	Palianti
★★★★★★★	Agathon	Sapin
★★★★★★★	Eratès	Girard
★★★★★★★	Cynèque	Lambert
Pauline Viardot	Sapho	Gabrielle Krauss
Poinsot	Glycère	Richard
★★★★★★★	Oenone	Duménil
N. Girard	Conductor	Gounod

LA NONNE SANGLANTE: Opera in five acts. Libretto by Eugène Scribe and Germain Delavigne after *The Monk* by Matthew Lewis.
Opéra, 18 October 1854
Role

Le comte de Luddorf	Merly
Le baron de Moldavv	Guignot
Rodolphe	Gueymard
Pierre l'Hermite	Depassio
Fritz	Aymès
Agnès	Poinsot
Agnès la nonne sanglante	Wertheimber
Arthur	Dussy
Anna	Dameron

LE MÉDECIN MALGRÉ LUI: Opéra-comique in three acts. Libretto by Jules Barbier and Michel Carré after Molière.

Théâtre Lyrique, 15 January 1858	Role	Opéra-Comique, 22 May 1872
Caye	Lucinde	Guillot
Faivre	Martine	Decroix
Gérard	Jacqueline	Ducasse
Lesage	Géronte	Nathan
Fromant	Léandre	Coppel

Meillet	Sganarelle	Ismael
Leroy	Robert	Palianti
Wartel	Valère	Bernard
Girardot	Lucas	Barnolt
*******	Conductor	Deloffre

FAUST: Opera in five acts. Libretto by Jules Barbier and Michel Carré after Goethe.

Théâtre Lyrique, 19 March 1859		Opéra (rue le Peletier) with recitatives and ballet,
	Role	3 March 1869
Carvalho	Marguerite	Christine Nilsson
Faivre	Siebel	Mauduit
Duclos	Marthe	Desbordes
Barbot	Faust	Colin
Balanqué	Méphistophélès	Faure
Reynald	Valentin	Devoyod
Cibot	Wagner	Gaspard
Deloffre	Conductor	Hainl

PHILÉMON ET BAUCIS: Opera in two acts. Libretto by Jules Barbier and Michel Carré, after La Fontaine.

Théâtre Lyrique, 18 February 1860 In 3 acts		Opéra-Comique, 16 May 1876 In 2 acts
	Role	
Fromant	Philémon	Nicot
Battaille	Jupiter	Bouhy
Balanqué	Vulcain	Giraudet
Carvalho	Baucis	Chapuy
Deloffre	Conductor	Constantin

LA COLOMBE: Opéra-comique in two acts. Libretto by Jules Barbier and Michel Carré after La Fontaine.
Baden-Baden, 3 August 1860

Role	
Sylvie	Carvalho
Mazet	Faivre
Horace	Roger
Maître Jean	Balanqué

LA REINE DE SABA: Opera in four acts. Libretto by Jules Barbier and Michel Carré after Gérard de Nerval.
Opéra, 29 February 1862

Role	
Balkis	Gueymard-Lauters
Benoni	Hamackers
Sarahil	Tarby
Adoniram	Gueymard

LA REINE DE SABA—*contd.*

Soliman	Belval
Amrou	Grisy
Phanor	Marié
Méthousaël	Coulon
Sadoc	Fréret

MIREILLE: Opera in five acts. Libretto by Michel Carré after *Mireio* by Frederic Mistral.

Théâtre Lyrique, 19 March 1864		Opéra-Comique, 6 June 1939, restored by Henri Busser
	Role	
Carvalho	Mireille	Jeanne Rolland
Faure Lefèvre	Taven	Madeleine Sibille
Faure Lefèvre	Andreloun (le berger)	Derenne
Reboux	Vincenette	Lucie Thelin
Albrecht	Clémence	Gaudinau
Méry	Une voix d'en haut	Martha Angelici
Morini	Vincent	Louis Arnoult
Ismaël	Ourrias	José Beckmans
Petit	Ramon	Etcheverry
Wartel	Ambroise	Clavensy
Wartel	Le passeur	Barbero
Ferrel	Un Arlésien	Ravoux
Deloffre	Conductor	Reynaldo Hahn

ROMÉO ET JULIETTE: Opera in five acts. Libretto by Jules Barbier and Michel Carré after Shakespeare.

Théâtre Lyrique, 27 April 1867		Opéra, 28 November 1888, with ballet
	Role	
Carvalho	Juliette	Patti
Daram	Stefano	Augussol
Duclos	Gertrude	Canti
Michot	Roméo	Jean de Reszke
Puget	Tybalt	Muratet
Laurent	Benvolio	Tequi
Barré	Mercutio	Melchissédec
Laveissière	Paris	Warmbrodt
Troy jeune	Gregorio	Lambert Descilleuls
Troy	Capulet	Delmas
Cazaux	Frère Laurent	Édouard de Reszke
Christophe	Le duc de Vérone	Ballard
Neveu	Frère Jean	Crépaux
Deloffre	Conductor	Gounod

CINQ-MARS: Opera in four acts. Libretto by Paul Poirson and Louis Gallet after the novel by Alfred de Vigny.
Opéra-Comique, 5 April 1877
Role

Le marquis de Cinq-Mars	Dereims
Le conseiller de Thou	Stephanne
Le père Joseph	Giraudet
Le vicomte de Fontrailles	Barré
Le Roi	Alfred Maris
Le chancelier	Bernard
De Montmort	Lefèvre
De Montrésor	Teste
De Brienne	Collin
De Montglat	Chenevière
De Château-Giron	Villars
Eustache	Davoust
La princesse Marie de Gonzagues	Chevrier
Marion Delorme	Franck-Duvernoy
Ninon de l'Enclos	Périer

POLYEUCTE: Opera in five acts. Libretto by Jules Barbier and Michel Carré after Corneille.
Opéra, 7 October 1878
Role

Polyeucte	Salomon/Sellier
Sévère	Lasalle
Felix	Berardı
Néarque	Auguez
Albin	Menu
Siméon	Bataille
Sextus	Bosquin
Un Centurion	Gaspard
Pauline	Gabrielle Krauss
Stratonice	Calderon
Conductor	Lamoureux

LE TRIBUT DE ZAMORA: Grand opera in four acts. Libretto by Adolphe d'Ennery and Jules Brésil.
Opéra, 1 April 1881
Role

Xaïma	Daram
Iglésia	Janvier
Hermosa	Gabrielle Krauss
Une esclave	********
Manoël	Sellier
Hadjar	Melchissédec
L'Alcade	Mermand
Un vieillard	Bonnefoy

LE TRIBUT DE ZAMORA—*contd.*

Ben Saïd	Lassalle
Le Roi	Giraudet
Le Cadi	Sapin
Un soldat arabe	Lambert
Conductor	Gounod

MAÎTRE PIERRE:
Libretto by Louis Gallet.
Unfinished opera.

INCIDENTAL MUSIC

Ulysse, tragedy in 5 acts by Ponsard, Comédie-Française, 18 June 1852.

Le Bourgeois gentilhomme (Molière) after Lully, Comédie-Française, 15 January 1857.

Les Deux reines, drama in 4 acts by Ernest Legouvé, Théâtre Ventadour, 27 November 1872

Jeanne d'Arc, drama in 5 acts by Jules Barbier, Théâtre de la Gaîté, 8 November 1873.

George Dandin, comedy after Molière, begun in February 1873, left uncompleted.

Drames sacrés, by Armand Sylvestre and Eugène Morand, Théâtre du Vaudeville, March 1893.

MASSES

1839	*Messe* (Église de Saint-Roch), unpublished.
1840	*Messe* (Rome, 1 May, 1841), unpublished.
1842	*Messe de Requiem* (Vienna, 2 November 1842).
1843	*Messe* (Vienna, 25 March 1843).
1846	*A son ami Gabriel de Vendeuvre.* Missa brevis. 4 men's voices, unacc.
	A l'Association des Sociétés chorales de Paris et du Département de la Seine. 4 men's voices, organ.
1853	*Messe à 3 voix d'hommes*
1855	*Messe solennelle Sainte-Cécile* Soloists, chorus, orchestra, organ obbligato.
1870	*Messe des Orphéonistes.*
1871	*Messe brève.* 3 men's voices, organ or harmonium acc.
	Messe des anges gardiens. 4 voices, organ acc.
1873	*Messe brève pour les morts.*
1876	*Messe du Sacré-Coeur de Jésus.* 4 voices and orch.
1883	*Messe no 3.* 3 voices and organ acc.
1882	*Troisième Messe solennelle (de Pâques).*
1883	*Messe funèbre.* 4 voices and organ acc.
1887	*A la mémoire de Jeanne d'Arc.* Soloists, chorus, organ.
1888	*Quatrième messe solennelle.*
1890	*Aux Cathédrales.* Soloists, chorus and organ or piano acc.
	Messe brève. Soloists, chorus and organ or piano acc.

1890   *Messe dite de Clovis.* 4 voices with organ acc.

       Messe de Saint Jean. 4 voices with organ acc.

1893   *Requiem.*

ORATORIOS

1866 (?)   *Tobie.* Text by H. Lefèvre.

1871   *Gallia.* For soprano solo, chorus, orchestra and organ. Text by Gounod.

1878   *Jésus sur le lac de Tibériade.* Scène biblique.

1882   *La Rédemption.* Trilogie sacrée.

1883   *Christus factus est.* Words adapted by Charles Santley. (Music taken from *La Rédemption*).

1884   *Mors et Vita.* A sacred trilogy.

MOTETS, CANTICLES, ETC.

1841   *Te Deum.* Envoi from Rome.

1843   *Hymne.* Envoi from Rome.

1843 (?)   *La Reine des apôtres.* Words by Gounod.

1853   *Domine salvum.*

       Ave verum.

1856   *O salutaris; Regina coeli.*

1855/6   *Dans cette étable.* Pastoral on an eighteenth-century carol; 4 voices.

       Bethléem. Arrangement of an eighteenth-century carol.

1855   *Les sept paroles du Christ sur la croix.* Mixed voices, unacc.

1856   *Regina coeli; Laudate Dominum.* Mixed voices, unacc.

       O salutaris; Inviolata. 4 voices.

       Laudate Dominum; Regina coeli. 2 voices.

       O salutaris hostia. Soprano, chorus, orch.

       Ave verum de Mozart. 4 voices.

       Cieux, fondex-vous en pleurs. Seventeenth-century canticle, 4 voices.

       Entr'acte et prière de Joseph de Méhul. Arr. for voices.

       Ave verum. Bass or contralto.

       Jésus de Nazareth. Words by A. Porte.

       O salutaris eternel. Orchestra and organ.

       Da pacem. 3 voices.

       Pater Noster. 4 voices.

       Inviolata. 2 voices.

1859   *Ave Maria* (Bach). Soprano and orchestra.

(?)   *Pater Noster.* 4 voices.

       Fixer ici ton sort. Seventeenth-century canticle.

1861   *Prière à Marie.*

       Près du fleuve étranger. 4 voices (Psalm 137).

       Tout l'univers est plein de sa magnificence (Racine).

       Ave Verum. 4 voices.

       Motets solennels: *Ave verum, O salutaris.*

1866   *Vendredi saint.* 6 voices, words by Alexis Badou.

       Noël (poem by Jules Barbier). Women's voices and organ.

MOTETS, CANTICLES, ETC.—*contd.*

1867   *Stabat Mater*. Words by abbé Castaing.

1868   *Tota pulchra es.* 2 voices.

       Sub tuum. 2 voices.

       Prière à la Vierge.

       Le mois de Marie.

       Le crucifix.

       Sicut cervus. Motet, 4 voices.

       Stabat Mater.

       Cantique pour l'adoration du Saint-Sacrement. Words by the marquis A. de Ségur.

       Le Ciel a visité la terre. Words by the marquis de Ségur.

1869   *Prière pour l'Empereur et la famille impèriale.* Words by Mme Baclen.

1870   *L'Anniversaire des martyrs.* Words by Ch. Dallet.

       Six cantiques.

1871   *Ave verum.*

       There is a green hill far away. Words by Mrs C. F. Alexander.

       Motet (Christus factus est).

       De profundis.

       O salutaris. 2 voices.

1872/3 *Angeli custodes.*

       Prière d'Abraham. Words by Jules Barbier.

       O salutaris. Soprano or tenor solo.

       Two Benedictus.

  (?) *L'Ave Maria de l'enfant.*

       To God, ye choirs above. Anthem, words by P. Skelton.

       Cantique pour la première communion.

       Bienheureux le coeur sincère, paraphrase by J. Barbier.

       La salutation angèlique.

       Ave Maria.

       D'un coeur qui t'aime. Racine (*Athalie*), duet.

       Le roi d'amour est mon pasteur. Words by Paul Collin.

       Glory to Thee My God, This Night. Words by Bishop Ken.

       Hymne à Saint-Augustin. Words by abbé Ribolet.

       Forever With The Lord. Words by J. Montgomery.

       Ce qu'il faut à mon âme. Canticle, words by abbé F. Sedillot.

1873   *Temple, ouvre-toi.* Words by Legouvé.

       Vexilla regis.

       On The Sea of Galilee. Words by Mrs Weldon.

  (?) *Te Deum.*

1879   *60 Chants sacrés.* Motets for various occasions. 3 vols.

1880   *Miserere.* 4 voices, solos, chorus, with organ.

       De profundis. (Psalm 130), solos, chorus, orchestra.

1886   *L'Hymne apostolique.*

       Quam dilecta tabernacula tua.

       Hymne de la patrie. Words by G. Boyer.

       Te Deum. Solo or small choir, chorus, organ, harps.

1886   *The Holy Vision.* Words by Frederick E. Weatherley.
1889   *La Communion des saints.* Soprano and chorus.
1890   *La Contemplation de Saint Francois au pied de la croix; La mort de Saint François.*
1892   *Second Ave Maria* (Bach).
        Je te rends grâce, ô Dieu d'amour. Canticle, words by P. Collin, 4 voices and organ.
        Toujours à toi, Seigneur. Hymn, words by P. Collin, 4 voices.
        Tantum ergo. Voice, violin, 'cello, organ.
        Pater noster. 5 voices, chorus, organ.
        Le jour de Noël. Chorus.

CANTATAS, CHORUSES, SONGS, ETC.

1837   Marie Stuart et Rizzio. Scène lyrique.
1838   La Vendetta. Scène lyrique.
1839   Fernand. Scènes lyriques for 3 voices.
1840/2   Le vallon (Lamartine).
1853   Hymne français (*envoi* from Rome).
1852   Ier prélude de Bach. Transcr. for piano, organ, violin and arr. as song.
1852–58 Quatre grands choeurs. With orchestra.
        Les pauvres du bon Dieu (?).
        La Chanson de Roland (Grétry). Arr. for 4 men's voices.
        Chasse; Ou sommes-nous ? (?).
        Vive l'Empereur! (?).
        Hymne à la France (?).
        L'Enclume (?).
        La cigale et la fourmi (La Fontaine).
        Le corbeau et le renard (La Fontaine).
        Bonjour, bonsoir (Spenner).
        Le rosier blanc (Spenner).
        Patte de velours (Spenner).
        La jeune fille et la fauvette (La Chauvinière).
        Cantate pour jeunes filles (Turpin).
        Un rêve (?).
        La distribution des prix (?).
        Paraissez, roi des rois (?).
        La reine des cieux (Turpin).
        Le géographie (Turpin).
        L'Action de grâce (Turpin).
        Le Catéchisme (Turpin).
        Le Benedicite (Turpin).
        Oú voulez-vous aller ? (Gautier).
        Primavera (Gautier).
1854/5   Marguerite (Pradère).
        Chant de paix (?).
        Les vacances (Bigorie).
        Le jour des prix (Scribe).

CANTATAS, CHORUSES, SONGS, ETC.—*contd.*

1854/5   Le temps qui fuit et s'envole (?).
La prière et l'étude (Turpin).
La récréation (Turpin).
L'écriture (Turpin).
L'arithmétique (Turpin).
Fêtes des écoles. For 4 voices.
L'hiver (Lully, arr.)
Chantons, chantons de Dieu le pouvoir eternel (Handel, arr).
En ce doux asile (Rameau, arr).
L'ange gardien (Quételard).

1855   Mon habit (Béranger).
Six mélodies.
Deux vieux amis (Véron).
Sérénade (Hugo).
Les châteaux en Espagne (Véron). Duet.

1860   L'âme de la morte (Banville).
L'âme d'un ange (Banville).
Chanson de printemps (Tourneux).

1861   Le juif errant (Béranger).
Six mélodies enfantines.

1862   A une jeune Grecque (Sapho, trans Yvaren).

1865   Medjé (Barbier).
Solitude (Lamartine).
Tombez, mes ailes (Légouvé).
Boire à l'ombre (Augier).
Déesse ou femme (Barbier, Carré).
Départ (Augier).
Donne-moi cette fleur (Gozlan).
Envoi de fleurs (Augier).

1866   Stances (Bertin).
Crépuscule (Bertin).

1867   Un rêve (Spenner).

1868   Au printemps (Barbier).

1869   A une bourse (Augier).
A une jeune fille (Augier).
Les pauvres du bon Dieu (Lebeau aîné).
Les martyrs.
Vingt mélodies.

1870   Absence (Ségur).
Chantez Noël (Barbier).
Je ne puis espérer (Delpit).
Chantez, voix bénies (Gallet).
Par une belle nuit (Ségur).

1871   La pâquerette (Dumas *fils*).
Chanter et souffrir (Delpit).
Mignon (Gallet).
Le souvenir (Collin).

1871   Oh, that we two were maying (Kingsley).
Beware (Longfellow).
Queen of Love (Palgrave).
The sea hath its pearls (Kingsley).
La siesta.
Boléro (Barbier).
Good Night (Shelley).
It is not always May (Longfellow).
The fountain mingles with the river (Shelley).
There is a dew (Hood).
Woe's me! (Campbell).

1872   Oh, happy home! (Maitland).
Le pays bienheureux (Hemans).
Perche piangi ? (Pavesi).
Prière du soir (Ligny).
Quanti mai (Metastasio).
Si vous n'ouvrez pas votre fenêtre (Dumas *fils*).
Biondina (Zaffira, cycle of 6 Italian songs).
Heureux sera le jour (Ronsard).
La fauvette (Millevoye).
La fleur du foyer (Ligny).
O, dille tu! (Zaffira).
Chanson d'avril (Coppée).
Chanson de la brise (Ligny).
The Maid of Athens (Byron).
Ma belle amie est morte (Gautier).

1873   Barcarola (Zaffira).
Blessed is the man (?).
Chidiock Tichbourne (?).
There is dew for the flow'ret (Hood).
English songs: Roy's wife of Aldivalloch.
                My beloved spake.
                Peacefully slumber.
                Welcome to Skye.
If thou art sleeping, maiden, awake (?).
Invocation (Pradère).
Loin du pays (?).
The Worker (Weatherley).
Prière du soir (Manuel).
Stanzas in memory of Livingstone (Houghton).

1874   Sur la montagne (Barbier).
A la Madone (Barbier).
Aimons-nous (Barbier).

1875   A la brise (Barbier).
Clos ta paupière (Barbier).
Mon amour à mon coeur (Barbier).
En avant (Déroulède).
Viens, les gazons sont verts (Barbier).

CANTATAS, CHORUSES, SONGS, ETC.—*contd.*

1876   Prends garde (Barbier).
           Prière (Sully Prudhomme).
           Compliment (Dumas *fils*).
           Les lilas blancs (Bourguignat).
           Ma fille, souviens-toi (Louise Marie B.).
           A toi, mon coeur (Barbier).
           Les jeunes Françaises (Legouvé).
           L'absent (Gounod).
1877   Vive la France (Déroulède).
1878   Jesus à la crèche (Barbier).
           La chanson du pâtre (?).
           Le départ du mousse (P. Barbier).
           La reine du matin (Barbier, Carré).
           Rêverie (Barbier).
           15 mélodies enfantines.
1879   Mélancolie (Coppée).
1881   Les châteaux en Espagne (duet, Véron).
1882   Marche funèbre d'une marionnette (Price).
           Réponse de Medjé (M. Barbier).
           Tu m'aimes (M. Barbier).
           Elle sait (Boyer).
           Ce que je suis sans toi (Peyre).
           Chant des sauveteurs bretons (Ségalas).
           Pauvre Braga, charmant garçon! (Nadaud).
1883   La chanson de la glu (Richepin).
           Déjà l'aube matinale (?).
           Dernières volontés (Veuillot).
           Les deux pigeons (La Fontaine).
           Memorare (?).
1884   Voguons sur les flots (?).
           A Cécile (Dubufe).
           Quand l'enfant prie (Boyer).
1885   La couronne des reines (D'Ennery, Brésil).
           Les adieux à la maison (?).
           Blessures (Turpin).
           Voix d'Alsace-Lorraine (Rousseil).
           Le temps des roses (Roy).
1886   Aria di camera (Hasse).
           Dieu partout (Plouvier).
           La travail béni (Plouvier).
           La fête des couronnes (Plouvier).
           Six choeurs.
1888   Ce qu'il faut à mon âme (Sédillot)
           Le temps qui fuit (?).
           Vincenette (P. Barbier).
           Gliding down the river (Farnie).
           Passiflora (Chambrun).

1889	Hymne à la nuit (Barbier).
1890	Aubade à la fiancée (D'Ennery, Brésil).
1891	A la nuit (Gounod).
1892	L'absent (Gounod).
1893	Tout l'univers obéit à l'amour (La Fontaine).
?	Au rossignol (Lamartine).

ORCHESTRAL WORKS

1837	Scherzo.
1840	Marche militaire suisse.
1855	Symphony No 1, D major.
	Symphony No 2, E flat major.
1865	Chant des compagnons.
1871	Saltarello.
1872	Marche romaine.
1873	Funeral March of a Marionnette.
1878	Marche religieuse.

SOLO INSTRUMENT AND ORCHESTRA

1886	Fantaisie sur l'hymne national russe. Piano and orchestra.
1887	Le rendez-vous. Piano and orchestra.
1888	Suite concertante. Pedal piano and orchestra.

CHAMBER MUSIC

1841	Quintet for 2 violins, viola, 'cello, piano.
1852	Méditation sur le 1er prélude de Bach. Piano, violin solo, organ.
1864	Hymne à Sainte-Cécile. Violin, piano, organ.
1885	Petite Etude-Scherzo. 2 double basses.
1886	Meditation on the song 'The Arrow and the Song'. Piano, violin, 'cello, organ.
1888	Petite symphonie pour 2 flûtes, 2 hautbois, 2 clarinettes, 2 bassons.
posth.	String quartet.

VIOLIN AND PIANO

1874	Peacefully slumber. Lullaby.
posth.	Souvenir d'un bal.

SOLO PIANO

1854	Valse.
1860	Valse caractéristique. 2 or 4 hands.
1861	La pervenche. Romance sans paroles.
	Le ruisseau. Romance sans paroles.
	Musette: les Pifferari. Impromptu.
1863	Royal-Menuet.
	Musette impromptu.
	Sérénade.

SOLO PIANO—*contd.*

1864   Le bal d'enfants.
          Georgina. Waltz.
          Mireille. Transcriptions.
          Six mélodies (song transcriptions).
          Eight melodies (song transcriptions).

1865   Le soir. Romance sans paroles.
          Le calme. Romance sans paroles.
          Valse des fiancés.
          Souvenance. Nocturne.

1866   Chanson du printemps. Romance sans paroles.

1871   Ivy.

1873   Dodelinette. Lullaby.
          Funeral March of a Marionnette.

1876   Maid of Athens (song transcription).
          La Venezia. Chanson sans paroles.

1877   La fête de Jupiter.
          Invocation.
          Prélude.
          Pastorale.
          Sérénade.
          Marche-Fanfare.
          Grand Waltz in D.
          Méditation.

1878   Saltarelle.

1879   Marche religieuse.
          Invocation and prelude.

1881   Valse caractéristique.
          Wedding March No. 1.

1882   Wedding March No. 2.

posth.   Six pièces pour piano.

PIANO DUET

1858   Menuet.
          L'Angélus.

1878   Marche religieuse.

1879   3 petits morceaux faciles.

ORGAN MUSIC

1858   Communion.

1871   La Melodia.

1876   Offertorium.

LITERARY WORKS

Books:

Autobiographie de Ch. Gounod et Articles sur la Routine en matière d'Art. Edités et compilés avec une préface par Mrs Georgina Weldon.

Published by Mrs Weldon, Tavistock House, Tavistock Square, W.C. 1875.
Mémoires d'un artiste. Calmann-Lévy, 1896 (posth.).

Articles:

Les compositeurs chefs d'orchestre. *Le Ménestrel*, June–July, 1873.
L'allaitement musical. *Le Nouveau-Né*, January 1882.
L'Académie de France à Rome. Institut, January 1882.
Le Don Juan de Mozart. Institut, 25 October 1882.
M. Camille Saint-Saëns: *Henri VIII. Nouvelle Revue*, 15 March 1884.
La nature et l'art. Institut, 25 October 1886.
Proserpine de C. Saint-Saëns. *Figaro*, 17 March 1887.
Ascanio de C. Saint-Saëns. *La France*, 23 March 1890.
De l'artiste dans la société moderne. *Revue de Paris*, 1 November 1895.

Prefaces:

Correspondance inédite d'Hector Berlioz. Calmann-Lévy, 1878.
Les soirées parisiennes de 1883, par un Monsieur d'Orchestre. 1884.
Les Annales du Théâtre et de la Musique. Noel and Stoullig, 1886.

Published correspondence:

Lettres de 1870–71. *Revue de Paris*, 1 February 1986.
Lettres à Georges Bizet. Ibid. 15 December 1899.
Lettres à Richomme. *Revue hebdomadaire*, 26 December 1908, and 2 January 1909.
Lettres de Rome et de Vienne. *Revue Bleue*, 31 December 1910 and 5 January 1911.

INDEX

243